BOLD THINKING CHRISTIANITY

Discovering Intellectually Vigorous Faith: One Man's Sequel to C.S. Lewis's *Mere Christianity*

By

MICHAEL PHILLIPS

MICHAEL PHILLIPS IS THE AUTHOR OF...

Practical Essential Christianity
George MacDonald and the Late Great Hell Debate
George MacDonald's Spiritual Vision: An Overview
George MacDonald's Transformational Theology
The Eyewitness New Testament in 3 Volumes
The Commands of Jesus
The Commands of the Apostles
Hell and Beyond
Heaven and Beyond
George MacDonald, Scotland's Beloved Storyteller
Make Me Like Jesus
The Eleventh Hour
Dream of Freedom
Rift in Time
God A Good Father
Jesus An Obedient Son

Bold Thinking Christianity
Copyright © 2013 by Michael Phillips

All rights reserved. No part of this book may be used or reproduced in any form or by any electronic or mechanical means, including information storage and retrieval systems, without permission in writing from the publisher, except by a reviewer who may quote brief passages in a review.

Print edition published 2013 by Yellowood House, an imprint of Sunrise Books

ISBN: 9780940652903

Therefore, gird up the loins of your mind...

1 Peter 1:13

It may be my reader will desire me to say how the Lord will deliver him from his sins. That is like the lawyer's "Who is my neighbour?" The spirit of such a mode of receiving the offer of the Lord's deliverance is the root of all the horrors of a corrupt theology, so acceptable to those who love weak and beggarly hornbooks of religion. Such questions spring from the passion for the fruit of the tree of knowledge, not the fruit of the tree of life. Men would understand: they do not care to obey;—understand where it is impossible they should understand save by obeying. They would search into the work of the Lord instead of doing their part in it—thus making it impossible both for the Lord to go on with his work, and for themselves to become capable of seeing and understanding what he does. Instead of immediately obeying the Lord of life, the one condition upon which he can help them, and in itself the beginning of their deliverance, they set themselves to question their unenlightened intellects as to his plans for their deliverance... Incapable of understanding the first motions of freedom in themselves, they proceed to interpret the riches of his divine soul in terms of their own beggarly notions, to paraphrase his glorious verse into their own paltry commercial prose; and then, in the growing presumption of imagined success, to insist upon their neighbours' acceptance of their distorted shadows of "the plan of salvation"...They delay setting their foot on the stair which alone can lead them to the house of wisdom, until they shall have determined the material and mode of its construction. For the sake of knowing, they postpone that which alone can enable them to know, and substitute for the true understanding which lies beyond, a false persuasion that they already understand. They will not accept, that is, act upon, their highest privilege, that of obeying the Son of God. It is on them that do his will, that the day dawns; to them the day-star arises in their hearts. Obedience is the soul of knowledge...

God forbid I should seem to despise understanding. The New Testament is full of urgings to understand. Our whole life, to be life at all, must be a growth in understanding. What I cry out upon is the misunderstanding that comes of man's endeavour to understand while not obeying. Upon obedience our energy must be spent; understanding will follow. Not anxious to know our duty, or knowing it and not doing it, how shall we understand that which only a true heart and a clean soul can ever understand...Until a man begins to obey, the light that is in him is darkness. [1]

George MacDonald

Contents

Foreword 1990, 2009   1
Introduction 2009   3

Part 1—Ongoing Revelation
Key Scriptural Concepts: *Walk, Think, Mind of Christ, Boldness, Drift, Tradition, Search*

1. Walking with God, 2001   13
   Reflections on lifetime priorities

2. Thinking for Ourselves—A Foundation to Get at Truth, 2001   23
   Assessing truth with humility, balance, and perspective

3. The World's Response to Superficiality, 2009   39
   What kind of boldness will the third millennium respect?

4. What is Bold Thinking Christianity?, 2004   51
   The cancer of religious "systems"

5. Halting the Drift of Reality Toward Dogma, 2003   61
   Are we immune from the pitfalls of our predecessors?

6. Historic Christianity, 2004   71
   Does "tradition" validate truth?

7. One Man's Journey Toward Bold Faith, 2004   85
   A mini spiritual autobiography

Part 2—Multi-Dimensioned Scriptural Truth
Key Scriptural Concepts: *Scripture, Faith, Truth*

8. The Word of God, 2004   105
   Literal, inerrant, infallible...or leaky human vessel through which God reveals his high λογος

9. Faith of Giants, 1993   133
   The two-edged sword of bold courage and humble trust

10. EIGHT PRINCIPLES OF SPIRITUAL TRUTH, 2005   149
    A deepening personal revelation toward obedient childship

PART 3—THE CONTINUING QUEST
KEY SCRIPTURAL CONCEPTS: *Growth, Humility, Discern*

11. THE DEVELOPMENT OF THE IDEAS OF CHRISTIANITY, 2005   167
    Truth grows and expands

12. THE OPEN-MINDED SPIRITUAL QUEST, 1998   181
    *Unity, openness, and the role of spiritual quest
    in understanding God's eternal purpose*

13. THE PENDULUM OF PERSONAL BIAS, 2004   195
    *The soil out of which emerge our ideas, choices,
    and conclusions regarding truth*

PART 4—DOCTRINAL STEPPING STONES
KEY SCRIPTURAL CONCEPTS: *Obedience, Diligence, Maturity*

14. THE TRINITY: A TRIAD OF RULE, OBEDIENCE, AND REVELATION, 2004   209
    *An exercise in bold thinking applied to Christianity's
    most widely held doctrine*

15. GUARD AGAINST SUPERFICIALITY, 2007   229
    Counterfeit parameters of spirituality

16. LET US GO ON TO MATURITY, 2007   247
    True indicators of growth in the life of faith

PART 5—GOD'S ETERNAL SYMPHONY
KEY SCRIPTURAL CONCEPTS: *Confirmation, Logos*

17. BOLD THINKING APPLIED TO SCRIPTURE, 1993   263
    *Four confirming fences to validate accuracy, prevent error,
    and lead to higher truth*

18. TOWARD THE HIGH *ABBA* LOGOS, 2004   281
    Learning to hear the symphony of eternity

Foreword

This book began twenty years ago. At the time I was slowly progressing through my fifth or sixth read of C.S. Lewis's *Mere Christianity*. While our family was spending a few days in Einigen, Switzerland, I wrote some notes to myself inside the back flyleaf of Lewis's classic. All these years later, they seem a fitting point from which to embark on this book, which I have entitled *Bold Thinking Christianity*. With a few changes to smooth out the stream of consciousness nature inevitable when jotting down notes to oneself, I said the following:

The day will come, paralleling what Lewis provided for his time with Mere Christianity, when a book of practical "theology" will be necessary for <u>our</u> generation. A new clarification is needed. Today's evangelical church is mired in <u>saying</u> doctrine rather than allowing Christianity to function as a fully balanced lifestyle that harmonizes belief and obedience. The Pharisees were bound by legalism. Evangelicalism is bound by knowledge, words, and a quarreling over doctrine. The chief segment of the spectrum where actions are emphasized seems to be on the Catholic/Episcopal side. Yet it is just as incomplete as on the evangelical side of the fence. There the ideas of Christianity are downplayed. Nowhere do I see the MacDonald balance—a vigorous attempt to study and think through the ideas <u>and</u> to practice them daily.

When that time comes, we must try to incorporate Lewis's practicality in addition to giving parallel emphasis to MacDonald's revolutionary ideas about God and his work—combining the two in a way neither actually achieved himself. Someday I would perhaps hope to produce something myself that reached a little higher theologically than Lewis, probing into questions he did not touch, yet which is written with a simpler mode of expression than MacDonald's. I should get away for an extended period of time to reflect, while reading and inundating myself in Lewis and MacDonald.

What particularly comes to my mind is that we of modern times (as opposed to the first century) are writing and thinking things that have equal validity with early Christian writings. Theirs were put in the Bible, but Paul was just writing letters. Lewis's and MacDonald's thought may be equally valid for teaching Christians about God. Their writings, like those of old, have to stand the test of time and be confirmed by the Spirit. But there is nothing intrinsically that excludes us (because we are modern) from keeping company with Paul insofar as our lives and thoughts with God are concerned, and the writings that result.

As Lewis says, the early Christians thought and reflected and "worked it all out," and the doctrine of the Trinity resulted. But it is not given to us as a fully completed "doctrine." They "worked it out."

In that ongoing process, our continuing to work things out may contain equal validity as the scriptural outworkings of the first century. That is why I believe MacDonald's writings may be on a level with the Epistles (as "may" be other contemporary writings—Drummond, Luther, Calvin, Augustine...who knows?...and only perhaps a very small percentage of such men's works; I can't say who and what they are). I simply feel that it is not intrinsically absurd for us to attempt (not to redefine, but) to <u>further</u> define and elucidate and clarify and "work out" God's ways in and among and having to do with men.

In "Making and Begetting" Lewis explains why—Theology must continue to be further clarified and defined because there are so many wrong ideas prevalent today, and especially in the church—the true Church. Godly people in the true Church, obedient people, nevertheless are filled with traditions and doctrines of men that need to be reexamined and taken to new levels. As Paul took Christian theology (as a new thing vis-à-vis the OT) to new levels, so we (paralleling the Judaism of Paul's day in which the early Christians were bound) need to take today's Pharisaic-infested traditions into new realms. Paul helped Christians of his day do that. Luther helped the Christians of his day do it.

Now is also such a day in the life of the Church. MacDonald may have unlocked the door. But now that door needs to be thrown open wide.

INTRODUCTION

Is *Mere* Christianity enough for a Christian generation rapidly losing its influence in the world?

Between sixty and seventy years ago, what has become one of Christendom's most beloved books, C.S. Lewis's *Mere Christianity*, came to be written.

I use that passive construction because its origins were different than that of most books. Assigning a precise date is impossible for the simple reason that the contents were first given by Lewis on the radio during the Second World War (in the period 1941-1944). When the weekly fifteen-minute addresses began, Lewis was not well known. He was but an obscure university professor of literature. He had not yet published his first bestseller, *The Screwtape Letters,* and was contacted by the BBC on the basis of his 1940 publication, *The Problem of Pain.*

Obscure as he was, however, the series was a "hit."

Lewis's talks were quickly committed to book form. They were published in three stages—the first aptly titled *Broadcast Talks,* followed by *Christian Behaviour* and *Beyond Personality*—in 1942, 1943, and 1944. A single re-titled volume including all three original short books was released in 1952. It was given the title *Mere Christianity* and included a new Preface by the author to the whole.

That was over a half century ago. During this time *Mere Christianity* has exercised a remarkable and singular impact in the Christian world. It has sold multiple millions of copies and been translated at last count into dozens of languages.

Mere Christianity has been influential in my own life and growth on many levels. To call it my "favorite" book describes in a superficial way something that probes far deeper than the enjoyment of what—for anyone interested in the logical underpinnings of the Christian faith—is undeniably a great read. I am not an avid *re*-reader. Most books I read only once. The fact that I have read *Mere Christianity* some six or seven times, at least double the readings I have given any other book (with the possible exception of Thomas Kelly's *A Testament of Devotion,* and George MacDonald's *Malcolm*) places it singularly at the apex of works that have fundamentally altered my outlook of what it means to call myself a "Christian." My primary copy has underlinings (many entire paragraphs!), notes, and annotations on 160 of its 180 pages. Not even my Bible boasts such a high percentage of marked passages.

Lewis's gifts of communication and logic have proved as stimulating as his spiritual insights. His seamless blend of simplicity and profundity has been not only inspirational to my walk of faith, but also illuminating as a wonderfully effective method of communicating truth. Over the years, the example of Lewis's style (working in harmony with the theological depth of his mentor George MacDonald) has been ever before me. I have often thought that if people lived by the principles set forth in *Mere Christianity,* and then followed Lewis's counsel and moved on from *his* writings to feed on those of MacDonald, the man he called his "master," there would never be a need for me to write books at all. Lewis and MacDonald, I felt, said all there was to say. And said it better than anyone else could possibly hope to say it.

MOVING BEYOND "MERE"

A number of years ago, however—as the notes in my copy of *Mere Christianity* quoted in the Foreword attest—I began to revise that assessment. I realized that there was indeed more that needed to be added, as an *addendum* or a *postscript,* to Lewis's groundbreaking work.

In the 1940s, Lewis was addressing a vastly different spiritual climate and cultural milieu. His broadcast talks on the air of the BBC were directed to a "general" audience. In his *The Case For Christianity* (the American title of *Broadcast Talks*), Lewis spoke out of his own experience—to which he liberally referred and which added veracity to his arguments—as one who had come into Christian belief from lifelong *un*belief. His perspective was as an observer, an outsider, attempting to evaluate concisely, rationally, logically, and practically whether or not Christianity was true. That done, he turned to "What Christians Believe." Even here he maintained the same "outsider" vantage point. Such is the flavor of his book, and contributes to the forcefulness of its content. While it is probably true that over the years more "Christians" have read *Mere Christianity* than "non-Christians," in tone Lewis consistently conveys the impression that he is addressing the *unbelieving* world. It is a world he understands well. He gives the impression by implication that he actually feels a closer affiliation with that world than the world of the Christian church. It is this *tone* of kinship with unbelief that contributes to the genius of the book.

One must not forget, as odd as the phrase sounds, that when Lewis drafted the talks that made up the contents of *Mere Christianity*, not only was he an obscure professor, he was still a relatively young believer. He had been an avowed "Christian" less than ten years when first contacted by the BBC. Most of his life had been spent as an atheist. The worldview which informs and gives substance to his progressions of thought are that of a man looking at Christianity from the *outside* trying to make sense of it. Even his use of the term "Christian" often carries the subtle implication that he, Lewis, is standing among the unbelievers trying to put into simple terms what "the Christians" believe.

For example, Lewis opens his chapter entitled Faith by saying, "I must talk in this chapter about what the Christians call Faith. Roughly speaking, the word Faith seems to be used by Christians in two senses or on two levels...it used to puzzle me...that Christians regard faith in this sense..."

He is not exactly admitting to what *he* believes about faith, but rather takes the position of an *observer* trying to weigh the evidence of what "the Christians" think. One notices this subtle use of language throughout. It is this fascinating perspective (sort of half in, half out), growing out of Lewis's life experience, that adds potency and vibrancy to his evaluation of the Christian faith. It is a brilliantly ingenious method. Lewis gives his readers room to maneuver by pretending to be more impartial than he really is.

Yet...though it seems a sacrilege to say about a book one admires so highly, some years ago I began to recognize an anachronistic element in this approach. With it came an awareness of a corresponding limitation inherent in the content of *Mere Christianity* as a whole. Don't get me wrong. I value that content as much as ever and will continue to re-read *Mere Christianity* every few years until the day I die. Eventually I may have notes and underlinings on *every* page! I recognize, however, that what Lewis has given us is not in itself *enough*.

It represents a beginning. A wonderful beginning. But once people come *into* the Christian faith, as Lewis did, what then? How do they *continue* to evaluate and sift and make sense of the ideas of Christianity—not from the outside...but from the *inside*?

As I began to ask myself that question, I began to reflect on the need for an addendum that picks up where *Mere Christianity* leaves off.

WHAT IS GOING ON INSIDE THE ROOMS?

The gulf separating the times in which Lewis wrote and our own is no mere gulf of sixty or seventy years, it is a chasm of altered outlook and perspective that might as well be centuries wide. It is a tribute to the timelessness of Lewis's writings that they ring with such vibrancy today. How many other Christian writers of the 1940s are still being read so enthusiastically in our time? Lewis is not just being read, his books continue to sell in the millions! His ongoing appeal is astonishing and diverse.

Yet too, we must recognize how vastly different things are today—both *outside* and *inside* faith. If he was just starting to write in today's climate, as an unknown, *without* a surging worldwide fifty year legendary reputation behind him...if no one had heard of him, would Lewis's witty, humorous, occasionally sarcastic cheek play so well to a world, not only more lost in its unbelief, but far more cynical than that of two generations ago? Would non-Christians throughout Britain tune in to their radios, unwilling to miss a single episode of his broadcasts about the existence of God and the elemental doctrines of Christianity? Would Lewis in today's societal climate be found on the cover of *Time* as he was in 1947?

Maybe so. But I think the question legitimately arises whether the non-Christian world would even take notice. A radio show about God and Christianity *today*...it would be lucky to get a 1% market share. I doubt if modernism would so easily laugh, or find Lewis's folksy treatment and syntax—*on the level with the man who says he is a poached egg, idealistic gas, Christianity and water, morality and mousetraps, our old friend the devil—hoofs and horns and all, the atonement and vitamins, crazy old tubs, an ordinary decent egg*—so convincing. *We* love it, of course. But it is very possible that the non-Christian world would ridicule Lewis rather than admire him.

Within Christendom it is different. This is clearly where Lewis's greatest impact over the past half-century has been felt. Christians adore his style and his shrewd, simple, intellectual, inclusive vision of Christianity. And if he was ridiculed by the general public, it would make him all the *more* popular in the church...as if he could be any more popular than he already is! His unique style has helped Christians understand the fundamentals of their faith in ways too numerous and penetrating to enumerate and continues to do so. Yet those rational foundations by Lewis's own admission, though profound, are extremely basic. He makes little attempt to carry any discussion into much theological depth as did his Scots mentor. Repeatedly Lewis emphasizes (protesting a little *too* much) that he is *not* a theologian. He prefers, he says, to leave the theological profundities of Christian ideas to "more talented authors" than he.

Fair enough. But what of those areas where more help is needed? Once inside the great "house" of Christianity Lewis describes in his Preface, how *does* one evaluate between the ideas in the various "rooms?"

> ..."*mere*" *Christianity is here put forward...*" Lewis writes, "*more like a hall out of which doors open into several rooms. If I can bring anyone into that hall I shall have done what I attempted. But it is in the rooms, not in the hall, that there are fires and chairs and meals. The hall is a place to wait in, a place from which to try the various doors, not a place to life in...and, of course, even in the hall, you must begin trying to obey the rules which are common to the whole house.*" [2]

If Lewis's intent is merely to bring people into the outer hall, which he has done admirably and effectively, how are we to move beyond "mere" (that is, *basic* or *fundamental*) Christianity into deep and bold and practical lifelong Christianity *in* the "house?"

Another aspect of Lewis's approach also necessitates renewed scrutiny and evaluation.

The needs of today's reader are radically different than those Lewis was addressing when he spoke on national radio to the secular population of Great Britain 65 years ago. While any generalization is dangerous, it can safely be said that the church of today, in both Britain and the United States, is filled with millions of people who have been Christians, been in the church, been in Lewis's "house" of belief most of their lives.

Having come into belief from the outside and thus addressing his audience from that perspective, Lewis spoke as if addressing non-Christians. But he is now, through our written record of his talks, speaking primarily to *Christians*. His astonishing book sales every year (with the exception of *Narnia*) are selling predominantly within the *Christian* community and its fringes. I have not once in forty years seen a C.S. Lewis title on the shelves of an airport bookstore. Clearly the sheer volume of Lewis's sales insures that many of his books do find their way into the hands of non-Christians, and many of these turn to Christianity as a result. Yet it remains undeniable that *most* of Lewis's readers have been raised in an environment of a lifetime's familiarity with Christianity's ideas. Their need is not to know whether or not Christianity is true. They accept that. They need to know how to evaluate between the myriad theologic orthodoxies of the many camps of Christian thought.

Even more importantly, they need to know how to evaluate their *own* beliefs with intellectual profundity and sagacity. This is something Christians are simply *not* taught to do...in any of the rooms.

Building upon Lewis's foundation, that is my purpose: To help those who have been Christians for years, perhaps all their lives, to evaluate the ideas of their faith in fresh ways.

I think of it as bold Christian living beyond the box.

In that "beyond the box" living, I identify five principles that serve as road markers on the quest toward bold Christianity:

1) Ongoing Revelation,
2) Multi-Dimensioned Scriptural Truth,
3) The Continuing Quest,
4) Doctrinal Stepping Stones,
5) God's Eternal Symphony.

These five, and the scriptural words and concepts associated with them, will be our focus as we progress together.

Lewis addressed those who were in similar circumstances to his own. I am addressing those who are in similar circumstances to *my* own—who have been in the church a long time and who need encouragement (as I did) to think through the parameters of their belief system beyond the learned boundaries of the particular "room" of the great house where they happen to find themselves.

In that sense, the undergirding rationale of this book is exactly the same as was the foundation for *Mere Christianity*—to examine the ideas of Christianity logically and with an open mind and common sense. But whereas Lewis began outside the house to examine the veracity of the structure as a whole, I take as my starting point that most of you reading this book are probably Christians. The task before us is to try to figure out how much truth, and how much error, exists within the specific precepts and doctrines of our rooms of belief.

To accomplish that takes what I term "bold thinking" Christianity.

PART 1

ONGOING REVELATION

God's revelation is neither fixed nor static. It is dynamic, progressive, and expanding in every successive generation.

Key Scriptural Concepts:

WALK, THINK, MIND OF CHRIST, BOLDNESS, DRIFT, TRADITION, SEARCH

ONE

Walking With God

Reflections On Lifetime Priorities

"For we are his workmanship, created in Christ Jesus for good works...
that we περιπατησωμεν (should walk) in them...Therefore, be imitators of God,
as beloved children, and περιπατειτε (walk) in love,
as Christ loved us and gave himself for us, a fragrant offering and sacrifice to God."
—Ephesians 2:10; 5:1-2

περιπατεω: PERIPATEO — *Walk*

PERIPATEO can signify to walk in both the literal physical or the figurative sense. In that it is just like its English counterpart. In its nearly one hundred appearances in the New Testament, it is used about half and half. The majority of its figurative uses come from Paul and John. In its figurative sense, it is simply synonymous with the conduct of one's life, or *live*, which is the rendition given in Ephesians 4:17: "...you must no longer PERIPATEIN (live) as the Gentiles do." PERIPATEO is translated in a variety of ways in 1 Corinthians 7:17. The Revised Standard has it: "Let every one *lead the life* which the Lord has assigned to him, and in which God has called him." The King James more accurately renders it: "As God hath distributed to every man, as the Lord hath called every one, so *let him walk.*" Perhaps the highest New Testament challenges to the Christian to PERIPATEO with God are found in Galatians 5:16: "But I say, PERIPATEITE (walk) in the Spirit..."; 1 Thessalonians 2:12: "PERIPATEIN (walk) worthily of God,"; and 2 John 6: "And this is love, that we PERIPATOMEN (should walk) according to his commandments."

MY MOTHER AND I USED TO PLAY A LITTLE GAME. I wouldn't consider her *old* until admitting I was *middle-aged*. And likewise, she wouldn't call me middle-aged until she was ready to consider herself old.

We both went along with it. And actually neither of us ever fully owned up to the facts.

But time does pass.

Several years ago my mother said, "I look in the mirror and I can hardly believe it. I remind myself of my mother when *she* got old."

I have to admit a similar sensation when I see pictures of myself from twenty years ago, or even ten, and realize, "Hey—what's happening to me? I don't look like that anymore!"

My mother is now gone, and I am well past sixty. No doubt many young people would say I had bypassed middle age altogether, and would call me positively *ancient*.

I was aware over a decade ago that a transition occurred when I stepped beyond the threshold of the half-century mark. I could not help becoming pensive about the years spent and the pathways trod in reaching such a symbolic point. I knew I was standing at a crossroads. I looked back as well as forward, wondering if I had lived my first fifty years well, and wondering, too, what the future might hold.

When I passed that milestone, that thing we call old age seemed neither so old nor so remote. Nor did it seem quite so odious. I found myself, in fact, more and more anticipatory of what age truly signified—not the approach of *death*, but the preparation for *birth* into eternal life.

Most young men and women in their teens and twenties, when vision is unbounded, energy high, and no goal seems impossible, dream of great accomplishments and worldwide impact. As the years pass, reality causes such dreams to grow quieter and more inward. And hopefully more eternal. In my own life, a sense of my failings has played an intrinsic role in that process. Perhaps failure is a necessary component in the equation of growth. How else can Christlikeness come to outweigh worldly objectives in one's value structure?

I once wanted to change the world. Like Winston Churchill, I wanted to change the world before I was thirty.

But I didn't. Reality always comes calling. Maturity helps you gradually view your life and the person you are with increasing perspective. The years make you slowly less blind to your own faults. As a result, the main world I now want to turn upside down lies within myself—the world of my own inner being...my choices and attitudes and character.

Though my old man still exerts itself with annoying vigor, my ambition now is well summarized by my mentor George MacDonald: "It is enough that the man who refuses to assert himself, seeking no recognition by men, leaving the care of his life to the Father, and occupying himself with the will of the Father, shall find himself, by and by, at home in his Father's house, with all the Father's property his."

Saying that, however, does not change the fact that passing sixty was an even more sobering experience than passing fifty. One can cross life's other milestone birthdays, from eighteen and twenty-one, to thirty, and even forty, still maintaining the bravado, and declare, "My best years are still in front of me."

But when you round the corner of fifty, then sixty—and how quickly I will be inserting the words *seventy* into this sentence—those words don't fall quite so easily from the lips. When you realize how quickly forty gave way to sixty, and realize that seventy is bearing down like a freight train, suddenly you recognize what for some is a very chilling fact:

You're looking in the distance toward the end of life's road.

WHAT SHOULD LIFE MEAN?

Sure, there's plenty of time. Perhaps your best years *are* ahead. But you can no longer pretend that old age will *never* come as we all did during the hubristic days of youth.

It *will* come.

And it *is* coming at a more rapid pace than any of us feel completely comfortable with. The sun may still be high in the sky, but there's no pretending it is still on the rise. The apex has been reached and it's heading down toward the horizon.

If you're a fatalist, then the response is typically along the lines of, "Everybody ages, so what. You're going to get old and eventually die. You and me and everybody else. Nothing you can do about it. So deal with it."

An adequate response, I suppose, if it satisfies you to think that way.

But I want to know what it's all about, what it *means*.

I want to make sure, when I get to the end of that road and the inexorably sinking sun finally sets on my earthly days, that my life has counted for some of the right things.

I have always been of an introspective bent. I suppose when one tends toward the shy and melancholy, that goes with the territory. It's probably also an occupational hazard for writers who spend their days trying to discover what life is all about. So the threshold of fifty plunged me into a season of evaluation—looking at where I'd been, where I was going. It sent me on a new search, as it were, for the *meaning*, the *essence*, of life.

And now, looking back over *sixty* years—that's enough to give a sense of perspective that is not possible when you're younger. The years still ahead, of course, will add to that perspective geometrically with every passing year. I am keenly aware, therefore, that my reflections now represent a focusing that will continue the older I get.

Yet though the process may never be complete, there are times when it is beneficial to pause for a thoughtful glance around, to take stock of the journey thus far, and perhaps, if needed, make adjustments on the roadmap leading toward the future.

What does life really mean? Or perhaps the question ought to be: What is life *supposed* to mean? And: Are we or are we not falling in with that purpose?

I have thought about such things before. I am a writer. I work with ideas, thoughts, life-themes. If I happen to tell stories in the process, it is only because the story of *life* itself intrigues me. This involves growth, the operation of spiritual processes upon heart and brain, decisions and choices and their impact upon the paths an individual's feet take. Above all it involves the attempt to understand and chronicle that most delicate and hidden mystery within the human story—the quiet, personal, invisible response of the heart and soul to its Maker, its Savior, its Lord.

Therefore, as a writer I have long asked the kinds of questions that have filled me recently. But when you turn the questions upon yourself, the nature of the inquiry suddenly changes. I now find my *own* life caught up in the very themes and cross currents till now reserved for my characters. It is *my* existence whose purposes and meanings I hunger to understand. I have become a character in my own drama. What else can I do with *this* life's story but try to get to the bottom of it?

Michael Phillips

THREE INCOMPLETE PRIORITIES

There's nothing new in wondering about the meaning of life. Every high school and university commencement speaker addresses what we call "priorities in life." But I think most of our efforts and reflections tend to be short-sighted. What do I want to get done, achieve, work toward now, next week, next year? Where do I want to be five years from now, ten...even twenty?

Not only are we short-sighted, we are *accomplishment, experience,* and *pleasure* driven. Affluent western modernism has infected us with a false sense of what is good and worthwhile. These three elements bring that faulty imbalance into stark clarity.

What can I get done?

What do I want to experience?

How can I carve out more time for personal leisure and pleasure?

These are the three pillars of twentieth and now twenty-first century mankind's frame of reference toward life—*doing, experiencing, enjoying.*

These also undergird our *spiritual* perspectives when we talk about goals and priorities. The religion of present-day western Christendom is a *do, experience,* and *fun* religion—be it conservative or liberal, evangelical or Catholic, Pentecostal or Anglican, Mormon or Orthodox, Baptist or Presbyterian—to varying degrees across the spectrum. It isn't too often these days that we hear evangelists say, "Come...join the cause—become a Christian and die with me." More often it's along the lines of, "Come join the party!"

During my season of introspection, I have looked at my own values, especially with the first two of these three factors in mind that have led to our culture's imbalance. To what degree, I have asked myself, has my own life been infected with a false sense of the lasting significance of my *doings,* my *experiences,* and, to a lesser degree, the *enjoyment* I have had in life. And if these three incomplete priorities do not represent the *summum bonum*—the supreme good—what then instead should represent one's life-priority on a higher and more permanent plane?

As a Christian, there might have been many ways I would have answered the question of ultimate "priority" at various stages throughout my life. *To serve the Lord* is a favorite expression that describes how many would sum up their goal in life. But immediately one observes the *do*-focus. I therefore wonder if it falls short of giving us an adequate grip on a truly summital perspective.

To *experience* God...to *minister* to others...to enjoy *relationship* with the Lord...to *know* God more intimately...to *love and be kind* to those around me...to be Christ's *disciple*...to live in *fellowship* with God's people...to *study* the Word...to do the *Lord's will*...these and many such phrases express aspects of what we call our faith. I have used many of them myself, and still would. Doing the Lord's will...being Christ's disciple—of course these remain pivotal in my thinking. To an extent they certainly represent high scriptural objectives.

But I find myself asking if even these rise to the apex. Can we not see the emphasis, again—hidden between the words—on the personal experience, the blessings received, the enjoyment of corporate fellowship with others on journeys similar to our own, the *active* life of western modernism's particular brand of this thing we call Christianity.

THE ULTIMATE GOOD

I find myself hungering for a deeper foundation of meaning than any of these three passions of modernism quite fulfill. Many of them may be worthy objectives for the immediate and even intermediate future. But will they matter when I am lying on my deathbed?

What I learned, what I read, the marginal notes I added to the underlinings in my Bible, the knowledge I gained, the scriptures I memorized, the material I gave away, the church activities I was involved in, the hours I spent in ministry, the meetings I attended, the possessions I owned, the insights the Lord gave me, the lives I influenced, the Bible studies I was part of, the prayers I prayed, the places I visited, the sermons I heard, the quiet times I enjoyed, the music I listened to, the leisure I enjoyed, the time and money I gave to the Lord's work, and in my own case the books I wrote...will any of it matter then?

Some of these *may* matter.

I suspect many of them, however, will not. How can we discover the difference? How can we make sure that we are investing our time and energy now in those things that contain *lasting* import?

A WORTHY TOMBSTONE AMBITION

What is the scriptural bedrock that *will* matter during those last days of life? What perhaps will turn out to have been the only thing that ever mattered at all?

In other words...what of *lifetime* priorities?

Not the interim goals with which I was consumed when I was 25 or 33 or at present in my 60s. Not where I want to be in five years or ten. But where do I want to be when all life's five-year plans are gone—when those that were accomplished have become dust along with those that were not...when successes have vanished along with failures, when all life's experiences and knowledge and blessings have faded into memory?

Perhaps the question in its starkest form reduces to this: What is the single thing I could most hope to appear on my tombstone?

When Judy and I are in Scotland, because most cemeteries have traditionally surrounded churches, we literally walk through a conglomeration of graves and tombstones, crooked and slanted, some half falling over, every Sunday as we make our way through the churchyard to the church door. Some of them are two and three hundred years old, their inscriptions completely gone. But the stones that can still be read always cause me a moment or two of pensive reflection about the lives represented. Some of the inscriptions are so touching and speak of lives of devoted service and dedication as Christians. Actually the whole mystical aura of a church rising high in the middle of two hundred or more grave markers is rather wonderful—the great cloud of silent witnesses is a visible truth every moment. You get a sense of history, spiritual history, the history of individual lives, that is not possible anywhere else.

It is a nostalgic and sobering experience to ponder: What will *my* grave marker say? How will those left after me sum up *my* life?

There will be no room to tell the story of my life. All that will be gone. What legacy is left? What is the one thing that sums up a worthwhile existence?

The Bible gives just such an epitaph. May we be worthy to have it said of us.

"Noah was a righteous man...and he walked with God." (Genesis 6:9)

He walked with God.

The words themselves echo with the strength and dignity of a life well-lived on this earth. All the little things that we made our concerns through the years are suddenly dwarfed into insignificance alongside those mighty words of lifetime stature.

Say those four words slowly aloud. Do they not positively convey the strength of a rock ten times the size of Gibraltar, a lasting rock of purpose anchored in the foundation stone of eternity itself. Of all the things that life eventually strips away, for one to whom they apply, those words remain untouchable.

Will that be able to be said of you...of me? Will they think to put it on our tombstones?

We often say that there is nothing you take with you. But that's not completely true. Having walked with God *is* a treasure that goes with you beyond the grave.

Surely such was the purpose in God's heart when he created us—that he would have beings to walk in fellowship with him in the full magnificent maturity of their created manhood and womanhood. This is exactly the injunction Paul reaffirms when writing to the Ephesians. He tells us to "imitate" God by *walking* in love and good works. It is a *walk* identified by the sacrifice of Christlikeness, which is a "fragrant offering" to God.

Can you imagine anything more precious at the end of your sojourn on earth than for it to be said of your life that it was a *fragrant offering* to God!

Sadly, it will *not* be said of most of the race of created human beings that it walked with God while on the earth, and offered him the fragrant perfume of sacrificial Christlikeness. We are a race that has decided to live on its own terms rather than walk in obedience to our Maker. Many will not learn to know and walk with God until they cross through the doorway of death. It may be said of them ten thousand years from now. But it will not be said that the process began now, in this life, where God purposes it to begin.

However...it *will* be said of a few of our number—they of that rare and singular breed who chose a different path—when the days of their earthly lives draw to a close: "There is a man, there is a woman...who *walked with God*."

It is a lofty goal to think about. I am not sure it will be said of me. At present I am aware of far too much of my self to think such a thing possible. But the hunger after such a high calling fills me with a hopeful energy to focus the eyes of my spirit on lifetime objectives rather than passing ones, and upon the foundational priority of walking with God most of all.

THE FIRST STEP

The imagery of *walking* as descriptive of a spiritual life lived in daily harmony with one's Creator is significant on so many levels.

To be able to walk at all requires being able to take the vital first step. The initial step in any endeavor is always the most important, the most frightening, the step that requires the most decisiveness and courage. That first step in the spiritual life is the step of setting oneself to know God aright—to understand who he is, who we are in relation to him, and why we are here and how he expects us to live.

It is a step that requires bold *thinking*.

No one learns to περιπατεω with God by accident. No one discovers who God truly is and where they stand in relation to him by accident. The men and women of history who indeed learned to walk with God took their first forays into such a life by learning to *think* correctly about him and about themselves.

Every revered man and women in the spiritual annals of humankind—from Noah and Job to Moses and Elijah to Peter and John, even Jesus himself, as well as all those intrepid Catholic saints and Protestant thinkers and Orthodox Fathers—learned to walk with God by thinking boldly about his nature and his ways.

They did not simply absorb the doctrinal tenets of a learned faith by rote. They were well-practiced in what Peter calls "girding up the loins of their minds."

They were bold thinkers.

God calls us to follow in their footsteps, and thus take our first steps in learning to walk with him.

Learning to Know God Aright

In 1942, C.S. Lewis wrote: *"It is no good asking for a simple religion. After all, real things are not simple. They look simple, but they are not...And if you are prepared to stop there, well and good. But if you are not...then you must be prepared for something difficult."* [3]

The challenge before Christians in the third millennium A.D. is to take Lewis's words seriously. But many do not. They intellectualize his brilliant logic, but pay little personal heed to the content contained within that logic, and the imperative of obedience toward which Lewis continually points.

Lewis follows the above quote: *"Very often...this silly procedure is adopted by people...who, consciously or unconsciously, want to destroy Christianity. Such people put up a version of Christianity suitable for a child of six and make that the object of their attack."*

Sadly, however, in the generations since, it has been the Christian world as much as the non-Christian that has "put up a version of Christianity suitable for a child of six." Christians in our time have forgotten the vital first lesson of our spiritual forebears of generations past—how to gird up the loins of the mind to *think* boldly about God and his ways.

In these observations may be discerned the faint echo of Lewis's spiritual mentor George MacDonald, who in 1885 wrote, *"How have we learned Christ? It ought to be a startling thought, that we may have learned him wrong. That must be far worse than not to have learned him at all: his place is occupied by a false Christ, hard to exorcise! The point is, whether we have learned Christ as he taught himself, or as men have taught him who thought they understood, but did not understand him. Do we think we know him—with notions fleshly, after low, mean human fancies and explanations, or do we indeed know him—after the spirit, in our measure as God knows him? The Christian religion, throughout its history, has been open to more corrupt misrepresentation than ever the Jewish could be, for as it is higher and wider, so must it yield larger scope to corruption:—have we learned Christ in false statements and corrupted lessons about him, or have we learned himself? Nay, true or false, is only our brain full of things concerning him, or does he dwell himself in our hearts, a learnt, and ever being learnt lesson, the power of our life?"* [4]

TWO

THINKING FOR OURSELVES—
A FOUNDATION TO GET AT TRUTH

Assessing Truth with Humility, Balance, and Perspective

> "Do you not yet νοειτε (understand)? Do you not remember...?
> How is it that you fail to νοειτε (perceive)?
> —Matthew 16:9, 11

νοεω: NOEO—*Think*

The Greek verb NOEO means literally "to direct one's mind to." It is active not passive, capturing the accountability of personal and decisive engagement required. To *think* in this active sense one must *direct* the mind with force and energy, a far different thing than passively allowing the mind to fill with random non-thoughts, or with only the ideas and opinions of others. In the New Testament, NOEO and its forms is often translated *perceive* or *understand*.

The noun form, NOUS, is "mind" as distinguished from the physical brain. The brain may be a mere reactive or passive portion of the body that happens to be located in the head. The *mind*, however, notes the power of the brain that is engaged by the will and directed to think, analyze, make decisions, weigh alternatives, form judgments, draw conclusions...and perceive and understand. Both the noun form (NOUS, mind) and the verb form (NOEO, think) are active, and intended as integral ingredients of vigorous Christianity.

Overlooked by many is the frequency in the gospels where Jesus exhorts his listeners (more than mere "exhortation," *commanding* it) with some form of: *Listen carefully, be clear-minded, apply yourself to* think, learn, and understand. Along with *Be watchful and alert,* these commands are given by Jesus with more frequency than the command to love. Jesus knew that his disciples had to learn to *think* with clarity. His oft-used "Behold" indicates far more than seeing with the eyes but always implies "inner vision"—look earnestly, contemplate, regard, perceive, apprehend. Passive, unthinking, unperceiving, lazy non-thinking discipleship does not exist in the New Testament. Thus the clear frustration with his disciples evident in Jesus' tone in Matthew 16: "Do you not yet νοεῖτε (perceive)? How is it that you fail to νοεῖτε (perceive)? He *expected* them to think. Wise thinking was part of the package.

E*VERYONE HAS HEARD PEOPLE QUARRELLING. Sometimes it sounds funny and sometimes it sounds merely unpleasant; but however it sounds, I believe we can learn something very important from listening to the kinds of things they say.* [5]

With these words, C.S. Lewis introduced himself to the British public on the air of the BBC one Wednesday evening in the first week of August of 1941. They are also the words millions of readers since have encountered upon opening to Chapter 1 of Lewis's immortal classic *Mere Christianity*, the book that grew out of Lewis's wartime radio addresses.

These two sentences, and the shrewd sequence of ideas which follow, tell us several extremely interesting things. Most obvious is what they tell us about Lewis himself. They reveal a master, nay, genius, at work, subtly combining profundity and simplicity with devastatingly penetrating insight. For in the pages that follow, Lewis parlays this everyday observation into one of the most incisive arguments for the existence of God ever devised. Philosophically unexcelled, Lewis yet takes his listeners through a series of logical progressions with a clarity and lucidity that anyone can understand. The interweaving of wit and humor provide the icing on the cake. It is simply a remarkable display of perception and communication skill.

TWO ERAS...TWO KINDS OF PEOPLE

Lewis's opening salvo and what follows also reveals something about the time. Christians and non-Christians alike *did* follow his train of thought, and many were persuaded by his argument. They followed the logic and were convinced of its truth because absolutes held sway as an undergirding basis for the way people thought.

Lewis's apologetic was based on absolutist thinking. When he adds in the next paragraph, "The other man very seldom replies: 'To hell with your standard,'" Lewis is acknowledging this fact—that absolutes existed in the 1940s as a foundation for logic, dialogue, and reason. This is reinforced by the title of the first series of his talks, "Right and Wrong as a Clue to the Meaning of the Universe." The words *right* and *wrong* meant something. There were, as Lewis goes on to explore, "absolute standards" everyone was aware of.

Seventy years have gone by since. Everything has now changed. Absolute standards in the general secular culture have vanished with the wind. Ours is an age of relativism in every field and discipline. This relativism pervades morals, ethics, politics, logic, personal accountability, finances, entertainment, government, advertising, education, law, justice, relationships...you cannot look at *anything* in our society without seeing relativism at work.

There remain but a few isolated segments of society where absolutist thinking still has meaning. Some Christians, and those hungry hearts who have begun to perceive the bankruptcy of modernity's secular relativism, are still able to read Lewis's argument and absorb its powerful truths. But on the streets of New York, San Francisco, London, Paris or Berlin where moral and ethical relativism reigns supreme, where hearts are too self-absorbed to hunger for God, where absolute concepts like *right* and *wrong* no longer contain practical meaning...modern men and women *would* say, "To hell with your standard." Whether they could even follow Lewis's ratiocinations is doubtful. But even if modernists could follow his logic, Lewis's conclusions would mean nothing to them. Absolute truth in their world is a non-existent mirage.

Christians facing this titanic shift, and the assumptions it brings to modern discourse, are in a precarious position, though most don't realize it. Because Christians aren't being taught to think with acumen themselves, these trends have also infiltrated the church like an invisible fog. That is why I said above that *some* Christians are able to make sense of Lewis's arguments. Many would not be able to. They are relativist thinkers too. Relativism exists throughout Christendom no less than in the general culture, with equally lethal results.

That is the reason for this book—because the challenge for Christians to equip themselves to think boldly about the precepts of their faith has never been so imperative as at this critical hour.

Having taken a glance back at the imagery Lewis used to begin his treatise on *mere* Christianity, let us move forward in our discussion of *bold* Christianity, taking the liberty of borrowing his idea and a few of his words to present a new image. It is one you will recognize as surely as Lewis's listeners recognized his:

Everyone has stood at a store counter watching a clerk punch buttons so that his or her cash register will automatically tell what change to give you from your $20 bill for a $19.75 sale. It looks funny to see them wait for the .25 on the screen rather than just hand you a quarter, but however it looks I believe we can learn something very important from such incidents that take place all around us.

It is the difference between these two images that we must ponder with insight. People listening to Lewis's words seventy years ago were able to think. People today can't. Lewis's image addressed his listeners' logic and ability to follow an argument and draw intelligent conclusions. Today's cash registers are designed to address the fact that people *can't* use logic to draw intelligent conclusions. The two images illuminate what we're up against. The momentum of our times is moving with unstoppable force in the opposite direction from perceptive thought. The moment we try to actually start *thinking* about things, we will be swimming upstream against our entire culture.

How many times have you encountered a picture or symbol or icon (on a traffic sign, some computer or other electronic instruction, or trying to make sense of the installation sheet—"Some assembly required"—for the cabinet you bought at Wal-Mart) that actually makes it *more* difficult and *less* intuitive to understand than had old-fashioned *words* been used? More than once I've sat bewildered in an unfamiliar rental car, staring in perplexity at the controls, unable even to get the thing turned on! Television remotes are the worst for their iconic confusion. Who can make sense of even half the buttons?

(I suppose one might ask who *I* am to be talking about clear headed thinking when I can't even turn on a car or use all the features of a remote control! Maybe they have a point!)

In our time, words are no longer used to convey information. They're too complicated.

This is the difference between Lewis's era and ours. In his time it was assumed that people could read and use their brains. That assumption, like absolutes and right and wrong, is gone with the wind.

Christians are caught in the crosshairs of this decline. Because in large measure they are getting their beliefs and doctrines just like customers get change at a convenience store—from spiritual cash registers. Push the button and out pops the doctrine intact.

Michael Phillips

CHRISTIANITY LITE

We live in a lethally superficial age. Contrary as it seems, in this era of almost superhuman technological achievement, the facility to *think* judiciously is on the endangered skills list. Our computerized culture has rendered us dependent on machines to do our thinking for us. With a few deft keystrokes, literally the whole world can be brought up on screen in front of our eyes.

It's called the information age. All the data anyone could ever want is instantly accessible. No need to engage the mind to figure things out, weigh ideas, and arrive at conclusions. Computers and calculators do it for us. Raw knowledge has replaced introspection. Our culture has made a god of this tidal wave of information. People don't even *try* to νοεω anymore. They don't have to.

This doesn't mean that modern men and women are any better or worse than the people of other eras, only that influences are changing us in ways we do not recognize. The multiplication tables are a defunct requirement in our schools. Why bother when calculators are allowed when taking tests. It won't be long before young people no longer have the ability to read a roadmap. Will atlases be the next thing to go, following word-instructions and the multiplication table?

We are losing our little gray cells from atrophy. We are taught (in school and in church) to solve equations by formula...but we are not taught to think for ourselves.

The world is full of intelligent people. The world is full of gifted people. The world is full of knowledgeable people. The world even contains a surprising number of compassionate people. But as Richard Foster clarifies, the desperate need of our time is for *deep* people, what he calls "genuinely changed" people. [6]

People who can *think*...Christians who refuse to be content with spoon-fed formulas of belief.

Such cognitively forceful men and women are few and far between. It is a genuine treasure when you discover one. Yet when you do, the religious community eyes his or her bold convictions with suspicion. They would rather have status quo spirituality. Perhaps we should not be surprised. Over a century ago the Dane Soren Kierkegaard wrote, "When a man more powerfully stirred than the rest steps forward in our age, a man who sets the price of being a Christian at only a fifth of the price the gospel puts on it, everyone cries, 'Look out for that man! Do not read what he writes...do not talk with him...he is a dangerous man.'"

Because of my work with George MacDonald, through the years I have encountered this mindset more than once, including churches and schools where, if not actually banned, the leadership has *warned* its flock against reading MacDonald's work. Why? Because he challenged the status quo of 19th century Scottish Calvinism and asked if there was more in God's heart to accomplish than what was revealed by the formulas of Calvinism's memorized catechisms. How intriguing that C.S. Lewis's books have sold 200 million, yet his spiritual mentor, the man he called his "master," is banned in some circles. That gives you something to think about!

In the hundred and five years since MacDonald's death, even in the forty-five years since that of C.S. Lewis, the state of affairs has worsened. We have become a generation of Christians almost incapable of the level of brainpower necessary to understand either ourselves or truth on a larger scale. We have succumbed to the same drift and decline as has the culture around us. And because we have allowed ourselves to become shallow non-thinkers, spiritual formulae is very appealing. It eliminates the need to think, or turn the light of self-reflection inward where it is most desperately needed of all.

Nowhere has this modern shift away from vigorous thinking caused more misunderstanding about who God is and what are his purposes than in the two almost diametrically opposite wings of the church represented by evangelicalism and Catholicism. Personal inquiry that deviates from the standard model of formula-doctrines is nearly unknown in the ranks of evangelical and Catholic Christendom. Though they are not quite so officially codified, evangelicals have their own learned catechisms as surely as did the rigid Scottish Calvinism of MacDonald's youth 175 years ago.

Add water and you don't even have to stir...instant prophecy, instant salvation, instant sanctification. Look it up in a book by your favorite theologian and read "What Evangelicals believe," or "What Catholics believe." Learn the formula and *voila*—a fully intact belief system, no mental work required. No wrestling with ideas, no struggling with doubts, no implicational reasoning, no tireless research to resolve scriptural inconsistencies, no study of apologetics, no humble contemplation to root out one's own blind spots and immaturities, no intellectually rigorous engaging of the culture around us, no pushing suppositions to logical conclusions.

None of that is necessary. The average Catholic or evangelical believer doesn't know what the words *apologetics* and *logical conclusions* even mean. The Apologetics shelf in many Christian bookstores has been replaced with How-To, Self-Help, and Twelve Step books to meet every need. *Christianity Lite.*

The creed possesses an answer for everything. Don't *think*...just consult the formula.

Thus the vicious cycle: Spiritual formulae breeds shallow thought... shallow thought leads to more formulae.

It may be that this dearth of spiritual depth is more than a little responsible for the current wave of interest and conversion into the relatively new "American" expression of ancient Orthodoxy. A friend recently commented to me of his own fascination with this phenomenon: "People are hungry for something *deeper* with God. I've been in the evangelical church for twenty years, but the superficiality is just finally too much. I need more."

Yet one cannot help but wonder if an expression of the Christian faith so dependent on ritual, and which attaches such significance to a reverence for icons, however justified its reasons for using them to remember the saints of history, can ultimately provide the reality people like my friend are seeking. That it is doing so for many at present is undeniable. Time will tell what will be the long term impact within the church at large.

A FACADE OF INTELLECTUALISM

We don't recognize the trap for what it is because the onslaught of information and technology to which we are exposed, like superficial thinking, *also* breeds formulae, adding to the vicious cycle a subtle masquerade of intellectualism.

Because we know so many scriptural facts *about* our faith (whether it be Catholic, Evangelical, Orthodox, or whatever else), and because the seeming scriptural proofs are so apparently convincing, and because their proponents speak with such dignified authority, we assume an intellectualism that isn't there.

Much of our doctrinal dogma is in fact not intellectually solvent at all, but logically deficient and even scripturally erroneous. Yet those who should be combating such trends most strenuously flatter themselves that *they* are immune from the problem. Pastors and priests, teachers and evangelists, yes, and even we who author books to enlighten God's people—all who claim to have the tenets of the canon down cold, who defend them with scriptural precision, and who pass them on with apparent authority...these urgently need liberation from formula-thinking for the sake of those who hang on their every word. Yet it is often those most dependent on the rote recipes of spirituality who remain most unaware that *formula*, rather than an intellectually integritous exploration of Scripture, undergirds what they call their faith.

How sadly indicting are George MacDonald's piercing words from his era, warning us to learn what the passage of more than an entire century has failed to teach us: "If those who set themselves to explain the various theories of Christianity had set themselves instead to do the will of the Master, how different would the world be now." Thus, MacDonald goes on, "Theologians have done more to hide the Gospel of Christ than any of its adversaries." [7]

The result has been extreme...and invisibly ruinous to Christianity's witness. Behind a facade of prosperity, vibrancy, church expansion, political clout, and exuberant liveliness, Christians have lost sight of the necessity to *think*. And the world recognizes this atrophy of intellectual muscle, even if we do not. Evangelicals see *Left Behind* advertised on network television and given a few seconds of air time on "60 Minutes," or see *The Prayer of Jabez* or *The Purpose Driven Life* or *The Shack* on secular bestseller lists, and flatter themselves that the world is listening, that a "witness" is going out.

We don't stop to consider what the world thinks about it. Nor do we pause to consider the horrendous implications *against* our witness and the cause of Christ if the messages contained within such publications, as a few examples among many, *aren't* accurate indicators of self-denying Christlike discipleship.

How much damage to the cause of truth and to the cause of Jesus Christ will we have done by allowing and encouraging such phenomena without pausing to subject them to truth on a larger scale? How great will be the stumbling blocks in the way of truth from the circulation throughout the world of hundreds of million of books of formula-doctrines...*if their foundations are faulty!*

Catholics flatter themselves with equal shortsightedness to see how the whole world revered Pope John Paul II and paid tribute to his life after his passing, and assume a vibrancy and reality to Catholicism as a whole that doesn't exist at all. Sadly, the discipleship-faith of the humble man known as John Paul is not being lived by 99% of his ardent admirers. Nor were the uncompromising standards voiced by Pope Benedict admired and embraced by Catholicism as a whole. Thank God for the 1%! But Catholics must not be naïve any more than evangelicals about the cancerous superficiality of its overall programme and focus.

In light of such trends in evangelicalism, and perhaps the emptiness of the average lifelong Catholic's rote response to ritual, the current wave of interest in Orthodoxy is understandable. To be honest, I found far more reality of commitment to gospel truth, even with icons surrounding me, in a recent visit with a group of converted Orthodox Christians, than I see in evangelicalism's worship of its *Left Behind* and *Jabez* icons of false doctrine. We might as well call it *The Purpose Driven Shack* and we might be closer to the truth. Better a silent revered image on the wall of a saint of old who gave his or her life for the faith than a truth-poisoning image in the heart of a false god of Mammon or a false christ returning to bring a man-invented vengeance to the world.

A CRIPPLING DEPENDENCE ON FORMULA

The mindset caused by modernity's worship of knowledge, formula, easy answers, add-water-and-stir religion, and dependence on ritual, doctrine, and dogma has created a generation of Christians content to sit in church and accept what they are told, go through their exercises of worship, and peruse their favorite books and devotional aids with the same mentality they bring to their computers—mindlessly absorbing input from others without thinking about where *truth* is represented and where it is not. Spirituality is no longer viewed as an energetic life of *growth* of heart and mind—probing and questioning, pondering and praying in fresh and ever deeper ways, even occasionally saying to the naked theological Emperor, "Hey, hold on a minute,"—but rather the process of accumulating more and more data to add to one's so-called storehouse of wisdom whereby to bolster the precepts of the formulae.

More than ever what we call *belief* in this computer age is comprised of scriptural lists, memorized prayer-promises, theologic recipes, prophetic timetables, and doctrinal clichés, supported by proof texts, outlining the correct hermeneutical view concerning every aspect of spirituality. This policy can be seen among Christians of every brand and stripe. These prescriptions are passed on from week to week in pulpits across the land, and reinforced in Bible studies and books and conferences and television programs, all accomplishing for the faithful believer just what the computer does—dishing out the information, defining the parameters of dogma, memorizing the verses that support the model, while *discouraging* the need to think and reflect and question.

Free thinking has become the most serious taboo of all. It might cause you to step outside the formula. Take what you are taught, therefore, memorize it, catalog the proof texts with which to combat falsehood, heresy, and liberalism (if you are an evangelical), or fundamentalism (if you are a Catholic)...but never, *never*, say the gurus of formula, question the doctrine.

Prayerfully probing the heart and purposes of God—starting not with a file of learned axioms with which to dispense spiritual quandaries with a wave of the hand, but rather with an approach to the throne of grace on bended knee, with mind awake, heart open, and senses eager to stretch the boundaries of one's concept of God—is sadly not a priority that is stressed much these days.

We have changed Jesus' words to the synagogue ruler in Mark 5 from, "Don't fear, only believe," to, *Don't think...only believe.*

The gospel of experience and worship (of many varieties) is alive and well. But the gospel of dynamic intellectual vigor, and unpretentious critical engagement with the world, absent pomposity, has almost entirely disappeared from Christendom's programme.

When did you last hear your minister or priest say: "I'm not going to give you an answer this time. Go to the Scriptures and find out for yourself. Don't just read the surface words or pick up a book and automatically accept what someone says. God gave you a mind—you can think as well as a theologian, bishop, abbot, or cardinal. Therefore, probe the limitations of the traditional explanation. It may not offer as thorough a biblical solution to the conundrum as you suppose. Do so not to challenge or debunk, but to *find truth*. Don't merely dredge up what you have been taught. The Holy Spirit invites you to approach God's Word with an open mentality and a large view of the Father's purposes. Be not afraid of honest interrogation. Fear of question is not to be found in the New Testament. Jesus *encouraged* spiritual inquiry. So dig and think for yourself, even if in the end you come to a different conclusion than someone else, or even a variant view from mine. Diversity of opinion is healthy—it forces us to think. We'll talk about what you find next week."

I'm not sure about you, but I do not recall *ever* hearing such a charge from the pulpit. Instead, preachers, priests, and teachers outline every detail to make sure no one falls into the dreaded pit of scriptural error. They seldom encourage you to think for yourself.

Take notes, get the formula down, make sure you know the verses clearly that prove the conclusion. But don't probe too deeply. The Bible commands us to νοεω, but you don't have to worry about that.

And because we possess such an abundance of information, so many books and Bibles and devotional tools and manuals and cathechismic guides, all read and re-read and underlined—we are unquestionably the most *knowledgeable* generation of Christians that has ever lived—we delude ourselves into thinking that such formulae is intellectually robust. In fact it is shallow, fat, and lazy.

It has even come to the point where most new Bibles coming out now do your thinking for you. The new generation of "marginal notes" are not intended to encourage you to dig for yourself, but rather to *tell* you what the Scriptures mean.

Doctrinal formulae...the lifeblood of evangelicalism, Catholicism, Orthodoxy, Anglicanism, and of Protestantism. It has bred anything but the sort of Christianity that turned the first century world upside down.

REMOVING THE STRAIGHTJACKET OF SUPERFICIALITY

Modern men and women are sophisticated enough to recognize superficiality when they see it, and they want no part of it. The world is hungry for vitality and reality. The world is hungry to see spirituality harmonized with life as we experience it. The world is not closed to faith as many suppose. In some ways the world has never been more open to spiritual things. But the world *is* closed to dogma without life. And everywhere, it seems, that's exactly what religion is dishing out. What many within it don't realize is that seemingly "vibrant" Christianity is dishing out dogma and formula too.

These days the world isn't observing Christians like C.S. Lewis on the cover of *Time* magazine. For the last thirty years of the twentieth century as the previous millennium drew to a close, it saw instead men like Jerry Falwell and Jim Bakker and Pat Robertson and Benny Hinn and other evangelical spokesmen making their regular appearances on the round of television talk shows, repeating back the formulae of fundamentalism, with its accompanying political, prophetic, and social thrust. Whatever the question, whatever the topic, a predictable response was at the ready. At the same time Catholicism took a terrible beating from one priesthood scandal after another, calling into question (in the world's eyes) the repute and future of the entire historic edifice. John Paul and Benedict, men of stature, were unable to stem the negative tide. No wonder, as the third millennium A.D. moves forward, many are heralding Christianity's decline. From both sides of the spectrum, it seems that influence is slipping away. Obama declared that the U.S. was no longer a Christian nation, relegating Christianity to secondary status in his vision of a new world order.

The world is hungry for *real* people, *deep* people, *changed* people. But where are today's Francis Schaeffers, George MacDonalds, C.S. Lewises, and Dietrich Bonhoeffers, who took their Christianity into the world with boldness, meekness, honesty...and without formula? To be sure, there are a handful who are trying to challenge Christians to think outside the formulae of churchy platitudes. But they are voices crying in the wilderness. How many hear them? Their books hardly sell. They are not invited to speak. Their voices grow silent.

No one cares, because no one *wants* to think. It is more comfortable being spoon fed by our priests.

An invisible straightjacket has enclosed itself about Christendom's self-satisfied and inward-focused culture, squeezing and narrowing its theological focus, ever more tightly defining what comprises "doctrinal correctness."

Thus, the gospel we present to a world hungry for meaty spirituality is an incomplete gospel. It is a true gospel, but not a *whole* one, offering an experiential interaction with Christ or the church, but in the way of *ideas* presenting little but a re-marketed tradition of the elders.

George MacDonald wrote, "The message of the good news has not been truly delivered." [8] Little has changed in a hundred years.

It is not that the church has grown entirely ineffective. The gospel contains a power that its adherents can never completely dilute because of the centrality of Jesus Christ himself—whose very being and character will always keep the gospel alive with life-changing potency.

So some, of course, continue to listen. But a constricted formularistic version of the truth is not what the Son of God died to bring the world.

The point is...we have a problem. What do we do about it? I can only speak for myself. And in my case, I came to the point in my walk with God when I recognized that good honest *thought*—even fresh, bold, formula-challenging thought—was not a spiritual bogeyman. God had given me brains, and he expected me to use them. The questions I asked of God were attempts to liberate myself from formula-thinking. I did not engage in this process to prove this view or that opinion *wrong*. I was simply hungry for truth in those areas where I discovered the precepts and elder-traditions wanting.

HUMBLY DISCOVERING THE BALANCE

A foundation, therefore, of getting at truth must be wisely laid. Its building blocks are boldness of prayerful inquiry, scriptural truth, and historical perspective. The mortar of such foundations is mixed with a combination of balance and humility.

Boldness...humility?

Inquiry into the *new*...respect for the *old*?

Do such seeming opposites really go together?

They must. It is what the *balance* of truth is all about.

Our own sons have discovered deeper spiritual reality in formal and traditional expressions of Christianity in which the authority of the church and its leadership are foundational. Though rigid structural formality does not particularly feed my spiritual being any more than does loose Pentecostalism or hip worldly evangelicalism, I admire their respective spiritual sojourns as highlighting the required balance in one's search for meaning between the individual and corporate, between "thinking for oneself" and taking what you are taught by those in spiritual authority over you "in faith."

The pastorate, the priesthood, and the so-called professional ministry has not traditionally attracted through the years the wisest, most balanced, most unbiased, most selfless seekers after truth. That it has attracted many such, and continues to in every era, given the tremendous inertia of its structure and orthodoxy, is one of the wonders of God's church. We count a number of humble pastoral seekers after truth among our dear friends and our admiration for them is great. But such men of truth are sadly in a great minority, and face an uphill struggle in a church full, rather, of leaders, pastors, priests, and spokespersons pushing their own agendas and opinions rather than the Will and perspectives of God.

So how does one know when to trust a received teaching and take it "in faith" as true, and when, on the other hand, to launch out and seek deeper truth from God himself rather than from his would-be spokespersons?

It is a delicate and difficult balance to find, and one in which one must walk humbly, always humbly.

To step out from under the umbrella of "accepted church orthodoxy," and say, "God, what truth do you have to show me?" is an exercise in which we must engage with prayerful and humble caution. And yet...if that umbrella of teaching is riddled with holes from tradition, doctrinal rigidity, theologically erroneous interpretation, a misreading of God's character, along with ambiguity and scriptural inconsistency...what else can we do?

It has then become no umbrella at all but a false covering which allows ideas of untruth to rain into our lives without the protection truth is meant to afford.

My own first steps in such directions were tentative. Breaking free from that bondage was no easy task. Yet what should I discover but that thinking through matters of faith for myself did *not* send me into doubt, despair, unbelief, or off the edge of the one-dimensional theological world into heresy.

Just the opposite. I discovered the Father *more* omnipotent and intimate, the Son more relevant and alive, and the Bible *more* precious, practical, and true than ever before. My entire framework of belief, far from weakening, has been immeasurably *strengthened* by this inner pilgrimage of heart and mind, thinking and praying through the tenets of faith for myself, not because someone told me what I was *supposed* to believe.

Therefore we can be both cautious and bold, fearless to humbly search for *more* truth, even as we revere the tradition of the church as a conduit for God's life through the ages.

And thus do we discover the delicate balance: Thinking for oneself with *bold humility* in an environment of *respect and honor* for what has come before.

Applying the Brain to Know God

The challenge to *think* is emphasized over and over in the writings of C.S. Lewis, including this memorable and oft-quoted passage:

"Prudence means practical common sense, taking the trouble to think....In fact, because Christ said we could only get into His world by being like children, many Christians have the idea that, provided you are 'good,' it does not matter being a fool. But...as St. Paul points out, Christ never meant that we were to remain children in intelligence: on the contrary, He told us to be not only 'as harmless as doves,' but also 'as wise as serpents.' He wants a child's heart, but a grown-up's head. He wants us to be simple, single-minded, affectionate, and teachable, as good children are; but He also wants every bit of intelligence we have to be alert at its job, and in first-class fighting trim...The fact that what you are thinking about is God Himself...does not mean that you can be content with the same babyish

ideas which you had when you were a five-year old." [9]

George MacDonald carries this theme yet further in voicing the imperative to know God correctly:

"...everything depended on the kind of God believed in.... He wondered how many ideas of God there might be, for every one who believed in him must have a different idea...He had not yet come to consider the fact, that the best of men said he knew God; that God was like himself, only greater; that whoever would do what he told him should know that God, and know that he spoke the truth concerning him; that he had come from him to witness of him that he was truth and love.... no man is a believer...except he give his will, his life to the Master...no man, in a word, who does not obey him, that is, who does not do what he said, and says. It seems preposterous that such definition should be necessary; but thousands talk about him for one that believes in him; thousands will do what the priests and scribes say he commands, for one who will search to find what he says that he may do it—who will take his orders from the Lord himself, and not from other men claiming either knowledge or authority. A man must come up to the Master, hearken to his word, and do as he says. Then he will come to know God, and to know that he knows him." [10]

Three

The World's Response to Superficiality

What Kind of Boldness will the Third Millennium respect?

"But we have νουν Χριστου (the mind of Christ)."
—1 Corinthians 2:16

νουν Χριστου: Noun Christou—
Mind of Christ

Paul's bold assertion in his first letter to the Corinthians that "we have the mind of Christ" is one of the most intriguing, complex, thought-provoking, and commented-upon passages in the New Testament. The widespread implications are positively extraordinary on the face of it. What did Paul actually *mean*?

I think it likely that he meant all (and more) than we can hope to imagine. The intricacies of application are many, but for the purposes of our discussion we can simply remind ourselves of Jesus' shrewd encounters with the religious leaders, his logic, his forceful challenges. He did not speak in platitude or cliché but with dynamic mental and spiritual precision. He engaged the world of his day (spiritual, secular, political) on a far more incisive, challenging, probing, and compassionate level—as did the Apostle Paul—than has most of Christendom in the years since his time. Therefore it is safe to assume that Paul meant no sort of supernatural E.S.P. when he spoke of the mind of Christ, but rather an eternal outlook and perspective on life and the world that translated into a dynamism of spiritual and intellectual engagement not seen before nor since.

Probably the most accurate rendition of the actual words used by Paul in 1 Corinthians 2:16, NOUN CHRISTOU, would be "judgment" or "wisdom"—perceiving things, judging things in the same way Christ would...right thinking.

THE NECESSITY FOR CHRISTIANS of long (perhaps lifelong) faith to examine the precepts of their beliefs with fresh gallantry and stout hearts is made imperative in our time by the radical and dramatic changes that are sweeping through the world like a societal hurricane. The 21st century truly is becoming a brave new world before our eyes. In many respects Christianity as a whole is not showing itself particularly well-equipped to meet the challenge. Though many will vehemently disagree, I think it possible that Christianity could be approaching a time when it may find itself almost entirely losing its potency as a world force.

Some hard-hitting, brutally honest reevaluation of what is going on inside our house is urgently pressing upon us as it has not been since the end of the fifteenth century. Christianity's survival is not at stake, but certainly our effectiveness in the world is.

In his 1952 Preface to *Mere Christianity*, Lewis went to great lengths to clarify what he meant by the words of his title. In some ways, that Preface represents one of the most insightful chapters of the whole book.

As "mere Christianity" was a phrase that Lewis recognized could have been misunderstood, so too are the words of my title. Therefore, I will likewise attempt to explain.

I do not mean boldness of action but boldness of *thought.*

It is natural to equate "boldness" with brazen arrogance, with bluster and outspokenness. That is the very opposite of what I intend by the words. We are not talking about *in-your-face* Christianity, but bold *thinking* Christianity.

I happen to believe with all my heart that *this* is exactly what Paul meant when he coined the term, νουν Χριστου *the mind of Christ.*

It is a private boldness, an inward fearlessness. It is the courage to face the foes of political tolerance and learned platitudes and religious clichés that sap the vitality and water down the life-changing truth of the Christian message. It takes courage to buck the pressure to conform to the indoctrinated status-quo beliefs of everyone else in one's denomination or faction or church or study group. It is hard to question the majority view. It takes guts to say, "I know we have all been taught to believe such-and-such. But I have been thinking and praying and studying about this matter strenuously. I have come to see that some deeper principles may be involved than we previously assumed."

Statements of this kind are not well received in the religious world. *Any* religious world. Such, however, is the rare valor of the bold-thinking Christian.

TWO MISCONCEPTIONS

Talk of "meeting the challenge" and "reevaluating" our beliefs probably already has some readers squirming!

Expressions such as these will immediately prompt two erroneous responses. We need to clear them away at the outset so we don't get off on the wrong foot.

Misconception one—that this reevaluation of certain Christian ideas is a mere responsive accommodation to modern secularism and will thus threaten or diminish traditional belief.

Many are so fearful of change that they will reject the call to bold thinking out of hand. I have no intention, however, of rewriting traditional doctrine as a mere feeble adaptation to modernism. That would be a grievous mistake. But neither do I want the challenges of modernity to make me cling to doctrines that are *untrue* because I am fearful and too hidebound to examine them. That's flat-earth thinking. We are therefore trying to recognize the need to weed the garden of our ideas so that its precepts can flourish more effectively in the deep soil of biblical truth. If a so-called "traditional" idea is *wrong*, let's weed it out and get rid of it. If a traditional idea is right, let's add nourishment and nutrients to the soil so that it can grow and bear yet more fruit. The purpose of reevaluation is to eliminate *wrong* ideas so that Christianity's *right* ideas and timeless *truths* can spread with increased power throughout the world.

Misconception two—that meeting the challenge of our times can be accomplished societally, culturally, or politically.

There may be a place for Christians to respond in such arenas. Many are addressing those needs already. That aspect of Christendom's collective challenge, however, is not the subject of our query here. For the remainder of *this* book, put social, cultural, and political Christianity out of your minds altogether.

CHRISTIANITY IN TODAY'S WORLD

With these two potential fallacies concerning our purpose behind us, then, we need to look realistically at where Christendom as a world religion presently stands.

Christianity's impact in today's world is difficult to measure. It clearly depends on who you ask. Also on what you mean by impact. Catholicism has fallen on hard times recently, while Orthodoxy in America is undergoing a surprising renaissance. Talk to a pastor of a ten-thousand member evangelical mega church and you will likely be told that the impact of the evangelical message has never been greater. In government, in the court system, in the media, on high school and university campuses, and in Hollywood, however, the shrinking cultural influence of Christianity has become almost negligible. All about us are voices declaring the end of the Christian era.

So we are confronted with two opposing views or theories of Christianity at this moment in the history of western civilization—one, that Christianity as a world force is dying; and two, that Christianity is vibrant and healthy and is continuing to mightily influence the world for good.

Most Christians meet this dichotomy without much intellectual rigor. All across the spectrum, we either ignore the fact that the rest of the world isn't paying much attention. Or we flatter ourselves that in our *own* experientially vibrant mega church everything is hunky-dory and that the world is listening with as much interest as ever. At Saddleback on a Sunday morning, it's pretty easy to loose sight of the fact that Christianity is *losing* the battle on just about every front in the world at large.

That there are pockets of vibrancy here and there cannot obscure a sobering reality: The war for the souls of mankind and the heart of western culture is going very badly.

In my opinion the reason can be traced directly to the decline of bold thinking among serious Christians. We are *not*, as a body of God's people, thinking with Christ's mind.

Objections to that statement will be immediate and vociferous. But if we are going to get on together you had better know where I am coming from...and that *is* where I am coming from. Many Christians have lost the capacity to think courageously about their beliefs. That is my conviction and I stand by it.

We fall back on the Bible and give answers to the questions of modernity that smack of platitude and provincialism. The Bible is my guide too, but we must present its truths through the prism of keen intellectual acuity and honesty, not black and white anachronism. We must meet people where they are. Most of them aren't where we think they are. Our responses resemble political press conferences. It doesn't matter what question is asked, we answer with a pre-packaged formula. Thus we *don't* generally meet people where they are. The disconnect between the church's method and message and the concerns and outlook of modern progressivism is stark and glaring. We are speaking different languages.

Too easily we lay off blame for today's runaway unbelief and anti-Christianity on liberalism, on the rise of Islam, on the homosexual movement, on the increasing sinfulness of the end times, on political correctness, on progressive secularism in government and education, on nonsensical social tolerance, on the anti-Christian bias of the media and academia and intelligentsia, on the breakdown of the family, on the social engineering agenda of the judicial system, even on the stranglehold of evolutionary theory on science and education.

What we're not so adept at doing, however, is asking how much of Christianity's declining influence is our own fault.

DUAL BLIND SPOTS

In many ways today's average men and women are inanely ignorant and ill-informed. The world's literacy rates are higher than ever. Yet American presidential politics has degenerated into a high-school popularity contest, where an unthinking electorate is appealed to at the most base and unsubstantive levels. We might as well be voting for homecoming king or queen or president of a vacuous sophomore class. The heartbreaking truth is that this "style before substance" methodology *works*. That seemingly intelligent people are incapable of seeing through the smiling personality-facades is positively astounding.

Modern men and women can *read*...but they cannot *perceive*.

Remarkably, however, in other arenas, the world demonstrates a discrimination and discernment that Christendom has been woefully ill-prepared to meet. The blatant hypocrisy of congressional and journalistic personalities claiming to be "good Catholics" or "good Methodists" or "good Episcopalians," or whatever, is all too clear as they endorse political agendas that represent the very antithesis of Christian values. Though right and wrong is clear and unambiguous according to its teaching, tradition, and sacred writings, Christianity's truths are regularly cast aside in favor of modernism and expediency.

Abortion and homosexual "rights" represent but two of a host of issues where progressive politics trumps the spineless so-called "christianity" of such media and political leaders. The only reason the world doesn't laugh in their faces at their pretended faith is because the secular progressivism of such liberal Christianity dovetails so nicely with its own biases. So it conveniently endorses this foundationless form of "christian values," while turning its attacks on *conservative* Christianity for its attempt to do the unthinkable—actually adhere to the teaching, tradition, and scriptural truths upon which Christianity (and America's Constitution, legal system, and fabric of society) is based.

This hypocrisy is easy enough for the intelligent and unbiased to see in the political, cultural, and social arenas. What is not so easily recognized by the church at large is the world's response to its, the church's, doctrinal and theological narrowness and sectarianism. Believe it or not...*we* have our own blind spots too. While the world is not generally sophisticated enough to recognize the biases and hypocrisies of political liberalism, it *is* sophisticated enough to spot the flaws apparent throughout the Christian world.

This is due in part to a devastating anti-Christian swing in public opinion over the last generation. It isn't fair, of course. And the double-standard by which the world judges liberal and conservative outlooks only reinforces its *own* hypocrisy. Still, these perceptions exist, logical or not, fair or not, and Christendom has to deal with it.

We're not dealing with it very well.

We see the world's blind spots. It sees ours. Standoff.

The trouble is, we ought to be able to see the world's *and* our own. We ought to be skilled, wise, intelligent, objective thinkers on all sides of every issue, spiritual or secular. Our wisdom and objectivity should be an example to the world, providing the leadership in every discipline and area of endeavor. But this is clearly not the case. Christians are one-dimensional thinkers like everyone else.

If the mind of Christ doesn't give us the capacity to think with more wisdom and clear-headedness than the world Paul described in Romans 1 as lost in its own foolishness and darkness, then something's not working as it should.

THE IMPERATIVE TOOL FOR THE TIMES

Many Christian responses exist to the changes the world is hurling at us. As I have tried to make clear, but it bears reemphasis—

this book will not call for a frontal assault against abortion or the homosexual hijacking of the political agenda, or a campaign to reinstate creationism and prayer in schools or elect a born again president to the White House. However others may be led toward such efforts is their concern. Our objective here points in another direction.

To strengthen the undergirding fiber of Christianity's power and truth, and to meet the anti-Christian bias that has infected the world like a fog of moral, ethical, and relativistic decay...we have to look *inward*.

It's time we *do* learn to think with the mind of Christ. It's time we discovered the wisdom, objectivity, and multi-dimensionality that ought to have characterized Christian thinking long before now.

Rather than expending valuable energy on external social and cultural tangents, the tool we need to learn to use more effectively is the *mirror*.

As Christians we have not been self-evaluative or self-correcting. We have grown doctrinally lazy and stagnant.

It is no secret (to us at least) that the world is not thinking clearly. The unbelievable influence of the homosexual lobby, is all the evidence one needs that the world has not merely lost its moral compass, it has lost all capacity to think with logic and acuity. *Everything* has been turned upside-down. Black is white. White is black. Deviancy is normal. Believers in morality are shunned as intolerant.

But we Christians aren't thinking clearly at every point either. We may be thinking correctly about certain social issues. But within our house, we remain insular, shallow, formula thinkers. We discern the world's inconsistencies...but not our own.

This is why the world has ceased to respect Christianity as a force. It is not because, in the decay of its rationalism and morals, the world has put forward homosexuality and abortion, for example, as "normal" and entitled "rights," and is mad at Christians for calling homosexuality aberrant, and insisting that no woman has the right to kill an unborn fetus. These are red herrings to the central crux of the problem. They are important issues, to be sure. Life and death is at stake in both. I am as infuriated as the next man by modernity's unthinking promotion of an institution as absurd, repellant, and disgusting as "gay marriage."

But I am also a practical man. I recognize that such issues as these, or the illegality of a Christmas crèche or Ten Commandments plaque on public property, or a liberal bias on the bench that outweighs fairness and justice, do not represent the true battle line in Christianity's polemic war for relevance on the world stage at this critical hour. Our stark differences on such points (maddening, yes...but not germane) do not in themselves explain why the world has largely stopped listening to Christianity's central message.

The problem lies deeper.

As Christians, we have to look at *why* the world respects our viewpoints so little.

It's not because we oppose gay marriage or abortion rights. It is because we have lost the ability objectively to scrutinize ourselves.

It is because we are not cutting-edge *thinkers*. It is because we do *not* as a body of people demonstrate the mind of Christ.

Our ineffectiveness in communicating the reality of the Christian faith into the brave new Orwellian world of the 21st century is rooted in a lack of *bold thinking* on the part of Christians about the precepts of our faith. Our reluctance to examine inconsistencies within our *own* belief systems, in the world's eyes, justifies not listening to us at all.

WHAT THE MIRROR REVEALS—FORMULARISTIC FAITH

We are a people far too satisfied with clichés.

The vast majority of Christians are fearful to engage in a thoughtful, knowledgeable, prayerful scrutiny of belief. Their *own* beliefs. They are eager and quick to pick apart those of everyone else. There are few things they enjoy so much!

But scrutinizing their *own*...that's an unpracticed discipline within Christendom.

It is exactly this reluctance that makes us appear as non-thinkers to the modern world. Catholics are afraid to think outside their boxes. Evangelicals are afraid to think outside their boxes. Liberals are afraid to think outside their boxes. Mormons are afraid to think outside their boxes. Pentecostals are afraid to think outside their boxes. Baptists, Seventh Day Adventists, Presbyterians, Anglicans, Methodists...superficial thinking infects Christendom everywhere. So we all circle the wagons and hole up within the safety and security of our own well-entrenched orthodoxies...and gradually the world stops listening.

When unbelievers do not accept our formula-prescriptions as truth, we tend to write them off as closed-minded and unspiritual rather than look within ourselves to see whether certain aspects of *our* dogma might require a more probing look.

Remarkably, it is not primarily the *content* of the Christian message the world objects to. It is rather put off by the clear demonstration of *sectarianism* in a religion whose impact is supposed to be measured by unity, and the palpable *close-mindedness* to ideas outside the confines of each little private camp of tightly defined orthodoxy.

A solution, therefore, does not begin by trying to outlaw abortion or gay marriage, but learning to be shrewd Christian *thinkers*. We may still vote against such obviously flagrant violations of gospel truth. But we can't deceive ourselves into imagining that doing so will change the world's view of Christianity. The world won't start listening until they see us thinking with objective rigor, and then being willing to *live* by the ideas of our faith not just talk about them, debate them, argue about them, and judge those who disagree with us about them.

Don't get me wrong here either. I am not contending that the world *can* think and Christians *can't*. Good heavens, the world is worse at bold thinking than we are. If self-scrutiny is not practiced by Christians, it is altogether unknown in secular progressivism. One of the best kept secrets of our time is that greater narrow-mindedness and bigotry per square inch exists in political liberalism than anywhere else on the planet. Its intolerant and prejudicial clichés are *far* more lethal to the future of our society than any clichés of conservatism.

That is why *we* have to lead the way with bold thinking. The world is so far gone in liberal insanity (I use that word not bombastically, but in its technical sense: a complete inability to judge rationally) that it is incapable of sound judgment at any level.

But we have to grasp with sobriety that bold thinking begins at home. Attacking the other side accomplishes nothing in the end. It's fine if one relishes in the continuing clash of opinion but doesn't really care if there's ever any progress. If we truly care about a solution, however, and far more importantly, if we care about Christianity's long-term impact and effectiveness, it's time to silence the guns of attack, argument, and self-defense...and pick up the mirror.

If the world sees that we cannot think with acuity about our own doctrines, it has every right to ignore us when we speak on issues related to the culture. It may seem like creation and Noah's ark and the trinity and evolution have nothing to do with abortion and homosexuality and the slide of western civilization into an abyss of moral relativism.

But they have *everything* to do with it.

The world is watching us. If we are knee-jerk, formula thinkers, unwilling and unable to examine ourselves keenly, and if we offer little more than learned maxims about the dating of *Genesis*, salvation, the afterlife, God's character, the meaning of the atonement, hell, the nature of Jesus, science and the Bible, and a hundred other points of uncertainty and debate, they won't listen to us about *anything*.

REEVALUTION IS PART OF OUR TRADITION

Many will of course reject the call for reevaluation and self-scrutiny. There are always those in any movement or enterprise so entrenched in the methodologies and doctrines and perspectives of the past that they cannot budge.

So the familiar jargon and formulas of Christianity's separate and divided mini-orthodoxies will persist. Those steeped in the orthodoxies will always march under banners that proclaim, *If it was good enough for Paul...if it is good enough for pastor...if it is good enough for the Pope...if it was good enough for Luther and Calvin...it is good enough for me.*

This illuminates a *third* misconception—that the orthodoxies of Christianity have always been set in stone.

It is not so. Paul had to reevaluate some things too, just as Christian theologians and thinkers continued to do long after Paul was gone. Christianity has since its inception been a *developing* faith. What are we afraid of in allowing that process to continue?

The Christians of the first century were taught that Jesus would return in their lifetimes. It was a false teaching. Even Paul was swept into it. Gradually the apostles and everyone else had to come to terms with the fact that it wasn't true. That reevaluation of a widely held orthodoxy didn't compromise the supernatural foundations of their faith. They simply realized that they had misunderstood the timetable. They had to interpret Matthew 24 through different eyes. There were deeper meanings involved. Their interpretations of the second coming had to adapt and change and develop and evolve. Most Christians have little idea to what extent the tenets of their beliefs derive more from Augustine or some ancient church council than from Jesus himself.

This is exactly our challenge today—to find the *deeper* meanings to some of the important doctrines of Christianity. In other words, to remove the weeds from our garden of truth.

HUMBLE EXAMPLE NOT ARGUMENT OR PERSUASION

In my opinion...this is where we are.

Over the last thirty to forty years we have largely presented Christianity as a series of doctrinal, experiential, social, and political clichés. We *haven't* continued to grow as a wise and objective thinking people of faith. And predictably the world has stopped listening.

To be honest, I don't know whether even bold thinking within Christendom is capable of slowing the runaway train of liberal secularism that is careening western civilization toward a wreck of epic proportions. No one can see into the future. Maybe we are thundering toward Armageddon, who can tell.

One thing I do know is that Christians will never "convince" the world to abandon secularism and return to the values and absolutes upon western civilization was founded by *persuasion*. Such is the failed methodology of the past.

Example changes culture, not argument.

Christians will increase the reach of their voice only by wise, integritous, and incisive *thinking* and humble *example* within its own ranks. When the world observes Christians speaking with intelligence, open-mindedness, and wisdom and humility rather than formula, pomposity, and cliché, it will stand up and take notice. Where the world will be by then, and what will be the effect, is anyone's guess.

C.S. Lewis's Challenge

C.S. Lewis brings *Mere Christianity* to a triumphant conclusion with words we need to remind ourselves of daily:

"The Christian way is different: harder and easier. Christ says 'Give me All...I have not come to torment your natural self, but to kill it. No half-measures are any good...'

"That is why He warned people to 'count the cost' before becoming Christians. 'Make no mistake,' He says, 'if you let me, I will make you perfect. The moment you put yourself in My hands, that is what you are in for...Whatever suffering if may cost you in your earthly life, whatever inconceivable purification it may cost you after death, whatever it costs Me, I

will never rest, nor let you rest, until you are literally perfect...This I can do and will do. But I will not do anything less...'

"*As a great Christian writer (George MacDonald) pointed out, every father is pleased at the baby's first attempt to walk: no father would be satisfied with anything less than a firm, free, manly walk in a grown-up son. In the same way, he said, 'God is easy to please, but hard to satisfy.'...*

"*This is the fatal mistake. Of course we never wanted, and never asked, to be made into the sort of creatures He is going to make us into. But the question is not what we intended ourselves to be, but what He intended us to be when He made us...The job will not be completed in this life: but He means to get us as far as possible before death...*

"*I find I must borrow yet another parable from George MacDonald. Imagine yourself as a living house. God comes in to rebuild that house. At first, perhaps you can understand what He is doing...But presently he starts knocking the house about in a way that hurts abominably...He is building quite a different house from the one you thought of....You thought you were going to be made into a decent little cottage: but He is building a palace. He intends to come and live in it Himself.*" [11]

Inspired and uplifted as we may be by these passages...time passes. Things drift into old patterns. Inspiration is difficult to sustain. Life, as we say, goes on. Years gradually slip along. Before we know it, we have been living what we nebulously call a "Christian life" for ten, twenty, even thirty or more years. We wake up to realize that we haven't *thought* deeply about much of the teaching we have received during those years. At least we haven't thought about them in the way Lewis challenged us to. Without noticing, we have settled into some spiritual, intellectual, and doctrinal ruts.

Lewis concludes with the words:

"*The principle runs through all life from top to bottom. Give up your self, and you will find your real self. Lose your life and you will save it. Submit to death, death of your ambitions and favourite wishes every day and death of your whole body in the end: submit with every fibre of your being, and you will find eternal life. Keep nothing back. Nothing that you have not given away will ever be really yours. Nothing in you that has not died will ever be raised from the dead. Look for yourself, and you will find in the long run only hatred, loneliness, despair, rage, ruin, and decay. But look for Christ and you will find Him, and with Him everything else thrown in.*" [12]

This is Lewis's bold challenge. They are timeless words. But have we grown with them? Christianity is facing threats on every side. Is our Christianity, yours and mine, courageous and astute enough to meet the challenge...not only with *mere* Christianity, but with *bold* Christianity?

Can we take up where Lewis left off, and bring his message and vision more effectively into our era? Let us commit to move beyond *mereness* into *boldness*. Let us inquire together how to be courageous thinkers that C.S. Lewis and all the great men and women of faith who have preceded us would be proud of.

They were bold in their eras. Now we must be bold in ours.

We are at a critical crossroads time in our history. It is time for bold thinking within Christ's Church.

FOUR

WHAT IS BOLD THINKING CHRISTIANITY?

The Cancer of Religious "Systems"

> "Joseph of Arimathea, a respected member of the council...τολμησας (took courage) and went to Pilate, and asked for the body of Jesus."
> —Mark 15:43

τολμαω: TOLMAO—*Boldness*

The Greek TOLMAO means to dare to do or bear something difficult, dangerous, even terrible. Its root is to *lift* or *carry*, as enduring a burden. From this it can occasionally mean *suffer*. More often, however, it implies more than the merely physical, but a personal boldness and daring and courage to undertake what is difficult. In Greek, most verbs have two basic forms, one a stronger form of the other. In this case, the related APOTOLMAO is the stronger form of TOLMAO, and indicates extreme boldness.

In light of this chapter's discussion, two other Greek words, also translated as "boldness," highlight interesting differentiations. THARREO is generally rendered *courage*, as in the phrase, "Be of good courage," and is often associated with personal confidence, or the confidence and courage that comes from temperament or personality. The distinction between "confidence" and TOLMAO's summoning of boldness to undertake a difficult task is clear.

CHRISTIANS ARE CALLED UPON TO WALK MANY TIGHTROPES. Any number of difficult balancing acts are required as we navigate our way through life. Christianity is neither a simple religion to understand correctly, nor an easy life to live.

Probably one of the most difficult of such balances to discern is the distinction made by Jesus when he said that we were to live *in* the world, but not be *of* the world.

On numerous occasions he emphasized to his disciples that they were not of this world any more than he was of this world. "My kingdom," he told them in dozens of settings and illustrating the principle in many different ways, "is not of this world."

But here we are. We are self-driven fallen creatures that are born into this world. We possess an intrinsic nature that is rooted in this world. And we must live our whole lives in this world with that worldly nature clinging closer to us than our skin.

AN OTHER-WORLDLY CITIZENSHIP

What, then, does it mean to be not *of* this world? What does it mean *practically*? There are many ways to spiritualize such questions. Most of us have a ready stockpile of answers that our mental cash registers have taught us with which to meet such questions. But how *real* are those answers—how functional, workable, practical?

When you and I walk out of the house every morning to begin our day's activities, what does it mean that we are not *of* this very world in whose midst we will be busily engaged all day? Does it merely mean that we "believe" certain things about God, Jesus, and the Bible that many of those around us do *not* believe? Does it mean that our outlook and perspectives on life and the world are more "spiritual" because of those beliefs?

Or does the difference go deeper? Surely it *ought* to go deeper. Yet for how many Christians does it?

As can be said for the adherents of other world religions, Christianity is for many a system of belief. Though Christians view it as the *truest* faith, it is nevertheless for them a "religion."

Many Christians never perceive to what an extent the mentality of a religious system infects the theological dogmatism accompanying what they call their beliefs. Even the most lively and apparently energetic Christianity—whether Orthodox, Evangelical, Protestant, or Catholic... whether liberal or fundamentalist—is invisibly subject to the universal human propensity toward systematizing spiritual perspectives into doctrinal rigidity.

Christianity, however, does not merely place us in a uniquely personal relationship with God the Father and his Son Jesus Christ—something no other religion offers or can produce. Christianity is not merely defined by its ideas or by various spiritual experiences. It is not comprised of study, service, evangelism, knowledge of Scripture, good deeds, ministry, church attendance, or fellowship with others of like mind. Nor are its truths plumbed by regular practices and a continually renewed sense of worship, devotion, and prayer. The totality of the Christian faith cannot be understood even on the basis of the fact that God offers to live, by his Spirit, in our hearts.

Christianity may incorporate all these into it. But its foundations lay elsewhere.

The fundamental essence of the Christian faith reduces to how one thinks and behaves.

How one *lives*.

To be a disciple of Jesus Christ involves a revolutionary way of ordering one's thoughts, attitudes, priorities, perspectives, actions, responses, and moment-by-moment affairs. Only in the daily practice of obedience and a dedicated commitment to selfless Christlikeness does it avoid the fatal tendency toward religiosity.

It is this *life* of Christianity—an applied, practical, obedient life—which Jesus taught and exampled to us.

To be his disciple—and thus to call oneself a *Christian* (literally, "a follower of Christ")—is to make oneself, by daily conscious decision and accompanying lifestyle, a citizen in a kingdom that is not of this world.

NOT BRASHNESS...BUT BOLD THINKING

Because of its revolutionary nature, and the revolutionary worldwide impact of its Founder, the man who claimed to be God's Son and who rose from the dead to enforce that claim, from its earliest days Christianity has been a vigorous thinking man's religion. Many of the greatest minds in history have been Christians. Through the years, however, its precepts have too often drifted into dogma, with the result that many of its followers have forgotten how to think, and to think with that same vigor, about their faith. This is one of the predictable and unfortunate results of religiosity in all forms—the loss of the capacity to *think* with originality.

An even more grievous hallmark of the religious mind usually accompanies such religiosity—fear of ideas that fall outside the theologic borders established by the traditional orthodoxies that inevitably grow up around originating *Belief.* Such doctrinal orthodoxy (aka, OC: "Orthodox Correctness") is rooted more than we have allowed ourselves to recognize in occasionally erroneous traditions passed down by the elder-gurus of our "rooms" of faith. There are Catholic orthodox correctnesses. There are Pentecostal orthodox correctnesses. There are Evangelical orthodox correctnesses. Even such fringe movements as Liberation Theology, which pride themselves on liberality and progressivity, have their own correctnesses of orthodoxy from which those under its sway also fear to deviate.

We are all influenced by the constraints of OC...wherever on the spectrum we find ourselves.

In learning to think boldly about Christianity, therefore, this fear is probably the first boogieman many encounter. But the courageous thinker must not be afraid to ask hard questions and explore thorny issues. We have to do so even when they perhaps go against certain cherished dogmas that have come down through the years but which may not reflect the intended teaching of the Founder of the Christian faith, Jesus himself.

Scripture becomes one of our chief guides (not the only one, but near the top of the list,) but not always as interpreted by theology, church doctrine, or by the opinions of those who would inhibit bold thinking. We seek truth, practicality, and reality. We do not necessarily seek what is taught by tradition, dogma, or indoctrinated church formula.

The word bold and the phrase bold Christianity will likely prompt three incorrect assumptions.

Ask any ten evangelicals what is meant by "bold Christianity" and you will probably get ten uniform answers equating it with outspokenness. Ask any ten non-Christians the same thing and probably eight of the ten will roll their eyes and bring up the tendency of certain fanatical types to preach and proselytize at the drop of a hat. Ask ten Catholics or Presbyterians or Episcopalians the same question and you will likely wind up with thirty more answers to add to the list.

Many of us have felt that we ought to be more assertive in speaking out in defense of our faith. Yet at the same time, most have experienced the discomfort of being preached at when we neither asked for it nor wanted it.

This is the first erroneous assumption that must be discarded before the notion of bold thinking can be rightly understood—that boldness characterizes an outspoken witness to the non-Christian world, whether a sensitive one or not, an outspoken defense of Christianity, a forward willingness even combativeness to debate and confront and challenge ideas contrary to Christian principles. And though most of us are a little uncomfortable with street preacher types, deep inside we can't help wondering if there ought to be a little more fearlessness in our response to the world's drift away from Christian principles. This quiet guilt has infiltrated our thinking with the damaging foolishness that has been promoted in our time associating boldness with being sufficiently obnoxious as to get in people's faces whether they have any interest in hearing our opinions or not. I call it *damaging* because few things so undermine a witness that is supposed to be based on Christlikeness of character more than verbal preaching. I call it *foolishness* because of how at variance it is with the Lord's clear command about how the world will come to recognize the truth of his teachings.

NOT ACTIVISM...BUT BOLD THINKING

This is the personal side of the mistaken assumption about boldness. There is also a corporate side, which views "boldness" within the Church as taking an assertive, forward, pro-active stance to engage the world culturally, socially, and politically.

Clearly this can take many forms and is often good and necessary. The late Pope John Paul II was one of the most forcefully "bold" pontiffs within recent memory in this regard. Not long before his death he came under strong criticism for speaking out concerning Poland's vote whether or not to join the European Union. His entire pontificate was characterized by what many would call a boldness to insert himself and the weight of the Catholic Church into the arena of the world's political affairs. His successor Pope Benedict XVI proved equally bold in his stands against abortion and homosexuality. Though the political left took profound offense, nearly all true Christians admired him for it.

Likewise, as the fundamentalist wing of the evangelical church gained political clout during the last half of the previous century, its leaders grew bold to speak out politically. They encouraged their followers to work actively for conservative causes and candidates and a pro-life social agenda. Pat Robertson and Gary Bauer both ran for

President. Jerry Falwell and Ralph Reed regularly appeared as television commentators. James Dobson was a major player in the political arena. Though he had not been nurtured out of its midst as one of its favorite sons, this movement might be seen to have reached its zenith in the election of George W. Bush in 2000. Its subsequent implosion (from internal forces in play long before) resulted in the election of a self-styled "Christian" of much different stripe in 2008. Only time and history will tell where evangelical political activism will go next...and with what result.

The church certainly plays a role in the world and ought to influence it, though it will never change its intrinsic sinfulness. No doubt it will take the clarity of eternity to fully distinguish between those things we have done to *further* the cause of Christ in the world, and those things we have done to *hinder* it. Obviously Pope John Paul II and Jerry Falwell, Pope Benedict XVI and James Dobson, Jimmy Carter and George W. Bush all took different positions on the specifics, and certainly impacted the world differently. But the word *bold*, viewed in this context, might be applied to each with respect to their engagement of the world on the basis of faith.

There is nothing intrinsically wrong with either individual outspokenness or the corporate assertiveness of the church and the political activism of its members—though we can speak out and engage the world in both beneficial and harmful ways. The point is only that our meaning when we speak of bold thinking Christianity here will be something else entirely.

NOT DEBUNKING...BUT BOLD THINKING

There is yet a third potential misreading of boldness."

Some consider debunking criticism a bold response to faith. Adopting a generally critical posture, many seeming intellectuals look at traditional faith as outmoded and eventually discard it altogether. They consider a secular outlook on matters of religion a boldly progressive response.

Philosophers throughout history, including an increasing number of theologians during the past hundred years, have devoted their energies to just such revisionism and critique. In attempting to *question* faith rather than *practice* faith, such otherwise intelligent men and women consider it their duty to challenge, reject, explain away, and discard rather than to find the deeper truth that Christianity may have to offer. They make of religion an intellectual exercise of analysis rather than a humble exercise of devotion and a practical life of obedience. Elevating their self-motivated intellects above the veracity of Scripture, in the end they *leave* faith rather than discover the deeper and more personal faith that prayerful bold thinking ought to produce.

In short, they do not make it their first business to know God. It is the difference between bold thinking *within* faith and challenges *against* faith.

Examples are numerous. Religious philosophers have been contending against Christianity ever since the advent of humanism and the enlightenment of the eighteenth century, a trend that might be said to have reached its zenith in the early 1960s with the announcement by modernist theologians that "God is dead." That this assessment struck such a worldwide chord in liberal circles shows to what an extent honest theological questioning had been replaced by the desire to debunk and reject historic Christianity. But such ultra liberal theology always fails to interpret Christian truth with insight and truth because its proponents throw the baby out with the bathwater.

None of these three—individual outspokenness, corporate activism, nor a debunking theology of rejection—represent the sort of *bold thinking* so vitally needed to reenergize third millennium Christianity.

BOLD DISCIPLESHIP ROOTED IN OBEDIENCE

If these are what it is not...what *is* it?

"Bold thinking Christianity" brings to daily faith a vigorous courage to search for spiritual truth, and to probe the depths of God's purpose, outside the box of learned dogma, cliché, and doctrinal formula. This does not assume that what we have been taught is *de facto in*accurate. There is no underlying predisposition to *reject* what have been learned doctrines. But neither do we take "as gospel" every specific and detail our pastor or priest tells us, or every jot and tittle our church teaches. We bring an open-minded humble hunger for truth to bear on all aspects of our belief system. Then we probe and pray and study and keep our mind open...and ask God to reveal truth.

The point made earlier bears repeating:

"We are therefore trying to recognize the need to weed the garden of our ideas so that its precepts can flourish more effective in the deep soil of biblical truth. If a so-called 'traditional' idea is *wrong*, let's weed it out and get rid of it. If a traditional idea is right, let's add nourishment and nutrients to the soil so that it can grow and bear yet more fruit. The purpose of reevaluation is to eliminate *wrong* ideas so that Christianity's *right* ideas and timeless *truths* can spread with increased power throughout the world."

The Christian who understands thinking with τολμαω seeks to know God intimately by the truth of his revelation as well as by common sense. He or she does not live by pat answers, proof-texts, or church catechism. Practical reality is life's code—a reality that engages heart and brain in a harmony of obedience to the instructions of Jesus.

The desire of the bold thinking Christian is not to devise an intellectual framework by which to analyze God and man, but to prayerfully probe the Scriptures and the mind of God in order that his nature, character, and eternal purposes are more clearly illuminated. The bold thinking disciple will thus be enabled to understand, obey, and fall in with God's purpose in a more dynamic and practical way.

The bold thinking Christian is therefore engaged in a spiritual quest moving in exactly the opposite direction from that of the debunking doubter. The critic engages in analysis that is primarily negative (what is wrong, what can be thrown out, what can be rejected, what parts of the Bible can be refuted and discarded, secularized, and termed outdated.) The result is intellectual and depersonalized, void of life-changing reality. The bold thinking Christian instead bases his or her spiritual growth on daily obedient discipleship where the ideas of faith are scrutinized to aid and enhance that obedience.

The process—including the reevaluative questions it produces—is altogether and entirely positive:

What are the *deeper* truths that spiritual formulae doesn't reach?

How much *more* truth can be illuminated from Scripture?

How much more *intimately* and personally can God be known?

How can the Bible's truth be *expanded* to fill yet more of life?

How can moment-by-moment obedience to the gospel life of Christlikeness be deepened by a wide awake mentality of common sense faith?

How much *more* alive is God than anyone knows!

To those whose comfort and security exist within learned orthodoxy and memorized cash-register clichés of doctrine, "bold thinking" after deeper truth may appear as "doubt." But only because they have so long contented themselves with being spoon fed formulas of belief rather than personally engaging in a vigorous tussle of ideas.

Bold thinking discipleship is not merely optional, it is vitally imperative if Christians are to engage the world in a way that makes people hungry for what they have to offer—a muscular gospel. Without it, we have little to offer but one more set of religious formulas. That will always appeal to certain types of people. But it will never influence the world mightily for Christ.

Only bold thinking Christianity has the potential and power to do that.

Courage

C.S. Lewis:
"Courage is not simply *one* of the virtues, but the form of every virtue at the testing point, which means, at the point of highest reality." (C.S. Lewis, *The Screwtape Letters*, Letter 29)

FIVE

HALTING THE DRIFT OF REALITY TOWARD DOGMA

Are We Immune From the Pitfalls of our Predecessors?

> "Therefore we must pay closer attention to what we have heard, lest we παραρυωμεν (drift away) from it."
> —Hebrews 2:1

παραρεω: PARARHEO—*Drift*

PARARHEO is used infrequently in the New Testament but is a concept full of potential meaning (and danger) for the Christian. PARARHEO again highlights the necessity for clear thinking and mental wakefulness. Literally," to flow or glide by," or "let carelessly pass," the meaning implies *mental* drift—the failure to give due heed and attention to important truths. Hebrews 2:1 contrasts bold thinking with lazy thinking in its two phrases: "Therefore we must *pay the closer attention* [προσεχειν: PROSECHEIN—literally, "to give heed more earnestly"] to what we have heard, lest we *drift away* [παραρυωμεν: PARARYOMEN] from it." (**RSV**) The King James renders the second phrase "...lest at any time we should let them slip." PARARHEO is also sometimes translated "slide," hence the word backslide.

IT IS A PRINCIPLE OF THE SPIRITUAL LIFE that movement is constantly occurring. There is no such thing as spiritual neutral. If we are not moving *forward* spiritually, we will inevitably drift *backwards*.

Thoughtless, mindless, growthless παραρεω is the lethal enemy of spiritual vitality.

There are times in the history of the church when debate over various specific doctrinal or theological issues opens doors to more general principles. The *specific* discussion prompts and stimulates *larger* trends and truths to become clarified. The results of such new focus are unpredictable and take God's people in new directions. As a result, the church is forever changed.

Sometimes for the better. But not always.

The church is a dynamic, fluid, incomplete, growing, and extremely human entity, not a perfect one. Thinking Christians of all ages have looked back during the two thousand year history of the church and said, "This was a positive development in our witness that furthered the cause of Christ…" while also admitting, "That was not such a good development…it may have set our witness back a few generations, if not centuries." The crusades are the classic and oft quoted example of the latter.

There is clearly much debate over which is which. Was the evangelical missionary fervor that accompanied the 19th century colonialism of the West a positive or negative influence? Was the lasting impact of the charismatic movement of the 1960s and 1970s positive or negative? With the advent of modern telecommunications as a tool for spreading the gospel, what has been the long-range impact of televangelism on the church and how it is viewed by the world? Has the obsession with prophecy over the final three decades of the 20th century added to or detracted from an accurate awareness of how God works in human life and in human history?

Obviously, it depends on whom you ask. Was positive growth occurring…or backward παραρεω?

Catholics are busy asking similar questions about the changes brought about by various Vatican councils and Catholicism's historic responses to cultural shifts. Are they positive or negative? Do they represent growth or drift?

The point is: The church is constantly changing, adapting to shifts in culture, modifying its approach, rethinking its doctrines, widening its scope. In general this is a healthy tendency. The church has to *grow*, and growth means change. Growth also means recognizing where we have drifted, where we have had it wrong, and making adjustments—whether it be in doctrine, in theology, in response to the world, or in response to one another—so as to get it right.

Change is part of growth. But we have to make sure that change is moving in the right direction.

We have adjusted our approach to missions. Adjustments have come to the charismatic wings of Protestantism and Catholicism. Most would agree that the excesses of televangelism need some tempering. Yet have we brought the eyes of intelligent scrutiny to bear upon our belief systems and doctrinal orthodoxies themselves? Many of those doctrines have roots in the middle ages and even earlier, and have not been subject to much scrutiny since?

Are we really satisfied that they tell all there is to tell?

ARE WE IMMUNE TO ERROR IN OUR TIME?

There is nothing so odious about admitting we've got something wrong. That's how growth occurs. The quickest way toward truth is to say, "I need *more* truth."

When Martin Luther nailed his *Ninety-Five Thesis upon Indulgences* to the door of the castle church at Wittenberg in October of 1517, he was attempting to address two primary specific issues in the church where negative drift had taken place—the system of indulgences, and the doctrine of justification by faith. But the debate sparked a revolution within the church of far more sweeping scope that changed Christendom forever. Indeed, his actions opened the door to a discussion of the very nature of how God relates himself to man. The *specific* discussion was of huge *general* import. By saying, "We've drifted...we have had it *wrong* on these two points," Luther led the church into an explosive reformation of needed growth and change.

It may be that the church of Jesus Christ, as it was in 1517, is at just such a critical crossroads in this third millennium since its Lord walked the earth.

An updated and more expansive perspective of what God wants and is trying to accomplish on the earth through his people, and by what means, may be required in our time. I believe God is anxiously waiting to illuminate this new perspective and bring the needed change to the church that will accompany it. This refocusing period of adjustment may in time represent so significant a turning point in the development of the church that Christians of the future will look back on this era of focus and debate as a Second Reformation.

LOOKING BEYOND ONE'S OWN DOCTRINAL CULTURE

A monumentally important principle— grasped by few, probably admitted by fewer—is that to grow in truth requires recognition that we do *not* possess full truth and need *more* truth.

Put more simply: To grow requires the recognition that we can drift in backward directions, that we can be wrong. It is the unusual pastor or theologian who can make such an admission about long cherished doctrines.

We are shortsighted. Steeped and immersed in the doctrines and traditions that surround us by our spiritual culture and environment, we make assumptions that are not necessarily accurate. The believers of Luther's day cannot all be written off as stupid, unenlightened, unspiritually responsive people. There were good, obedient, prayerful, Godly men and women alive then too, just as there have been in every era. And yet these good, obedient, prayerful, Godly men and women believed that God worked through the system of indulgences then prevalent in the church. They were too immersed in the tradition and doctrine of the time to be able to see beyond it.

That's an easy enough example to grasp. You and I are *not* culturally immersed in a spiritual environment where indulgences are the norm, so we can easily see beyond that particular doctrinal deficiency which bound the church at a particular time in history. What is not so easy to see is that we *are* immersed in a spiritual culture that produces blind spots of its own. Surrounded by that culture, we accept the teachings and doctrines of our own spiritual teachers, priests, and pastors without asking if there is more truth to be had out beyond the borders of the accepted theology that we have been fed all our lives.

Escaping the pitfalls of one's own doctrinal culture has been the Achilles heel of the church since the apostolic age. We can't discern our own limitations any more than we can smell our own bad breath. Objective self-analysis has never been one of the church's strong points. It is very difficult to recognize when your forward momentum has stalled and you've begun to drift.

The result is nearly always the same. History has proven it and re-proven it a hundred times. Spiritual realities fade. Drift sets in. Vibrancy is replaced by dogma and religious systems and institutions. That institutional dogma remains in place until another bold voice at some future time cries out against the drift and calls again for change and growth and a rebirth of reality.

Then the cycle begins again.

Are we really so very different than the people of Luther's day? We see the short-sightedness of *their* ideas about God's work. But we cannot see the shortsightedness of our *own*.

Our own realities drift into dogma too.

That's why a fresh debate is needed, just as it was needed in 1517. We've got to look up and out and beyond the blind spots and doctrinal errors embedded and ingrained and produced by the spiritual culture of our times. We are not so unique as we like to think. We are faced with the same need as Christians of all eras. We are not immune to the same pitfalls.

A KNEE JERK RESPONSE TO THE UNFAMILIAR

One of the remarkable and puzzling traits of the ordinary religious mind is its stubborn and argumentative inflexibility in the face of unfamiliar ideas. All my life I have found this tendency to be remarkable and bewildering. One would suppose that spiritual men and women would be *more* open to ideas than the average person of the world. But in fact, just the opposite is the case. Try as I might, I simply cannot understand this frustrating and, in my view, unChristlike phenomenon.

We reject what goes against the familiar. The response that springs to mind when confronted with a new idea isn't, "Wow, what if it's true?" but, "It's unfamiliar, therefore I don't like it and reject it without looking into it further."

Sadly, that's the kind of people Christians often are. We dismiss the new because we have been so saturated with the traditions of our various orthodoxies. As spiritual men and women, we are conditioned to argue against in automatic knee-jerk fashion anything contrary to what we have been taught. Our spiritual leaders have schooled us in this response by their example. It is how they respond to ideas outside their scope of reference too. We have watched them so long that we think it's the right thing to do. It is absolutely foreign to the knee-jerk mentality to respond to new ideas with, "Hmm...you make a fascinating point...I had not considered that before...perhaps I have not seen this issue as clearly as I thought I had."

When you have raised thorny questions or made probing suggestions about some controversial point to your Bible study leader, how often have you heard the above words?

How often has your pastor said, "You might be right, I might be wrong."

On the other hand, how many times do you see touchy questions responded to with ready-made answers—push a button and out comes a pre-programmed response. Our teachers and leaders and pastors and priests are positively full of answers. One cannot help occasionally wondering if they ask enough questions.

The dilemma before us really reduces to: What if the familiar doctrine is wrong? How ought we to respond? Should we respond with ready-made, push-button, knee jerk answers...or with openness to explore what might be God's deeper intent, mysteries hidden away in places that formula answers cannot penetrate? We mustn't forget the indulgences.

FEAR OF NEW IDEAS

The very suggestion of new ideas will no doubt have prompted some to put this book aside before now. Among them will be certain pastors, leaders, teachers, priests, and doctrinal expositors who will warn their people, "Do not read that man's words." Others, however, may have long felt an undefined queasiness in their spiritual gut prompted by the inadequacy of certain teachings in which they have been indoctrinated. These individuals may be excited by new possibilities. Those pastors, leaders, teachers, and priests among this latter group will be those not satisfied with formula responses, and who will challenge their hearers with important questions and principles seldom raised among their traditional thinking colleagues

There may not be many of you. In all times and in all ages the accepted doctrine, sanctioned, endorsed, and promoted by the theological hierarchy of the church, is a doctrine from which people are afraid to swerve.

In general, people have one of three reactions to thorny, controversial, and debated spiritual issues: They *ignore* them. They *fear* them. Or they become *angry* and defensive when presented with an idea that might threaten a viewpoint they espouse.

But all three are symptoms of spiritual drift not vibrancy.

Are *ignorance, fear,* and *anger* the models that the Apostle Paul exampled for us as he sought to come to grips with a new faith that went against nearly everything he and other first century Jews had been taught all their lives?

Hardly. Paul was a bold and courageous thinker, unafraid to explore beyond the boundaries of tradition and orthodoxy.

It is a sad indictment against those leaders and spokesmen and those in the clergy who make it their business to illuminate matters of faith, that they have taught Christians to ignore and fear the unknown corners of faith rather than to explore them boldly and enthusiastically. We should never be satisfied with the status quo of our lives with God.

Bold thinking Christians must do the opposite, not to satisfy the curiosity or the intellect with opinions on where Cain's wife came from, in what century the flood occurred, or what we are to make of Paul's statement that women should not speak in church. What's at stake is bigger than that. Bold thinking can't be reduced to small specifics. Our emphasis must instead focus on how we approach such issues, learning to take up the challenge to think for ourselves, perhaps by asking more questions than we answer.

It is our *methodology* that is crucial, not that we try to pinpoint specifics with doctrinal precision.

Do we bury our heads in the sand? Do we cling without logic and reason to knee-jerk explanations that do not probe the depths of Christianity's dilemmas and inconsistencies?

I have several books on my shelves with titles along the lines of "Answers to the Bible's Tough Questions." Invariably their authors attempt to explain those things in Scripture that we do not have enough information to understand adequately. The attempt to provide ironclad "answers," however, always strikes me as slightly presumptuous—as if we can know all there is to know about Scripture.

Many thrive on such attempts, expending enormous energy and study in the quest to discover the exact date and month of Jesus' birth, on archaeological proofs for various Old Testament stories, exploring every biblical conundrum, trying to *prove* the existence of Noah's Ark and *disprove* evolution, and on and on.

Such topics are interesting to me...but relatively unimportant. Study is a means to an end—which is to know God aright. We will never know God's heart by trying to prove the existence of Noah's ark. We know him by learning what kind of God he is, and by trusting him and obeying him.

The Christian church of today is far from homogeneous. It has many such hierarchies—Catholic, mainline Protestant, Evangelical, Orthodox, and so on—each promoting its own accepted doctrines. But they are all alike in that the leaders of these hierarchies teach their people to fear inquiry by calling diverse doctrines "dangerous," and attaching the dreaded label "heresy" to the most far-reaching of them. In our time, one of the most scathing critiques that can be leveled by evangelicals against ideas they find threatening is to call them *liberal*. From the other side of the spectrum, no more damning charge can be fired than by calling an idea *fundamentalist* in nature.

By a huge variety of subtle labels and tactics are believing men and women injected with fear toward any ideas other than what their own spiritual mentors deem appropriate. Most church leaders, pastors, teachers, evangelists, and priests, therefore, do not encourage their listeners to think. To do so might undermine the dependence of the people on their own words of wisdom given out from week to week. It has thus come to be assumed that teachings of doctrine and theology must never originate in the pew, they must only originate from the pulpit, whence springs all truth.

The specifics vary greatly, but in certain ways we are not so very unlike that church of 1517 before Martin Luther exploded it apart. We still look to our priesthood gurus to dispense our doctrines like spiritual pharmacists. We fear to think beyond the doctrinal boundaries they establish.

Can you be one of the few capable of looking beyond those boundaries, beyond the old paradigm, beyond the cultural milieu of our own time?

It is the bigger picture of who God is that we seek. I don't really care who Cain's wife was. But I care with all my heart who God is. So I will delve, and delve boldly, into Scriptural unknowns. Not so that I can fill in an informational matrix of scriptural data, but so that God's nature, character, and eternal purpose are more clearly illuminated, enabling me to obey and fall in with that purpose in a more dynamic way.

Can we be courageous and prayerfully open-minded enough to approach the Bible in the spirit of Paul, saying, "God, how big might you be! How expansive might be your plan! Blow open the doors of my faith to see beyond the boundaries of small-thinking men!"

COURAGE TO START A REVOLUTION

Those thinkers among you—both you who sit in the pew and you who occupy the pulpit—may be few. But you know who you are. You may not be many in number, but it is out of your courage to seek larger truth from God that a Second Reformation may well be born.

It takes courage to start a revolution...usually the courage of one. Can you be that one? Can you summon the humility to look beyond the familiar of what you have always believed? Can you summon the courageous humility to seek truth from God rather than from what those steeped in the culture of traditional but possibly erroneous thinking say you are *supposed* to believe?

Martin Luther began his exploration of the larger scope of God's work alone too. But fresh ideas that ring with truth—however unfamiliar they may be at first hearing—cannot be stopped. Luther opened the door in his time, and the groundswell grew until it was a flood.

So too, you few humble courageous souls who determine to explore God's larger purposes may face criticism and condemnation just as he did. Yet from your ranks the groundswell of bold thinking may grow in our time, as it did in Luther's, as one shares that truth with another, here a courageous pastor willing to put his future on the line, there a stout hearted Bible student eager to probe the larger intent of the Scriptures, until...the dike breaks and new truth from God breaks upon the church.

So take heart. God's Spirit is speaking. We must quiet our hearts and hear his Voice. The future of the church may be at stake. We have to hear him aright.

Drift...or Learn to Fly

One of C.S. Lewis's most familiar passages pinpoints the danger of spiritual drift by likening us to eggs. All movement is either forward into increasing life and vibrancy, or it eventually relapses into drift backwards toward spiritual stagnation and eventual death.

"When he said, 'Be perfect,' He meant it. He meant that we must go in for the full treatment. It is hard; but the sort of compromise we are all hankering after is harder—in fact, it is impossible. It may be hard for an egg to turn into a bird; it would be a jolly sight harder for it to learn to fly while remaining an egg. We are like eggs at present. And you cannot go on indefinitely being just an ordinary, decent egg. We must be hatched or go bad." [13]

Lewis was of course talking about the individual internal life of the Christian. He was speaking of the level of transformation we allow the Christ-life to exercise upon and within our hearts. But the same principle applies to our belief systems as Christians. They too must grow, expand, deepen...or they also will wither and die.

This principle of growth—whether in brain or heart—we find echoed in the words of George MacDonald:

"The love that enlarges not its borders, that is not ever spreading and including, and deepening, will contract, shrivel, decay, die." [14]

SIX

HISTORIC CHRISTIANITY

Does "Tradition" Validate Truth?

> "You have a fine way of rejecting the commandment of God,
> in order to keep your παραδοσιν (tradition)."
> —Mark 7:9

παραδοσις: PARADOSIS —*Tradition*

PARADOSIS is used by Jesus to describe what he calls "the tradition of the elders"—the teaching, ordinances, instructions, and tradition handed down generation after generation by the Rabbis, including *interpretations* of the Law that were then substituted for and elevated to the same authority as the Law itself. In Jesus' mouth, notably in Mark 7, the term is negative and is equated with the most blatant hypocrisy of the scribes and Pharisees. Paul uses it similarly to refer to Old Testament traditions (Galatians 1:14) and general traditions ("philosophies") of men (Colossians 2:8). But he also uses PARADOSIS in a positive sense to indicate his own teaching that he has passed on (1 Corinthians 11:2) and of Christian doctrine in general (2 Thessalonians 2:15).

MY WIFE AND I AND TWO OF OUR SONS stopped in Italy a few years ago en route to the wedding of a dear friend and spiritual daughter in Germany. We spent what time we had in as many museums and galleries as we could squeeze into our schedule.

We must have seen a thousand or more paintings, mostly pre- and renaissance era, on various religious themes. We were moved most of all by Michelangelo's work—the unbelievable Sistine Chapel and various sculptures in which he dared represent more wide-reaching themes than had any artist before him: God the Father, Moses, a nude David, a massive Mary holding the dead Jesus in her arms. Michelangelo was certainly a "bold thinker" of his time.

THE BIGGEST OF QUESTIONS

The many images of God and Jesus—from Michelangelo's enormous "Last Judgment," to tiny Byzantine icons of a mere two inches—have been swirling through my brain ever since. I have wondered what would be considered a representative picture that accurately characterizes what most Christians throughout history have thought of God.

Has historic Christianity truly envisioned Jesus as unsmiling and dour, who, with his Father, will wield thunderbolts of final judgment against humanity? Do these renaissance paintings in fact portray God and Jesus as they were thought of at the time, images so visually stunning that they deepened themselves into tradition in the coming centuries?

As we walked about the Sistine Chapel, I was drawn back and forth between the two most famous of its frescoes—the wonderful image of Creation in the middle of the ceiling, and the haunting array depicting the Last Judgment occupying an entire adjacent wall. Both are truly masterpieces of art and theology. Yet even bold-thinking Michelangelo could not escape the prevailing theological conception of God's ultimate judgment, which he made paramount over all other aspects of the biblical story. How could such a man, I wondered, who captured so tenderly the Father-love of creation, with God extending the finger of life toward Adam (a wonderful and beautiful image!), then portray such an angry Jesus sending half of creation away from him? The two frescoes seemed to represent a reversal of the modern theologic schizophrenia about God (a loving Jesus protecting us from a wrathful Father) presenting instead a compassionate Father and an angry Jesus.

Throughout our time in the Sistine Chapel, my head moving back and forth between the two contrasting images, I realized that Michelangelo had portrayed in that room a visual representation of the most significant question in the universe that man has been asking since the dawn of time:

Who is God?

This art of Christian tradition sent me reflecting yet further about "historic" and "traditional" Christianity on a larger scale, and the esteem in which many hold that "tradition." The question arose: What role ought tradition rightly to play in our doctrine and in our perception of truth? Is the historic *tradition* of Christianity—with its paintings, its orthodox theology, its portrayal of God's nature, its general interpretation of Scripture, its church structure—representative of Truth on a widespread scale?

HISTORIC...OR *TRUE*?

A book was released a few years ago with which some may be familiar—*If Grace Be True* by Philip Gulley and James Mulholland—setting forth a case for the universal salvation of mankind. This historically controversial doctrine (often also called "universal reconciliation") is not so scandalous an idea for those at the more liberal end of the Christian spectrum to handle. But within fundamentalism it represents heresy pure and simple.

The reaction by the evangelical media was knee-jerkingly predictable and patronizing: "...the book unfortunately goes beyond traditionally accepted biblical grace... Christianity as most evangelical Christians know it is severely compromised here." Another reviewer spoke of the authors' rejection of "the church's traditional doctrines of salvation and eternal justice."

My response was not one of surprise. You come to anticipate these things, and don't *really* expect Christians in officialdom to think in fresh ways about controversial topics. Orthodoxy *has* to preserve itself however it can. The means by which it does so is often with eyes and ears closed to potential revelations of truth from outside its own self-erected borders.

In this particular case it was evangelical and fundamentalist orthodoxy that was up in arms. For other debatable points the attacks might come from different quarters within Christendom. The two evangelical reviewers obviously felt that historic Christian "tradition" somehow stood as an overarching validation of scriptural accuracy.

As I pondered their words, I wondered when "the church's traditional doctrines" became such a bulwark to protect and preserve high truth.

The question I found myself asking was this: When did "historic Christian tradition" emerge as such a shining beacon of virtue, integrity, wisdom, Christlikeness, and scriptural purity?

I was a little confused. For I look back on the 2000 year history of the church with just the opposite perspective, with sadness and grief that God's people have so *poorly* carried out the instructions and followed the example of their Master. Because of that widespread lack of obedience, I grieve further that Christian tradition has so *inaccurately* portrayed Jesus and his Father, and has so thoroughly *mistaken* much of Scripture's truth.

If we look to what has been "traditionally accepted" through the history of the church, it seems we're going to find ourselves in trouble. What price the Crusades and many inquisitions and countless beheadings?

Are "historic Christianity" and "traditionally accepted doctrines," terms that we simply pull out of a hat when we want to stamp a certain point of view with an air of authenticity. Fundamentalists are great for doing the same with the terms evangelical and scriptural—investing the two words with the force of unassailable truth.

I doubt it's quite so easy. What do such terms really mean? Who is going to define what makes something "scriptural?" Does being historical make a doctrine right?

Speaking for myself, I don't care if an idea has been held by believers throughout "historic Christianity," or if it represents the "traditional doctrine" of the church. But I care with all my heart whether or not it is *true*.

There is a big difference. It is perhaps a difference to which church leaders within historic Christianity have not paid close enough attention.

HIGH TRUTH

It is my deep belief and conviction that the summital truth of the universe, and the essential and foundational message toward which Scripture points and in which history itself culminates in the person and teaching of Jesus Christ, is this:

That God our maker is not a mere "creator" in the abstract but is our very personal Father, our *Abba*, a good and patient and forgiving Father who desires to live in intimacy with all his creatures in a oneness of joy and mutually flowing and responsive love. His is a Father-love that is easy to please yet hard to satisfy until we submit to become fully his sons and daughters. He will rid both our hearts and the universe of sin because he will have us be his perfect and blessed children. His is a Father-love to which we have the opportunity as well as the duty to respond in the willing self-chosen obedience of childship. It is this Father-child relationship which Jesus came to example to us that we, his younger brothers and sisters, might learn how to enter into it, imperfectly but substantially, while yet in this life by yielding our own wills into the perfect will of the Father.

Think carefully about that last paragraph in which I have set down a brief statement of truth as I perceive it. My words are anything but representative of Christianity through the centuries.

If ever I stood outside "historic Christian παραδοσις," it is with such a statement of belief. This is anything but the portrayal of God's nature and purpose that his people have presented to the world.

LOW IMAGERY

Throughout the Old Testament, God was known as the great and terrible Jehovah of Sinai, a remote being of smoke and fire on whose face man could not look lest he die. It remains a mystery whether such was God's intent—to represent himself so differently than the garden life of Genesis 2 and than the reality Jesus later clarified—or whether such images were necessitated by so many centuries of superstition and unbelief that there was no way he could begin to reapproach a mankind that had become so depraved as to have forgotten him other than in such obscure forms. Fatherhood was apparent in the garden. Yet within a few short chapters of Scripture, it had all but vanished from the consciousness of men. Thereafter it appeared in a few brief glimpses through the occasional eyes of childlike prophets and kings. Then finally came that wonderful night in Bethlehem, after which all mankind would have the opportunity to know Fatherhood again in its fullness.

And yet the sad, indeed the heartbreaking reality that surely brings tears to the Father's eyes, is that since the time of Jesus, when God's Father-nature was so clearly and fully revealed *(If you have seen me, you have seen the Father,)* God's people—now calling themselves Christians as well as Jews—have continued to present a Sinai-picture (now infused with "Christian" symbolism but still based on old covenant principles) not an *Abba*-picture of God's nature to the world.

If one has any doubt of that, all he or she has to do is spend a day or two in Florence or in the Vatican Museum in Rome to see how God was portrayed to the world in the early centuries of the second millennium A.D. Nor did the Reformation do much to alter that imagery. The *style* changed. The imagery became more realistic and personal. But the essential *character* of God (with the exception of

Michelangelo's ceiling) remained substantially the same.

The God portrayed by the Protestants after Martin Luther was in most respects the same as what had come before.

The Sinai God of Moses became the vengeful God thirsting for retribution of the Prophets.

The vengeful God of the Prophets became the remote and distant God of the Pharisees.

The remote God of the Pharisees became the obscure God of Catholicism's Trinity who had no direct contact with man without a priestly mediator

The obscure God of early Catholicism became the holy, sovereign, unapproachable God of Calvinism who must punish sin to all eternity.

Traditional Christianity, in its portrayal of God, is succinctly summed up by Jonathan Edward's fiery sermon "Sinners in the Hands of An Angry God," and the sandwich board prophet proclaiming, "Flee from the wrath that is to come!" The familiar imagery may not always be permeated with fundamentalist hellfire-and-brimstone overtones. But the underlying doctrine remains pervasive throughout most of Christendom. The language of Catholicism moderates the doctrine. But an angry God, with hell lurking in the background, remains central to Catholicism's Prayer Book and Fundamentalism's altar call alike.

The God of Sinai—vengeful, remote, distant, obscure, sovereign, unapproachable, thirsting to punish sin—still dominates Christian theology three-and-a-half millennia later. The tradition continues. Little has changed but a softening of the imagery around the edges.

Meanwhile...where is the Father of Jesus Christ?

May God forgive the centuries of unbelief that the church (Catholic and Protestant, Orthodox and Anglican) has perpetuated since the radiant voices of Mark and Paul and John and Luke, and the Lord himself, were silenced, and the church lapsed into an old covenant interpretation of their words. May God forgive us for replacing the *Abba* of Jesus' heart with the fearsome Almighty tyrant of Sinai required by the unbelief of a stiff-necked and rebellious people both ancient and contemporary, both pre-Renaissance and post-Reformation—more intent on punishing sin than drawing his children to his breast—then mingling with that Sinai image through the years the election of Calvin and the misunderstood hell-fire of Jonathan Edwards, at length obliterating altogether the loving Father of Jesus Christ in favor of a grotesque and more than half-pagan image of fire, thunderbolts, and vengeance.

No wonder the Crusades and Inquisitions and untold religious wars and murders and burnings at the stake in the name of Christianity have so soured the world on our message that it is at length poised on the brink of rejecting Christianity *en toto* as the soul of Western Civilization:

We have not known who God is!

Do I stand outside historic Christianity in my worship of and obedience to the Father of Jesus rather than the false images of him that flow of history has produced?

The only answer I can make is, I hope so.

How could I possibly endorse the image of God represented by the four main streams of the organized church and their traditional theologic orthodoxies between 100 A.D. and the year 1824, when a new voice was born into the world to turn the eyes of many back to our gospel origins, there to behold a Father about whom Jesus said, *Now you may look in his face. Indeed, you must look into his face, for there you will discover the smile of love.*

I am proud to stand *outside* an historic Christianity which portrays an image of an angry and fickle God. I take my stand instead with our brothers David, Mark, Paul, Luke, John, Matthew, and a handful of others who have seen the Father as he really is, because they have beheld his face in the face of the Lord himself.

HISTORIC ERRORS

It will be obvious from the foregoing that, in my view, it can be argued that historic Christianity is in many instances an indictment *against* truth rather than a banner proclaiming it. Would we really argue that for most of its history the church has gotten it *right* and represented full truth about very much at all?

For three-fourths of the church's history, Catholicism and Orthodoxy *were* the church. When it comes to church structure, hierarchy, and priesthood, the Catholic and Orthodox churches are really the only segments of Christendom, certainly no protestant denomination, that can lay a legitimate claim to represent "historic" and "traditional" Christianity.

For more than half the church's history, it was considered wrong for the laity to read the Bible. Those of us who love reading the Bible for ourselves...we stand outside historic Christian tradition. There was a time we would have been heretics.

It would be considered as falling within historic Christian tradition to make war against one's adversaries and to pray to Mary.

Even anti-Semitism and other racial prejudice, sadly, has roots in Christian "tradition."

How many examples could we cite? It would not be mere dozens, but hundreds of traditions, doctrines, beliefs, and attitudes that millions of sincere Christians have adhered to...that have simply been *wrong*.

Many of those who led the church throughout its history in the focusing of its beliefs and doctrines were certainly devout, Godly, and prayerful men. However, within the historic flow of Christendom, for every leader who has truly apprehended truth about God's nature, there have been a hundred crusaders eager to see God through the lenses of their own passions, biases, and political aims.

Odious and terrible things have resulted...and they are indelibly linked in the world's eyes to "historic Christian tradition." Even the Enlightenment and Age of Reason and increasing secularization of the 18th and 19th centuries were in large measure responses to the horrific religious wars of previous centuries. Who can fault the world for rejecting our message when we have repeatedly gone to war with the banner of Christ waving in front of our legions? The thing is monstrous in its implications.

The church has only itself to blame for the rampant unbelief now threatening to sink western civilization altogether.

It is not only our tradition of atrocities that is culpable. We also have to look at many of our traditions of doctrines. Christian *practice* flows out of Christian *doctrine*. The two are inseparably linked. If our practice has been weighed and found so wanting, we must seek at least a partial explanation in the grievous misunderstanding of certain key doctrines.

I repeat: We mustn't forget the indulgences.

THE TRADITION OF THE ELDERS

Much of "historic Christianity" represents what Jesus called "the παραδοσις (tradition) of the elders."

A notable exchange between the Pharisees and Jesus occurs in Mark 7, to whose piercing truth in reference to itself modern Christendom remains almost entirely oblivious. If Jesus were to appear in our midst in the flesh today, would we really be so surprised to see a duplication of this exchange taking place with the very leaders and theologians who consider themselves his most faithful ambassadors upon the earth? To whom would he speak first—evangelical preachers, or the theologians of Catholicism at the

Vatican...or perhaps Jewish leaders in Jerusalem? Whether his probing words would be any more successful in opening the hearts of evangelical, Orthodox, Catholic, or Jewish leaders to more expansive truth than they were against the closed-mindedness of the Pharisees would be an interesting inquiry to consider.

As you recall, the Pharisees approached Jesus with the complaint that his disciples were eating with unclean hands, without having observed the proper ceremonial cleansing.

"So the Pharisees and teachers of the law asked Jesus, 'Why don't your disciples live according to the tradition of the elders instead of eating their food with 'unclean' hands?'

"He replied, 'Isaiah was right when he prophesied about you hypocrites; as it is written: 'These people honor me with their lips, but their hearts are far from me. They worship me in vain; their teachings are but rules taught by men.''" (Mark 7:5-7)

Were a similar conversation taking place today, I think Jesus would substitute for "the tradition of the elders" the phrase "traditional church orthodoxy."

"You have let go the commands of God," I believe Jesus would say, "and are holding on to your traditional evangelical orthodoxies. (Or substitute *Catholic, Greek Orthodox, Pentecostal, Anglican,* or *Jewish orthodoxies*.) You have a fine way of setting aside the commands of God in order to maintain your own doctrine...Thus you nullify the word of God by the orthodoxy that you have handed down. And you do many things like that."

CLEARING THE WATER AND INCREASING THE FLOW

Obviously no one is suggesting that we ignore the flow of truth that has come down to us through history. The church was intended as God's instrument for the transmission of life throughout the world. It has not *entirely* failed in its mission. Indeed, there have been notable and significant successes. The fact that God's Word has been so diligently preserved is a wonderful legacy to the medieval Catholic church in particular, for which we owe an enormous debt of gratitude to countless forgotten brothers who labored in cloisters and monasteries all their lives against huge odds to keep it alive. There are many such examples.

But in its portrayal of God's Father-heart, in spite of devout men who saw glimpses along the way, the church as a whole has utterly failed. Sadly, because of a fundamental misrepresentation of God's nature, the "flow" of life that has leaked out as a result of the church's ministry for 1900 years has been a dripping faucet more than the mighty thundering Niagara of living water God purposed his truth through the church to be to and for the world.

What true life-giving water has gotten through, we should rejoice in and pass on. But neither ought we to ignore to what an extent a Pharisaical tradition of the elders has infected historic Christianity no less than it had the historical Judaism of the first century, rusting the pipes of the church almost to the point at times of blocking the flow of truth through them altogether. Where the rust of tradition and wrong doctrine has impeded the flow of true gospel-water, we need to chip that rust away, vigorously if need be, in order that truth may gush out more freely.

It was this tradition-infested breeding ground of stagnation and self-righteousness that Jesus warned his disciples against. And thus it might well be said of many in our own time, "You have a fine way of setting aside the commands of God in order to maintain your orthodox tradition."

The fact is, the water from the rusty dripping faucet of historic traditional Christianity comes out through some doctrinal pipes brown and dirty. There are many instances where our predecessors have gotten it wrong. The revelation of God is ongoing and increasing. The mighty Niagara of living water will one day gush forth to the amazement of the world. But the longer we as a church are content with rusty pipes and dirty water, the further away that day will be. If our predecessors have gotten it wrong, it is a little silly of us to defend their errors because of some vague thing we call traditional Christianity.

I can hear the pious reviews of Martin Luther's *Ninety-Five Theses* in the 1517 issue of *Christianity Today*: "Ah, but the good Friar Luther has stepped outside the bounds of traditionally accepted doctrine."

I'm sure Martin Luther would have responded to such a charge with a vigorous, "Amen! That's why I nailed my theses to the door—because the historic Christianity of the church has grown corrupt and stagnant. I seek truth, not the tradition of the elders. Traditional Christianity has had it wrong all these years and it's time we redressed those centuries of error."

WHERE DO "NEW" IDEAS ORIGINATE?

In mentioning the book earlier and the knee-jerk response of evangelical reviewers to it, the intent was not to single out this one particular set of ideas, or any other, but to set forth a perspective to guide us in responding to bold and honest scriptural inquiries. Some ideas that seem "new" will be right, others will be wrong. But how can we determine where fresh water of truth is flowing unless we come at such inquiries openly, honestly, and prayerfully?

Throughout historic Christian tradition, being "a Christian" has, at different times and different places, been defined as:

—Being from a Christian nation,
—Being from a Christian family,
—Being baptized,
—Going to church,
—Being a good person,
—Believing in the tenets of Christianity,
—Trusting Christ for salvation,
—Publicly professing one's belief,
—Praying a prayer of repentance.

For 98% of the church's history, the concept of "accepting Jesus into one's heart" as a requisite to salvation was virtually unknown. It was not until the 1950's, and only within that particular segment of Christendom known as evangelicalism, that "inviting Christ into one's heart" was added to the above list. Billy Graham and "The Four Spiritual Laws" ingrained this "new" way of praying a salvation prayer so deeply into the evangelical consciousness that most now take it for granted that this is *the* primary means by which salvation is determined. In many minds this is the "historic" method for becoming a Christian...yet it is only sixty years old!

In fact, here is a *new* development within Christendom that does *not* represent "traditional" Christian orthodoxy. No New Testament writer employed the phrase about inviting Jesus into one's heart. When telling Nicodemus about being born again, Jesus never mentioned inviting him into one's heart.

It is truly a *new* doctrinal approach to salvation.

The question is a simple one, then: Why has *this* particular new interpretation (one not found in the gospels) been so readily accepted into the evangelical playbook, while the idea of universal salvation (for which the authors mentioned earlier *do* make a scriptural case) is summarily rejected? Inviting Jesus into one's heart goes beyond what has been "traditionally accepted" too? Where is the difference?

These are the kinds of questions a bold thinking Christian has to ask?

We need not pursue the subject of salvation further at this point. We're not trying to resolve specific uncertainties...we are trying to retrain ourselves to *think* about the doctrines of our faith with greater acuity and intellectual honesty than the quoted reviewers above demonstrated toward the book *If Grace Be True*.

Many so-called new insights are but the fresh flowering of gospel plants whose seeds have been so long encrusted over by orthodox elder traditions and grown too parched and dry from lack of wholesome water to germinate. When a new voice comes along to knock the rust from the pipes so that pure water again flows out to water God's garden and set the seeds growing in the sunlight of his true revelation, we should not reject the new flowers of wisdom because they have not been seen for generations.

Rather, let us rejoice that the gospel garden is bursting to life again.

All "new" ideas do not originate in gospel soil. There exist spurious, wrong, and heretical ideas as well as true ones. Our responsibility is to distinguish—on the basis of what Jesus said, not necessarily on the basis of learned orthodoxies—between weeds and flowers, between the false and the true, between the Mary Baker Eddys and the George MacDonalds of history, as well as to rightly divide the teachings even of the John Knoxes, John Calvins, John Pipers, and Jonathan Edwards whom some have made doctrinal icons but whose teachings may not at every point represent the flowering of the gospel truth of their namesake at all.

To potential new vistas of truth, some may say, "But brother, we mustn't deviate from the traditional doctrine."

If those new perspectives accurately reflect the spirit and words of Jesus, however, I heartily say, rather, "Let us explore the new so that we might discover more truth! These seemingly new flowers just might be growing from very old first-century seeds."

It may be, in these times of personal renewal when a few fresh voices are getting through to us about the imperative of obedience and the Father-heart of God, that because we are deviating from historic Christianity in certain ways, we are actually starting to get a few things that Jesus said about his Abba Father *right*.

The Two Sides of Christian Tradition

C.S. Lewis spoke of Christian tradition both positively and negatively. In doing so, as always, he hits the nail pretty closely right on the head, pinpointing both its value and its danger.

"Theology is like the map...Doctrines are not God: they are only a kind of map. But that map is based on the experience of hundreds of people who really were in touch with God...if you want to get any further, you must use the map...you will not get eternal life by simply feeling the presence of God in flowers or music. Neither will you get anywhere by looking at maps without going to sea. Nor will you be very safe if you go to sea without a map." [15]

"If ever the book which I am not going to write is written it must be the full confession by Christendom of Christendom's specific contribution to the sum of human cruelty and treachery. Large areas of 'the World' will not hear us till we have publicly disowned much of our past. Why should they? We have shouted the name of Christ and enacted the service of Moloch." [16]

He is here, of course, speaking not about the ideas of Christianity but its practice at many points during its past. But George MacDonald goes further. He also indicts much of Christianity's teaching, as well as those who have taught it, as contributing to that checkered history, which also causes the world not to listen to our message.

"The greatest obscuration of the words of the Lord, as of all true teachers, comes from those who give themselves to interpret rather than do them. Theologians have done more to hide the gospel of Christ than any of its adversaries. It was not for our understandings, but our will, that Christ came. He who does that which he sees, shall understand; he who is set upon understanding rather than doing, shall go on stumbling and mistaking and speaking foolishness." [17]

SEVEN

ONE MAN'S JOURNEY TOWARD BOLD THINKING FAITH

A Mini Spiritual Autobiography

> "The prophets who prophesied of the grace that was to be yours inquired (εξεζητησαν, sought out) and εξηρευνησαν (searched diligently) about this salvation....Therefore, gird up your minds..."
> —1 Peter 1:10, 13

εξηρευναω: EXEREUNAO—*Search*

The subject of the spiritual "search" appears throughout Scripture. Most are familiar with God's words through Jeremiah, "You will seek me and find me; when you seek me with all your heart." (Jeremiah 29:13). This highlights the essence of the spiritual pilgrimage—it is a quest to know God, to know him correctly. It is a search requiring diligence of heart. It is hard work, characterized by the determination to leave no stone unturned to know God as he truly is. It is the opposite of lazy, rote, formula spirituality. Thus, even in his occasional confusion and notwithstanding his outbursts of frustration, God honored Job while Jesus condemned the Pharisees. Job sought God *with his whole heart*. The Pharisees lapsed into dogma. This imperative is emphasized by Jesus repeatedly—seeking the pearl of great price and the treasure buried in the field, asking and seeking and knocking, the parable of the persistent widow. Humility and childlikeness are mental and personal conditions of heart which allows the bold search for truth to be successful.

Several words in the Greek New Testament shed light on the nature of the "seeking heart" that God honors. As noted earlier, most verbs in Greek have two forms. In the case of *search*, EREUNAO, is used both of God searching the heart (Romans 8:27) and the Old Testament prophets searching the Scriptures (1 Peter 1:11). The strengthened form is EXEREUNAO, to search diligently. Both words contain the general sense of "to search after" or "sniff out" or "look into." Philo and Plato used them to indicate the process of a philosophical inquiry.

Seek (EKZETEO) is used of seeking God (often translated *seek carefully* or *seek diligently*) and is found throughout the New Testament. Also related are desire ("yearn for"), ask, examine, question, and inquire. EXETAZO, to seek out and inquire thoroughly, is often rendered "examine." ZETESIS implies a questioning search and inquiry, sometimes translated in Acts 25:20 as "investigate." In 1 Peter 1:10-11, we find three of these words within a single sentence, emphasizing with great force the level of diligence required to apprehend and discover the high things of God. "The prophets who prophesied of the grace that was to be yours EXEZETESAN [inquired/sought out] and EXEREUNESAN [searched diligently] about this salvation; they EREUNONTES [searched/inquired] what person or time was indicated..."

THIS BOOK IS OBVIOUSLY NO AUTOBIOGRAPHY. Intrinsic to the challenge toward bold thinking faith, however, is the principle that learning to think beyond the confines of indoctrinated religious orthodoxies is intimate and individual.

It is a quest...an inward journey...a process...a pilgrimage of growth and deepening spiritual insight and maturity.

Two "P"s and two "I"s describe what we are about together—a *personal process* of *individual intimacy*.

Therefore, it seems appropriate that you know something of how this quest for deeper truth took place in my life.

It was not until some years after his own *Mere Christianity* that C.S. Lewis recounted what he called "The Shape of my Early Life" in *Surprised By Joy*. But as the topics involved in bold Christianity are by nature so individual, it seems that it will perhaps be beneficial of me to do so here in the context of this "personal process" of pilgrimage.

Your journey will be unique from mine. The specifics will vary. Yet hopefully my experience will encourage your own faith journey. Before we are done, you will be able to replace this chapter with your *own* story.

I grew up in a traditional protestant church of the 1950s. My best friend was the pastor's son. Both church and parsonage were like second homes to me, and the evangelical framework of belief gradually infused itself into me and came to represent my outlook on God, life, the world...and myself.

I found nothing in it so odious—though the sermons were dreadfully boring—nor did I have the sense of being indoctrinated into a dogma that represented but one slice of that vast thing called Christendom. The PK and I sought what adventures we could in the rooms, corridors, and on the grounds of the church, sitting together whenever it was allowed on Sundays, making the time pass with the snatched conversations and whispered diversions (aided by sign language, facial gestures, and scribbled notes) with which children for centuries, I presume, have made the tedious minutes of church drag by. My own more liberally minded parents sometimes let me take a book. But I didn't dare read during the sermon when seated down the pew from the pastor's mother-in-law. My friend's mother kept an eye on us from the choir but wasn't able to jab us in the ribs if we got the giggles. Her austere mother, however—the very image of Robert Falconer's grandmother—watched us like a hawk and let nothing pass.

My friend went forward to "accept Christ" at twelve. As he was forty-five days my elder and, in my view, the unspoken leader of our friendship, I was only a few months behind him heading down the aisle to be baptized. Though it was as meaningful as it could have been at the time, the chief significance baptism had on my immediate life were two: I was henceforth allowed to take communion on the first Sunday of every month, and when individual offering envelopes were set out the following January on a table in the foyer I found a box with my name printed on it as a church "member." I found both these developments pretty exciting—well worth the embarrassment of going forward, though not quite worth getting water up my nose when my friend's father forgot to put the handkerchief tightly over my nose when dunking me for the remission of my sins.

INITIAL QUESTIONS

You would have had to ask my parents, or my teachers of those early years, but I think I was generally a compliant and orderly boy. I wasn't a troublemaker or overly boisterous or loud. My friend and I were a couple of church-nerds. If we occasionally goofed off a little in Sunday school, who didn't.

I wasn't a rebel or doubter. But as I received my perfect attendance pin year after year, I began to tire of the pat answer formula-speak that our Sunday school teachers dished out every week from the teacher's manuals that accompanied our student workbooks. As I entered high school and as personal faith became more real, I increasingly reacted against clichés that sounded more and more trite with every passing year. It all struck me as just too convenient, a little too cut-and-dried.

In a good-natured though juvenile way, I gave a few Sunday school teachers a hard time during those years. I could not help myself—I found some of the jargon comical by its simplicity and lack of depth.

I began to raise a few questions—not concerning belief itself, but about the dogmatic answers to everything in the phraseology of evangelical-speak. An evangelically correct doctrine existed about what constituted salvation, the trinity, how often to go to church, about Christian political ideology, about the afterlife and the atonement and the judgment and the end times and the interpretation of every possible scripture. I simply did not respond well to this fill-in-the-blanks approach. It began to bore me just as sermons had in my younger years. I began to hunger for some reality, some meat, even some plain old common sense to go along with the drab memorized explanations.

This jargonistic evangelicalism was no mere product of the 1950s and 1960s which has disappeared in the vibrant renewal within evangelicalism today. Our church back then was pretty cutting edge and not so very different than most big, growing churches of today. I find the exact same formulas and clichés being served up all around me now, some almost word for word from what I was taught fifty years ago. I don't mind the old stories, but I do mind cliché interpretations.

I still find myself bored by most sermons I sit through, though perhaps for different reasons. I still find people communicating in evangelical-speak, a language that sounds like less than nonsense to the world at large we have been commanded to reach. And when the pastor calls upon the congregation to fill in the blanks for questions in the sermon outline provided in the bulletin and flashed on the overhead screen, I find myself wondering if anyone *else* is hungering for more. Half a century has passed. I still find a fill-in-the-blanks approach defining the evangelicalism even of most seemingly vibrant churches.

By the time I was eighteen, a few misgivings were creeping into my brain. In those days, the Billy Graham style moment of repentance and "turning from sin" (the sinner's prayer) was the standard means by which one became *saved*. Yet I was aware that my so-called "salvation" *hadn't* come via some experience of tearful repentance and "decision" *a la* the Graham team.

Subtly I began to wonder if I might have some problems in the salvation department.

Sure, I had gone forward in church during a closing hymn one Sunday morning when I was twelve. But there was no sense of repentance for much of anything, no sinner's prayer, no moment of "decision for Christ," no awareness of my sins, no wonderfully glorious new changed life.

I wasn't a sinner, I was just a kid. It was the carefully scripted means by which one "joined the church" and made a "public profession of faith." But I could identify no particular moment when Jesus "came into my life."

When the charismatic movement hit our church a few years later, my self-doubts deepened. It didn't take long for me to realize that I had even bigger problems with "the baptism" than with salvation. Here my personal experience was not just a little out of step, it was *way* out of step. Fireworks were happening to everyone else, but when I sat in the chair in the center of the room, the fuse was wet. I was a dud.

Everyone was going around talking about who was "Spirit filled." Inside I harbored a terrible secret.

I wasn't.

CRISIS

By the time I was twenty, I had sunk into a crisis of faith.

I wanted to be God's man. The years between my baptism and the age of twenty had been ones of steadily deepening growth toward genuine personal faith. I was praying, studying the Bible with some diligence, trying to practice my faith, witnessing when I had the opportunity, reading Christian books, and participating in several Christian groups. But I knew I was different. I was clearly out of step with the Christians about me who had glowing testimonies about both salvation and their experience with the Holy Spirit. Eventually I began to wonder if I was a Christian at all.

Now "crises of faith" take many shapes and forms. The salient question is whether a crisis occurs *within* faith or *against* faith.

When one begins to "question" and "doubt," what is the object of that *doubt*? What are the motives behind it? What resolution is one seeking? Is one trying to break away from faith and the church, or *deepen* one's Christian experience?

Is one doubting God *himself,* or is one doubting worn out jargon about him? Is one seeking an excuse to *abandon* God, or is one seeking to draw *closer* to God by clearing away the cliché-clutter with which his presence is obscured? Is one seeking to get free of obligation to God, or is one seeking *greater* levels of obedience to him?

In my younger years I had been taught that Jesus wanted me for a sunbeam. I had sung, "I've got joy, joy, joy, joy down in my heart," so many times that to this day multiple verses occasionally rise up unbidden from my subconscious to bang around inside my brain and hound me for days.

But the young man I was at twenty had little joy in his heart. I was anything but a sunbeam for him. Did that mean that Jesus no longer wanted me? Did *anyone* want me? Was there a place for me anywhere in God's scheme of things?

I honestly didn't know. The despondency of that lonely sense of not knowing whether I mattered to God made that twenty-something year old college student weep in broken-hearted sadness more than once.

TWO RESPONSES TO THE SIXTIES

One of my close high school friends was the most outspoken Christian I had ever known. He carried his Bible and witnessed and preached to any and all who would listen. And not in a phony or shallow or obnoxious way. It seemed very real to me at the time. I looked up to him. In a way he represented my ideal Christian. I wanted to be like him.

But I realize now that his was a cliché faith. He had a ready platitude for any occasion, a proof-text scripture memorized for every situation. And a year out of high school this same friend, encountering the rigors and intellectual assaults of 1960s college rebellion, lost his faith and has not walked as a Christian since. His faith wasn't bold in the right way. It had little depth or intellectual vigor that he had wrestled through and made his own. He was "bold" to carry his Bible through the halls of our high school (*long* before it was cool to do so!), and bold to speak out, bold to witness, bold to get in people's faces.

But he was bold with clichés. The deep founding ideas of faith capable of sustaining him amid the assaults of doubt had not been planted within him.

I encountered those same rigors and intellectual assaults against my spiritual training too. I met people whom the clichés did not fit. I encountered ideas the formulas could not combat. Reevaluative thinking leads many to a worship of ideas and their own intellects rather than into deeper truth. This was certainly apparent in the sixties. My friend and I discussed our different responses many times. There were questions *against* faith being launched on all sides by the rebels of the times. But there also exist legitimate questions *within* faith, and it was these that I was asking of my own beliefs and experience.

Unlike my friend, these challenges drove me *deeper* into the Bible, *deeper* into an investigation of God's being. I wanted to find the deeper truths represented rather than throwing out the prosaisms wholesale...and faith along with them.

I wanted to know God, to draw close to him, to obey him. I wanted to be his man. Thus, my so-called doubts were motivated toward the end of trying to get to know God better.

I always think of my friend when I draw the distinction between bold "thinking" faith and "debunking" faith and loud "preaching" faith. Only a *thinking* faith (a *toward*-God faith, not an *anti*-God reaction) will carry one through such times of stress. But this toward-God prayerful reevaluation may involve a challenging of narrow belief, a challenging of cliché doctrines, and indeed it may involve an occasional discarding of certain dogmas because they are found to be less scriptural than advertised.

HARRY AND DAVE

One example of this principle will illustrate the kinds of questions I was asking at the time.

There is a dogma within evangelicalism, an outgrowth of Calvin's doctrine of election, which views the human condition in terms of two exclusive humanities, one entirely lost, one entirely saved, with a clear split between the two. It was this doctrine of a cut-and-dried formulistic delineation that had been slowly suffocating me spiritually.

The reason it was suffocating me was simple: I obviously didn't fit the *salvation* and *baptism in the Holy Spirit* patterns registering in everyone else's lives I knew. If there were only two starkly separated options, *in* or *out*, sheep or goats, elect or non-elect, and if I wasn't "in" according to the formula...then I had a big problem.

It wasn't really fear of hell so much as simple confusion. Where in God's scheme of things did I *fit*?

Judy, my wife-to-be, and I were at the time part of a door-to-door evangelistic effort in our church. It reminded me of using the Four Laws to try to "lead people to the Lord" on the beach when I had been involved with Campus Crusade for Christ. Both programs were unbelievably rote. Every response we memorized to counter "possible objections" was a superficial cliché. And when we found ourselves witnessing one evening to a couple who were obviously already Christians, yet had nothing to offer but to spout back jargon that had no connection to their lives, I knew something was seriously wrong. The leader of our little trio of "witnesses" kept right on with the clichés by the book...I wanted to crawl into a hole and hide.

Two individuals wandered into my life simultaneously about this same time who in a sense represented the two opposite poles of this salvationary conundrum. I hardly realized it at the time, but they were tools God was sending to help me figure out my own place on that eternal spectrum of faith.

A fiery young street Christian by the name of Dave began coming into our little Christian bookstore, and, without anything better to do, hung around for hours preaching to the choir—mostly to me. Dave's "major" so to speak, was hell. He could talk about nothing else than his burden for the lost souls burning now and those who would later be sent to burn for eternity. He was consumed by thoughts of hell. It dominated his entire life's outlook. I do not recall hearing him talk about anything else. He could work himself into such a frenzy that he could yell and weep at the same time.

The other fellow who came to hang out in those days was a sweet, good-natured non-Christian. Gentle and somewhat simple-minded, Harry always had a smile on his face, and, as it struck me at the time, was incapable at that point of making the kind of salvationary decision or praying the sort of sinner's prayer that Dave would doubtless have pressed upon him had he known Harry's state. A press toward a "commitment to Christ" simply would not have computed in his heart and brain. All sorts of pat answers could be trotted out against such a conclusion. But I was there. I *knew* Harry. I knew how meaningless the evangelical phraseology would be.

Harry and I had known one another years before and, through his frequent visits, now rekindled that friendship. Because they met in our Christian bookstore and both were there talking to me (sometimes for hours!) I think Dave assumed Harry to be a Christian. Harry was simply one of those, like me and whatever customers he could corner, whom Dave badgered with ceaseless entreaties to get out onto the streets and get 'em saved and keep the lost out of hell.

The two young men passed like ships in the night. Sweet Harry never had a clue what Dave and his ranting was all about. Dave never had a clue that right in front of him was one of those lost souls he was so burdened for. He was so full of himself, so incapable of seeing people with Christlike compassion, that I doubt he even knew Harry's name.

Dave was one of the most imbalanced, insensitive Christians I ever met. He was like many I have encountered through the years—people who can preach and preach and preach, but who never *see* with the eyes of humble, Christlike compassion. After those few months when our lives chanced to cross, I never saw Dave again. Gradually Harry drifted away too.

Whenever I think of Harry, a smile comes to my face. I haven't seen him in years. I don't even know if he is still living. When I think of him, I am reminded of those dear ones in this life for whom the Father must have a special place in his heart.

As I juxtapose these two young men in my reflections all these years later, I still wonder what God thought of Dave's deranged obsession with hell and Harry's sweet, simply-minded lostness.

At the time, the questions raised by these two young men probed the deepest marrow of my belief system. Rather than simply memorizing "the wages of sin is death" to throw out when witnessing, I wanted to know on a deeper level just what salvation really *meant*. What was the difference between being a Christian and a non-Christian? Where did *Dave* and *Harry* stand at that moment in light of eternity? Was it really as cut and dried as the witnessing manuals presented it?

Had a plane suddenly come crashing into the bookstore killing all three of us there together, would Harry immediately be sent to the fiery doom of Dave's imagination, and Dave be welcomed into heaven, an instantly sanctified saint saved by grace?

Neither scenario computed in the calculus of my Protestant orthodoxy.

Did Dave really display what fundamental tradition called "saving faith?"

Was Harry really standing in "rebellion" toward God, the wages of which were hell and death? Or did that smile and cheerful countenance perhaps mean something on the eternal scale that bromide-interpretations could not account for?

What did *God* think about Dave and Harry?

And, too, lurking behind that question was a bigger one...what did he think of *me*?

THE LIBERATION OF GRAY AREAS

Those two young men brought gray-area thinking home with tremendous force. I point to my lengthy conversations with Dave and Harry as the time when pat-answer, proof-text Christianity began to unravel in my particular life.

I know the many responses that will be dished up to answer the dilemma for me in the letters I will surely get from those who consider me a biblical dunce for being confused about so elementary a doctrine—that goodness has no bearing on salvation, that only God knows each human heart, that we are all unworthy, that salvation comes only by Christ's blood, that in our human wisdom we cannot understand God's ways, that though we may want to find an excuse for good people like Harry, God's word makes clear that his holiness cannot live in the presence of sin, that there is no eternal life outside of saving faith no matter how good one's life. I've been around the block enough times to know how these things go. I'm certain the preceding section will also result in a flurry of salvation tracts being sent to help me out.

I regularly receive mail from readers trying to help me understand some issue or another, full of knee-jerk clichés and lengthy proof-textual passages of scripture which they think I am unfamiliar with. I can only assume there to be no Daves and Harrys in the lives of such individuals. Any honest thinking person who looks deep into the eyes of a Harry with the love of Christ has to wonder how little we must really know of the love God has for the lost ones of his world. There is something wrong with us if we do not raise probing questions to our Abba-Father about such dear ones.

Once I had encountered Dave and Harry, all the truisms of my upbringing were no longer satisfactory. I *knew* those two young men. Proof texts were no good anymore. They could not resolve the dichotomy that said, in spite of Harry's good nature and sweetness, that he was on his way to an eternity in hell if he did not go through a certain process of mind and utter certain rote words which, as it seemed to one who had known him for many years, he would have been incapable of uttering with intellectual clarity and honesty. To have put the sinner's prayer in front of him would have been like asking him to recite a paragraph in an unknown foreign language, a procedure which would have left him in as big a fog as before.

The prayerful scriptural inquiry that resulted over the course of the next several years drove me into a prayerful study of the essence of salvation itself. It was not a search merely to resolve the questions raised specifically by Harry and Dave. It was the much larger question whether the maxims I had been spoon-fed were big enough to contain the full implications of a hundred other important queries about the Christian faith.

Did the formulas satisfactorily answer the quandaries? Or had the ship of my Sunday school platitudes sprung a leak?

It was fundamentalist Francis Schaeffer who helped me see that the dogma of two exclusive humanities was insufficient to explain the human condition. Schaeffer clarified that there exist gray areas in humanity which most evangelical-speak and Calvinist predestination-speak, does not address. He helped me see that salvation was not always purely black and white. A clearly definable *moment of conversion* was not the only means for measuring spiritual reality.

What a help this was to me in my attempt to understand my own salvationary dilemma. I had long been frustrated at being able to locate nowhere amid the pigeon-hole definitions to place *myself*. I didn't fit the formulas. Schaeffer's insight was similar to the point Lewis makes when he says in *Mere Christianity*, "The world does not consist of 100 per cent Christians and 100 per cent non-Christians. There are people...who are slowly ceasing to be Christians but who still call themselves by that name: some of them are clergymen. There are other people who are slowly becoming Christians though they do not yet call themselves so." [18]

This alerted me to the equally important truth that gray areas existed *within* salvation too, and that not everyone necessarily came into relationship with God, or lived out their relationship with God, in exactly the same way.

In both Lewis's and Schaeffer's calculus of spirituality, there *was* a place for me even though I was not a Billy-Graham-formula Christian.

Eventually I discarded my belief in the "two exclusive camps" view of humanity—one entirely saved, the other entirely lost. There will no doubt be some who will seize upon that phrase "discarded my belief" and run with it. *Ah, ha!* they will think. *He was losing his faith! That explains what all this re-evaluation of belief is about!*

I can anticipate the salvation tracts on their way to me already.

But hear my words with TOLMAO and NOEO and discern their import. I only discarded a *lower* untruth in order to embrace a *higher* truth founded in the discovery that God is bigger, more encompassing, higher, broader, and more Almighty than any narrow formula can define.

I traded in a cash register cliché about humanity and salvation for a bigger, broader, more expansive, and *bolder* view—a new view full of mountains and streams and snowy peaks and sunrises and sunsets and ocean vistas...and all the nuanced magnitude of God himself!

This wider outlook about salvation infused me with more tolerance and love for those around me. No longer were they merely sheep and goats, saved and unsaved, according to a precise formula of final judgment. Now they were *people*, into whose eyes I could look with compassion and patience and understanding, and perhaps a little more of the feeling Jesus had when he looked upon the multitudes and saw them as sheep without a shepherd.

Abandoning the formula led me closer to the heart of God.

In discovering *more* of God's nature we always find ourselves living *less* by rote dogma and proof-text. God himself, one finds, is not so neatly boxed up as many orthodoxies would have him. Bold thinking, as I came to define it at least, always looks to *more* of God, not less.

My high school friend, however, did not follow that path. Like many who pride themselves on their intellectual prowess, he made the fatal error of throwing the baby out with the bathwater.

THREE AREAS OF RESOLUTION

The initial areas in which I began to look beyond the orthodox-formulas of my indoctrinated training were three—salvation, the Holy Spirit's work, and my own temperamental uniqueness.

I *had* to look beyond the boundaries in these areas for sheer spiritual survival:

I had to know if I was a Christian though I didn't fit Billy Graham's formula.

I had to know if the Holy Spirit was part of my life though I didn't fit the charismatic formula.

I had to know if God had made me as I was and thus accepted me and loved me as I was, or was I destined to life as a second class Christian because I was not bubbly, outgoing, and perennially joyful?

I had to know. My εξηρευναω for higher truth was underway!

That God flooded me with his love and answered these three personal quandaries, was an ongoing and progressive work over several years. Most of God's best things do not happen all at once. My growth into bold thinking Christianity didn't either. Things take time.

God gradually brought me out of my crisis *within* faith, and the two-year depression that accompanied it, by showing me the simple truth that I had already begun to stumble on years before in Sunday school—that evangelical clichés did not tell the whole story.

Salvation couldn't be contained in a formula box. It didn't come to everyone in the same manner. If my experience did not coincide with a single-moment decision formula as urged by so many evangelists, that fact did not invalidate my own unique walk that perhaps God had begun differently.

Neither could the work of the Holy Spirit be contained in a formula box. If the fireworks did not ignite for me, that did not invalidate the Spirit's quieter, less visible and ongoing work within me.

And finally, if my personality did not produce outwardly visible Christian cartwheels and constant smiles, and even if mine was a temperament prone to bouts of depression (maybe I got to be a raincloud rather than a sunbeam; plants need both sunshine and rain to grow) God was still with me. My temperament did not make me a second class Christian. God had created me as I was, after all. I could actually thank him for my introverted personality. I could even learn to discover *strengths* of personality that might accompany the weaknesses that had till then spiritually crippled me.

These realizations were unbelievably liberating.

THE QUEST WIDENS

What began as a search to understand God's outlook, purposes, and methods as pertaining to my own particular life in the above three areas, gradually became a quest to discover more truth about God in other areas too.

From the realization that there was more to salvation, more to the Holy Spirit's work, and more to the Christian life, than clichés and sunbeams, I drew a life-changing conclusion. There must be more to God's purposes and methods in *all* aspects of revelation.

It was a startling thought.

If evangelical-speak had so simplified these truths of God as to gut them of their essential power, then I had some work ahead of me. And what an exciting prospect I now considered it!

The Bible became, no longer a book of proof-texts, but a multi-layered mystery of revelation. Its truths could not merely be memorized like sentences from a phrase book and then activated by remote control when looking up: "Where to find help when..." or

"How to respond to..." or "Scriptures to give when non-Christians say..."

The mountainous truths of the Bible could never be apprehended in such a way. Its wisdom had to be mined like precious ore. It would only be accurately revealed to one who had probed deep into the mineshaft called *Abba* not those who tried to scale the mountain along the path called *Sinai*.

Only that one tunnel leads to the riches of the Father-lode.

Once the way into that mineshaft began to reveal itself and I began to find truth buried deep inside it, the process of discovery could not be stopped. Truth became its own reward. Never again could platitudes satisfy my hunger. I wanted to know who God was and how he worked beyond the phrase-book mentality.

As I gradually emerged from under the cloud of spiritual self-doubt, I discovered within myself a desire to communicate this more expansive outlook. I wanted to tell people that God was bigger than a single methodology of salvation or of the Holy Spirit's work. I knew it because I was living proof of it.

Two more jargon-heavy theologies eventually came under my prayerful scrutiny—the role of church in the life of the believer, and the widely accepted outlook on the end times, in those years popularized by Hal Lindsay's *The Late Great Planet Earth*.

The former query produced a very painful result. I was essentially labeled *persona non grata* in the congregation where I had grown up. The questions that I was bold to raise concerning reality in church life were too disconcerting. I have not taught, spoken, or been involved in church leadership since. The pain of this rejection, however, as did George MacDonald's ouster from his first pulpit, drove me yet more diligently onward in my quest to know God beyond what people said of him.

Before long—now being actively mentored by George MacDonald's prophetic voice—I was looking at everything with new eyes, eager to discover God's *more* amid the vast sea of evangelical rhetoric.

ENCOURAGING READERS TO THINK

When I began writing, I recognized that God's primary call on my life was to speak to Christians. I felt that call to be one of challenging my fellow believers to think beyond formula-faith. As I have already explained in some detail, it was a far different calling (because our backgrounds and personal stories came from such opposite directions) than that of C.S. Lewis in his writings.

Who in our day boldly says that the Father is greater than the Son? But for fear of offending the fundamentalist orthodoxy of the trinity, we keep our mouths shut. We are afraid to question and probe and explore God's heart.

Similarly, how many Catholics have the courage to step outside their orthodoxy and admit, "This worship of Mary simply isn't scriptural. Who ever came up with the idea that Mary never sinned?"

But we're wimps as well as non-thinkers. We haven't the courage to ask such questions or bring up any of a dozen other sacred cows. Those that do get their hands slapped by the Orthodoxy Patrol.

That is why in my books I have tried to raise thorny issues—to make people *think*. I consider it vital for faith to be *real*. I am in unending hot water with publishers and their editors who don't want their books to rock the boat any more than churches want their pastors to. But in my opinion, our boats need a little rocking!

Whenever salvation comes up, for example, I try to illustrate the truth that God breaks in on every life differently. I myself was such a victim of the untruth that all salvation must come according to the formula immortalized by the Four Spiritual Laws that I now want to encourage readers to view it from a larger perspective. My hope is that here and there I might prevent another young Christian from the suffering I experienced.

I desire to present no new formulas, but to point to the deeper truths toward which Jesus persistently urged his disciples about his Father and what it meant to be his son or daughter.

I am continually dismayed, however, to discover how little hunger exists within Christendom for *more*. Christians, I continue to discover, of every brand and stripe from Catholic to Pentecostal, are mostly content with formulas. They don't want their comfort zones upset. Dogma and orthodoxy are safe. If you never question and never think, you run no spiritual risks.

And thus we arrive full circle back to the challenge set forth in the Introduction—boldness guided by obedience, expansive thinking rooted in scriptural truth. It can be a difficult balance to find.

A NEVER ENDING QUEST

In the forty years since those early 1970's when I was forced to begin thinking about my faith in new ways as a matter of spiritual survival, the quest to understand God's character and know his heart has continued. In many respects it has been a solitary road. I will not say lonely for I have had the greatest life-partner imaginable with whom to engage in the spiritual and intellectual pilgrimage. We have wrestled through ideas, emotions, and spiritual struggles all these years together and it has been stimulating, challenging, and constantly invigorating to our joint-walk with God.

Most such tussles to understand God's ways originate with questions, and often involve pain. The quest to know the heart of God never takes place in a vacuum. The profoundest insights usually come through disappointment, heartbreak, sorrow, and sometimes deep personal anguish. We have been extraordinarily blessed. Our lives have not been nearly so difficult as many. But we have had enough of our share of trials to keep us progressing into the depths of the mountain.

But though not lonely, it has been solitary. We have found occasional pastors and teachers who for brief interludes have challenged us with life outside the formula-box. But we continue to be amazed how wedded Christians are, and *want* to be, to the jot-and-tittle interpretations they are fed. Most churches we have found are so content with doctrine–speak, so proud of their "ministries" and so puffed up about their "worship," that it seems all but impossible for the humble voice of Christlikeness to break through. It is too quiet a Voice for noisy congregations, busy patting themselves on the back, to hear.

So our quest has not discovered much camaraderie through the years. Nor do we find that many Christians even know how to wield the tools necessary to extract the most precious ore from inside the high mountains of an infinitely loving Fatherhood. Thus, we do not share these principles and our invisible inward journeys with many friends.

These are sad admissions. We have not made this a solitary journey by choice. But once you start talking about *more*, about God's being and purpose being *bigger*, one's fellow Christians start looking at you funny. Two roads regularly diverge in a yellow wood. Those seeking *more* will always be destined to travel the *less* traveled path.

What "religious" label would I now attach to myself. None, unless it might be: *Latitudinarian catholic (in the lower case) evangelical.*

Labels are of little interest to me. I would rather say that I am one who desires with all his heart to know God as he truly is. Beyond that, I would simply be known as one who is trying to be a *son of the Father* by attempting with faltering and imperfect steps to do his will, and as one who is a *follower of Christ*, a "Christ-ian" who is seeking to become an obedient child.

The Change That Leads to True Growth

"Mere change is not growth. Growth is the synthesis of change and continuity, and where there is no continuity there is no growth." [19]

"Humanity does not pass through phases as a train passes through stations: being alive, it has the privilege of always moving yet never leaving anything behind. Whatever we have been, in some sort we are still." [20]

Part 2

MULTI-DIMENSIONED SCRIPTURAL TRUTH

*God's revealed Word comes to us in the Bible
in an expansive interpretive tapestry
of many complex nuances and shades.*

Key Scriptural Concepts:

SCRIPTURE, FAITH, TRUTH

EIGHT

THE WORD OF GOD

Literal, Inerrant, Infallible...or Leaky Human Vessel Through Which God Reveals His High λογος?

"All γραφη (scripture) is inspired by God and profitable for teaching, for reproof,
for correction, and for training in righteousness,
that the man of God may be complete, equipped for every good work."
—2 Timothy 3:16

γραφη: GRAPHE—*Scripture*

GRAPHE is the noun related to the verb GRAPHO, to write. The evolution of the language of communication can be seen in both words in their similarity to the English "graph" or "graphic." The original meaning of the noun was a drawing or a painting, then gradually it came to indicate "characters" and thus, in time, writing. Interestingly, the verb form originally conveyed the meaning of *carve* or *engrave*, then *draw* or *paint*. A child *carving* his or her initials into the bark of a tree is touching something ancient in mankind's history, from which all writing eventually developed and the meaning of the word "Scripture" evolved. From writing, GRAPHE took on the sense of an entire *body* of "writings," then ultimate came to indicate the sacred Old Testament Jewish collection, which in its essence simply means "The Writings."

O<small>N A NATIONAL TELEVISION NEWS PROGRAM</small> a few years ago I watched one of evangelicalism's most prominent spokesmen pontificate in holy tones about his belief in the *literal* Word of God.

This minister-author of a major best selling series we are all familiar with consistently used the "literal" claim to validate and support his widely publicized fictional perspective of the book of *Revelation* which was then in its heyday. This same general outlook on the end times has held for over forty years. In that time it has been so solidified into the minds of its adherents as unquestionably *true*, that an entire generation of evangelical Christians is now unable to distinguish whether this orthodoxy originated on the Mount of Olives or the mountains of San Bernardino.

Though the end-times perspective that so took the country by storm prior to Y2K is one that needs to be critically and scripturally examined by bold thinking Christians willing to assess the damage that may have been done by an erroneous presentation of high and holy truths, this is not the place to do so.

But the good would-be prophet's comments on national television point to a larger and more disturbing misconception running rampant within evangelical ranks today, of which a potentially error-ridden second-coming theology is but one element. The question is not one of biblical prophecy *per se*, but rather of an entire approach, or outlook, or frame of reference to the reading and interpretation of the Bible as a whole.

<small>WHAT ARE EVANGELICALS CONVEYING TO THE WORLD—
HUMILITY OR POMPOSITY?</small>

I would help us, if I might, approach the Bible with more accuracy and insight—and more literality if and when it is called for—by understanding more clearly what kind of book the Bible actually is.

To do so, we need first to examine some common misconceptions.

The same man has publicly maintained that Catholics don't know how to read the Bible accurately. Underlying the self-righteous perspective of the famed author is the assumption, not unusual among evangelicals who have not investigated the matter in great depth, that Catholics do not view the Bible as *literal* and *inspired* and *infallible* and *inerrant* as they themselves do. The conclusion drawn from this assumption is that they, evangelicals, are more knowledgeable concerning the Bible's true meaning, secrets, doctrines, and interpretations, than others within Christendom who do *not* share this same adherence to and emphasis on literality.

The man's statement is not only an affront to serious Bible reading Catholics, it is an embarrassment to all of Christendom. During Pope Benedict's brief tenure, I conjectured on the possibility of a biblical discussion between our famed prophecy expert and Benedict. I drew the conclusion that I would put my money on the latter, the depth and erudition of whose books was profound. One wonders if either of them ever read the other's books?

The evangelical's monstrously judgmental outlook is based on an enormous misperception from which nearly all evangelicals suffer. Reading the Bible "literally" is viewed by most evangelicals as the Rosetta Stone of biblical interpretation, without which true scriptural understanding is as impossible as deciphering Egyptian hieroglyphics was prior to the discovery of the famous trilingual inscription near Rosetta, Egypt. Only to those who read it *literally* will the Bible unfold its true meaning. Upon this basis, evangelicals stake their claim to know the Bible's truths more accurately than other Christians.

There are a host of problems here, too many to consider in a single discussion. Not the least of these is the self-righteousness apparent in such a view, and the humility so glaringly absent. Spiritual self-confidence and boldness is one thing, arrogance is another. Jesus certainly stepped forward in the synagogue with confidence when he proclaimed, "Today is this scripture fulfilled in your hearing." He confronted the hypocrisy of the Pharisees, too, with bold self-assurance

The question is not being bold for God in one's approach to Scripture. Our interviewed brother certainly spoke forcefully about his vast knowledge of Scripture. The more important question, however, is what spiritual posture provides a more fertile ground for the growth of Pharisaism and pride, and what sort of attitude gives rise instead to humility. The latter, I might suggest, may be a far more vital ingredient to a proper, balanced, and truthful reading of Scripture than is pietism about one's own vaunted knowledge.

Now, indeed, Jesus knew something about the meaning of Isaiah's words that no one else in that synagogue knew. It is not unreasonable in itself to expect one person to be more knowledgeable than another in probing the depths of the Scriptures. Certain people *do* know the Bible better than others, just like some people know more about nuclear physics than others. The question is whether the parallel is accurate between Jesus (who knew the meaning of Isaiah's words better than his Jewish listeners) and today's evangelicalism (which claims to know the Bible better than other Christians) solely on the basis of *literality*?

As we will see, seeming literality may offer a flimsier foundation upon which to base biblical interpretations than most conservative Christians realize.

LABELS—PRO AND CON

The many labels so prevalent throughout Christendom are generally less than helpful—doing more to divide than provide positive benefit to the dispensation of the Christian message. In one sense, all denominational, fundamentalist, liberal, and conservative words are meaningless if they represent the attempt to define, pigeon-hole, and limit what Christianity is and how it functions. A "Christian" is one who follows Christ and obeys his commands, not one who has attached himself to any particular church, sect, group, or doctrinal persuasion, or who votes to the right or the left, or whose social agenda leans one way or another.

Father, what would you have me do? is the sole validation of working, practical, believing faith in He whom we call the Son of God.

Because of this foundational criteria, every church and Christian group of varying outlook and methodology is full of both Christians *and* non-Christians, including those, as C.S. Lewis says, who are slowly in the process of ceasing to be Christians, and others who are slowly in the process of becoming Christians. Being a Methodist, a Catholic, or a Baptist does not make one a disciple, it only makes him a Methodist, a Catholic, or a Baptist, who *may* or may *not* be a daily follower of Jesus Christ.

Such labels are especially meaningless in that evangelical is not a denomination at all, but a general outlook and perspective concerning matters of faith. There are "evangelical" Catholics and "evangelical" Lutherans and "evangelical" Episcopalians, and so on.

However, we may occasionally use labels because it helps us communicate practically. So we may speak of fundamentalist, liberal, conservative, evangelical. We do so judging no one but simply recognizing different outlooks—as we might identify day people and night people, shy people and outgoing people, and the unique outlook of Russians, Mexicans, and Hawaiians on the world. We are voicing practically that we are not all the same. As Christians we look at things differently. It is useful to be able to recognize those differences in a spirit of unity rather than using them as a basis for repudiation, debate, contention, and judgment.

Practically speaking, then, we recognize varying perspectives among us. There is a general *evangelical* outlook that is different than the general *Catholic* outlook, and both are different than the general Presbyterian, Brethren, Methodist, Amish, or Quaker outlook, and so on.

Similarities and disparities exist all along the spectrum. Catholicism and Orthodoxy, for instance, share a great deal in common, as do, perhaps, Baptists and Pentecostals. But *all* the lines within and between the various segments of Christendom overlap. That's what makes us a family. The true "Christian" will feel the bonds of kinship, brotherhood, unity, and affection anywhere he goes amongst his or her fellow believers, even though specifics of expression and outlook vary. Our local American Orthodox congregation, for instance, is largely made up of converts, so to speak, from other denominations, including many who once considered themselves evangelicals, and probably still do. Some of my closest friends, and one of my sons, are Catholic. These relationships provide rich fellowship and fertile spiritual discussion about deep spiritual matters. The lines between their "Catholicism" and my "latitudinarianism" intersect at dozens of places. My former pastor became Orthodox before his death. I have Latter Day Saint relatives whom I love dearly. My mother was an Episcopalian. Two of our other sons are elsewhere along the spectrum. Among my closest companions in the spirit, I count Lutherans, many Presbyterians, a good many Brethren, scores of Baptists, Mennonites, Pentecostals, and a number of believers who are members of no church at all. One of my prized friends is a complete and outspoken agnostic. My ancestral heritage has grown out of Quaker rootstalk extending back to the days of George Fox in England, and one of my spiritual mentors was a Quaker. George MacDonald whom I admire so greatly grew up as a Congregationalist and later became an Anglican, as was C.S. Lewis. All these labels blur and intermingle to make up what Paul so wonderfully called "the body of Christ."

So though I place no eternal significance upon them, I use labels simply to help us form a working familiarity with differing general outlooks that exist upon the spectrum of faith.

WHERE OUR DIFFERENCES LIE

Having taken this brief panoramic look at the many identifying distinctions which Christian believers affix to themselves, it could be argued that on the whole, active evangelicals are probably familiar with more of the Bible than is the average lay Catholic, Orthodox, mainline Protestant, Anglican, Lutheran, or Episcopalian. In a general way, one who considers himself an active evangelical is likely to have a greater personal working knowledge of the details of Scripture than is the average man or woman on the street who calls himself a Catholic or a Presbyterian or whatever else the case may be.

The reason implies no value judgment. It is simply a matter of emphasis. Knowledge of Scripture is more heavily stressed in an evangelical environment. Evangelicals (including Catholic evangelicals, Orthodox evangelicals, Anglican evangelicals, and Mennonite evangelicals) tend to place a higher priority on personal Bible study than do other more traditional church-based and/or liberal expressions of Christianity.

Catholicism and Orthodoxy, for example, base their belief system largely upon tradition, the teachings of the church, the creeds, and the pivotal role of the Eucharist and liturgy. Evangelicals would say their beliefs are based on Scripture. Because of this distinction, evangelicals feel a greater imperative to know the content of their Bibles. That is where their foundations lie. The average Orthodox or Catholic believer, on the other hand, will devote more effort to the study of church history or the lives of the saints, perhaps, and will likely know the historic creeds of the church more intimately than will most evangelicals. That is where *their* foundations lie.

In a discussion of church history, a catholic will likely trump his or her evangelical brother or sister in knowledge. In a discussion of biblical specifics, the fundamentalist will probably exceed his Catholic brother or sister in knowledge. Their differing strengths of knowledge reflect a different emphasis in the teaching each has received.

Thus, the average evangelical will more readily be able to quote passages from Scripture, will be familiar with the scriptural basis for his or her beliefs, will be able to cite scriptural references for various doctrines, and will be likely to know the differing themes of Romans and Ephesians and I Timothy. He or she has made such topics the focus of his study and reading. That same evangelical, however, may find himself in uncharted waters of ignorance if the discussion should turn to pre-Reformation church history, the development of the

Nicene Creed, or the lives of the martyrs and saints of the first 1500 years of Christ's Church. At that point the average Catholic or Orthodox believer will likely demonstrate greater knowledge because that has been the focus of *his* reading and study.

THE INFILTRATION OF SELF-RIGHTEOUSNESS

So far so good. There is nothing here so difficult to grasp. We know what we study.

People throughout the world speak different languages. There are two reasons: We grow up surrounded by the language of our parents. Later we may study to learn an additional language or two, even though we never escape the influences (and accent) of our primary language.

This distinction in the world of theology and doctrine, however, tends to bring in its wake a subtly divisive judgment on one side of the fence that does not exist on the other.

When confronting evangelicalism, the average Catholic does not generally say, "Ah, because I know more about the saints and martyrs and creeds of the church than most evangelicals, I, as a Catholic, am a more devout and obedient follower of Christ."

But when confronting Catholicism, as exemplified by the interview mentioned earlier, the average evangelical *does* often subtly think, "Ah, because I know more about the Bible, I, as an evangelical, am a more devout and obedient follower of Christ than most Catholics."

In more than fifty years in the church, I have encountered this subtle judgment of pride with regard to Scripture to a *far* greater extent within evangelicalism because of what it considers its own superior Scriptural knowledge. Usually this self-righteousness grows out of the assumption that evangelicals read the Bible as "literal," "inerrant," and "infallible," while others do not. Therefore, as they see it, they are able to interpret Scripture accurately and correctly.

This, however, is as ludicrous a conclusion as to say, "Ah, because I speak French and English, I am a better human being than someone who speaks Italian and Mandarin Chinese."

Greater scriptural knowledge may exist within the ranks of the laity of evangelicalism, but *less* humility toward the body of Christ also exists. It may be instructive to inquire to what extent the latter obscures the accurate eyesight of the former, and stunts the effectiveness and practicality of that knowledge.

DO INFORMATION AND KNOWLEDGE = WISDOM AND TRUTH?

The question thus becomes: Does greater scriptural knowledge indicate the possession of greater and more accurate truth at a high level?

It may be the case, in general, that evangelicals know the contents of their Bibles to a degree not emphasized in other segments of Christendom. But does this knowledge of data and content translate into a recognition of God's high Logos truth?

What if, rather, based on a series of misapprehensions and *faulty* assumptions, many evangelicals who know their Bibles, as it appears, inside out, actually do *not* grasp much of the high Logos truth to which Scripture points? What if an accumulated storehouse of biblical information does not necessarily yield the desired result?

It is not enough simply to read the Bible and amass its data. A computer can do that. To get at God's high Logos truth, the Bible must be read *correctly*.

Most Christians do not know how to do so.

That includes Catholics *and* evangelicals, liberals *and* conservatives, Pentecostals *and* Quakers. Most Bible teachers and preachers, authors and priests, yes, and so-called prophets as well, are only deepening in the minds of their listeners a long tradition of incorrect assumptions that *prevents* their followers coming anywhere near the lofty λογος that God intends his Word to convey into their hearts.

Startling though it will be to evangelical ears, one of the chief stumbling blocks to a right reading of Scripture, even one great *cause* of a spiritual dullness of which they are utterly unaware, is the Rosetta Stone—it would perhaps not be too strong even to call it an *idol*—of literality. It is such a stumbling block because it so easily leads to a formulistic outlook rather than a high-Logos personally obedient perspective.

FIGURATIVE AND LITERAL INERRANCY

What we are here attempting to clarify and illuminate is the misplaced self-righteousness that is based upon the false assumption that evangelicals possess the sole perspective necessary to read the Bible correctly.

The fact is, *no one* reads the Bible with perfect consistency of method or approach.

No evangelical scholar reads the Bible with uniform literality.

Nor does the most liberal agnostic read the Bible with consistent agnosticism. We are all literalists where we choose to be. We are all also agnostics where we choose to be. We focus our attention on scriptural passages that confirm our own biases and pre-held perspectives. Likewise, we explain away those that threaten our personal biases of belief.

This point will be a foundational watershed in the quest to understand "bold thinking" when applied to the Bible. The principle is a simple one. It can be stated thus:

The inerrant high truths of the Bible sometimes come to us literally and at other times interpretively.

This principle has an imperative corollary:

Inerrancy and the requirement of obedience are equal, whether the high truth is arrived at through a figurative method of interpretation or a literal one.

These principles dawned on my understanding over many years. Immersed in the teaching of evangelical tradition, I assumed—because this is what evangelicals are taught—that evangelicalism, with its rigorous adherence to literal inerrancy possessed the most accurate methodology for interpreting the Scriptures.

It came as a shock to realize, "Hey, evangelicals don't interpret the Bible 100% literally either."

The very nature of the Bible requires that it be read broadly, figuratively, and interpretively. A *literal* reading of Scripture under all circumstances is impossible. Everyone reads the Bible figuratively *and* literally, drawing the lines between the two at different points depending on their theological outlook.

The seemingly humble televangelist who pompously asserts, "I'm just a simple country preacher...no fancy theology for me...I just take the Bible as the literal Word of God," is deceiving no one but himself.

It sounds very pious, very spiritual...but it's not true. That televangelist who prides himself on his fundamentalist doctrine will become a closet liberal whenever his doctrine requires it—interpreting away the *literal* verbatim words of a passage and investing them with figurative meaning. He just won't broadcast the fact.

In the same way, the most progressive Unitarian, Episcopalian, or Catholic will become downright literal in his or her interpretation of some passage when an exacting rendition suits him, yet would positively disdain the "fundamentalist" label.

An intriguing example is presented by varying interpretations of the communion passages of Matthew 26, Mark 14, Luke 22, as well as

John 6:53-56: *"I tell you the truth, unless you eat the flesh of the Son of Man and drink his blood, you have no life in you. Whoever eats my flesh and drinks my blood has eternal life, and I will raise him up at the last day. For my flesh is real food and my blood is real drink. Whoever eats my flesh and drinks my blood remains in me, and I in him."*

How many evangelical country preachers and televangelists believe that in taking communion we actually partake in Christ's "literal" body and blood? Rather, it is in the Catholic segment of the Church where a literal view of the Eucharist is occasionally prevalent.

The interplay between literal and figurative reveals a sad fact within the broad and diverse body of Christ. We do not come to the Scriptures with open minds. We come to our reading of the Scriptures with an inward bent produced by doctrines and teachings, traditions and learned perspectives. These are constantly pushing, prodding, influencing, and urging us invisibly toward a set of pre-determined responses. We read the Bible thinking we are gaining meaning. But we are often merely reading back from the mirror of its words a reflection of our own predispositions.

This is a roundabout way of saying: We read in the Bible what we *want* to read.

We do not approach it so much from the unbiased perspective of *investigative research*, but for *confirmation* of views already ingrained. Most of our doctrinal persuasions are established before we even open our Bible's covers. We read the Scriptures according to whichever method of exegesis—allegorical, literal, moral, historical, etc.—most suitably yields that particular doctrine or end result we have been taught that the passage is supposed to produce.

THE OBSCURE LINE BETWEEN LITERAL AND FIGURATIVE

The constant interplay between the two methods, *literal* and *interpretive*, by which we read the Scriptures is sometimes easy to see and is at other times extremely subtle.

"I looked up, and there before me was a ram with two horns, standing beside the canal, and the horns were long. One of the horns was longer than the other but grew up later. I watched the ram as he charged toward the west and the north and the south. No animal could stand against him, and none could rescue from his power. He did as he pleased and became great.

"As I was thinking about this, suddenly a goat with a prominent horn between his eyes came from the west, crossing the whole earth without touching the ground. He came toward the two-horned ram I

had seen standing beside the canal and charged at him in great rage. I saw him attack the ram furiously, striking the ram and shattering his two horns. The ram was powerless to stand against him; the goat knocked him to the ground and trampled on him, and none could rescue the ram from his power. The goat became very great, but at the height of his power his large horn was broken off, and in its place four prominent horns grew up toward the four winds of heaven.

"Out of one of them came another horn, which started small but grew in power to the south and to the east and toward the Beautiful Land. It grew until it reached the host of the heavens, and it threw some of the starry host down to the earth and trampled on them. It set itself up to be as great as the Prince of the host; it took away the daily sacrifice from him, and the place of his sanctuary was brought low. Because of rebellion, the host of the saints and the daily sacrifice were given over to it. It prospered in everything it did, and truth was thrown to the ground. (Daniel 8:3-12)

Literal or figurative?

"But when Jesus turned and looked at his disciples, he rebuked Peter. 'Get behind me, Satan!' he said." (Mark 9:33)

Literal or figurative?

"And if anyone causes one of these little ones who believe in me to sin, it would be better for him to be thrown into the sea with a large millstone tied around his neck. If your hand causes you to sin, cut it off. It is better for you to enter life maimed than with two hands to go into hell, where the fire never goes out. And if your foot causes you to sin, cut it off. It is better for you to enter life crippled than to have two feet and be thrown into hell. And if your eye causes you to sin, pluck it out. It is better for you to enter the kingdom of God with one eye than to have two eyes and be thrown into hell, where 'their worm does not die, and the fire is not quenched.'" (Mark 9:42-48)

Literal or figurative?

"A sower went out to sow. And as he sowed, some seed fell along the path, and the birds came and devoured it. Other seed fell on rocky ground, where it had not much soil, and immediately it sprang up, since it had no depth of soil; and when the sun rose it was scorched, and since it had no root it withered away. Other seed fell among thorns and the thorns grew up and choked it, and it yielded no grain. And other seeds fell into good soil and brought forth grain, growing up and increasing and yielding thirtyfold and sixtyfold and a hundredfold...He who has ears to hear, let him hear." (Mark 4)

Literal or figurative?

"If I then, your Lord and Teacher, have washed your feet, you also *ought to wash one another's feet." (John 13:14)*

Literal or figurative?

"Then we who are alive, who are left, shall be caught up together with them in the clouds to meet the Lord in the air; and so we shall always be with the Lord." (1 Thessalonians 4:17)

Literal or figurative.

"So when the woman saw that the tree was good for food, and that it was a delight to the eyes, and that the tree was to be desired to make one wise, she took of its fruit and ate; and she also gave some to her husband, and he ate." (Genesis 3:6)

Literal or figurative?

"This is my commandment, that you love one another as I have loved you." (John 15:12)

Literal or figurative?

"Whatever you wish that men would do to you, do so to them." (Matthew 7:12)

Literal or figurative?

"Before him will be gathered all the nations, and he will separate them one from another as a shepherd separates the sheep from the goats, and he will place the sheep at his right hand, but the goats at the left." (Matthew 25:32-33)

It is obvious to our common sense that taking the Bible "as the literal word of God" is not a straightforward matter.

Do we literally possess *the mind of Christ*, as Paul indicates in 1 Corinthians 2:16? What does that actually mean? Does it not require some interpretive latitude to grasp how the Spirit of Christ works in and through our minds to conform our thoughts and attitudes and motives to his? In this case, perhaps there is a little heavier dose of literalness than with Daniel's vision of the two-horned ram, yet we have to add some interpretiveness to the mix as well.

Do we really read Jesus' words, "Leave your nets," as a text from which to build a case that discipleship is primarily for fishermen (and perhaps tax collectors).

Of course not. Such shallow interpretations miss the *spiritual* realities intended by a mile.

Teetotling fundamentalists have been explaining away the literality of the word *wine* throughout the New Testament for generations, and especially Paul's injunction to Timothy to "drink a little wine for your stomach." But who are Catholics to judge them when they equally disregard the command to diligently study the Scriptures.

So who is reading the Bible with more insight?

Finding deep levels of truth requires a balance. It comes down to how we *interpret* what we read on the pages of the Bible.

LITERALISTS AND NON-LITERALISTS TOGETHER

We are all literalists, we are all non-literalists. It just depends on where we happen to be focusing our attention.

The unbelieving skeptic brings his unbelief to bear on the resurrection, saying, "I don't believe it. It could never have happened. Therefore Jesus was not the Son of God."

The doubting Calvinist brings his skepticism to bear on Philippians 2:10-11, and in similar fashion "explains away" by means of certain theologic twists the literality of Paul's words in such a manner as to preserve the bias of his Calvinistic theology of eternal punishment.

We will all have to wait to discover the full scope of truth as eternity reveals it to us. For now all we can positively say is that pietism is both an illogical and an ignorant response to our differences.

We ought to have no complaint with this multi-dimensioned approach that blends literal and figurative interpretation. In its own way, it might be seen as validation of the vast breadth and complexity of the Bible. It may be indicative of a *correct* approach to Scripture's multi-layered and extremely diverse range of texts.

What I rail against is the self-righteousness with which the evangelical and agnostic and liberal and Catholic and Baptist alike imbue their *own* viewpoints with the stamp of God's approval as the supremely enlightened viewpoint.

It is such spiritual pride, not our inconsistency of approach, that dooms unity and damages our witness to the world. The world will not mind if we say, "There are perplexing aspects to the Bible we do not understand. In love and brotherhood we view them differently. But we do not allow them to diminish the unity of our brotherhood." The world will respect us for our honesty, and respect us even more for our unity in the face of tremendous diversity.

But when we puff ourselves up and claim alone to possess the full truth, the world will surely turn a deaf ear.

Entire social programs have been founded on a literal reading of Jesus' words in Matthew 25:35-36. Some who have based whole lifetimes of service upon the principle of this passage are not even Christians. Sadly, conservative evangelicals do not usually emphasize the literal imperative of Jesus' *feed the hungry, clothe the naked* words as a basis for salvation, which Jesus clearly makes it in this passage. Instead, they look to John 3:16 and Jesus' words to Nicodemus that "you must be born again."

Here we have two passages (John 3:16 and Matthew 25:35-36) in which, from the Lord's own mouth, we are given what appear to be categoric and unequivocal guidelines for salvation. Yet Christians read and interpret and emphasize these two salvationary passages differently.

The evangelical says, "Yes, of course, feeding the hungry is important...*but* the foundation must be urging unbelievers to be born again by a personal experience of repentance and faith in Christ in their hearts."

On the other hand, the liberal says, "Yes, of course believing is important as Jesus said in John 3:16...*but* without practical *feed-the-hungry* actions to accompany it, Jesus makes clear that such belief is meaningless. Being saved is doing what he said not a heart-experience."

Thus, we see our local Presbyterian Church spearheading a Food Endeavor campaign to care for the poor in our area, while a mile away the Baptist church sponsors frequent evangelistic efforts, door to door witnessing programs, and includes a salvationary altar call in every service. No one is encouraged to invite Jesus into their hearts in the Presbyterian church. There are no food or clothing collection boxes for the poor at the Baptist church.

And down the road we encounter a Pentecostal fellowship in which both John 3:16 and Matthew 25:35-36 pale under the gigantic shadow cast by the church message board as it emblazons the "full gospel" message of Acts 2:4. and 38 for all the town to see.

So where does true literality lie—in the *sinner's prayer* of evangelicalism, in collecting *food for the poor*, or in *speaking in tongues* as the true validation of belief? And Catholic readers may say, "All three miss it. Being saved, rather, is represented by—" and proceed to offer yet *another* scriptural emphasis of salvation.

HEAD COVERINGS AND MUTILATIONS

All Christians draw the lines of literality in different places according to their own personal views, scriptural interpretations, biases, church backgrounds, and learned perspectives. Examples abound.

Evangelicals and prophecy buffs base their outlook of the future on a *literal* reading of the rapture (1 Thessalonians 4:17) and a *literal* interpretation of temporal Israel's role in the end times drama. All the while, however, they ignore the massive Old Testament indicators, as well as Paul's words in Romans 9:6, 8, that "Israel" has become a *spiritual* and *symbolic* Israel, and that the Church is now *Israel*, rather than the 21st century secular nation going by the same name. *Symbolic* interpretations are the last thing an evangelical preacher wants to hear mentioned when teaching about the end times. It's all about literality—charts, graphs, wars, timetables, world governments, amphibious landings, crashing planes, and driverless cars.

When we change to the topic of communion and the Lord's Supper, however, visit any evangelical church and one will hear the terms *symbol* and *symbolic* as the pastor prepares his flock to partake of the elements (whose literal "bread" and "wine" have been changed to thin wafers and grape juice.) In this case it is Catholicism and Orthodoxy that read into the Lord's words a literal transubstantiation of the body and blood of Jesus. The Catholic has become the literalist, the evangelical the literalist skeptic.

Do any Christians seriously consider being "crucified with Christ" a *literal* text, or "circumcision of the heart" a *literal* requirement of faith? To follow such passages literally would require mutilation and death. Yet Paul speaks of them as components of our ongoing *life* in Christ. They are clearly and obviously *symbolic* images.

Who takes Jesus' words about sins of the hands and eyes *literally* and proceeds to gouge out the one or cut off the other?

The Bible's "immutability" and "unchangeableness" represents yet another misunderstood concept. All history is fluid and changing as it is being written—God's history included. Yet some fundamentalists hold to an illusion of unchangeableness that is no more founded in the fact of actual practice than is 100% literality.

In how many of today's churches are women "not permitted to speak," in literal adherence to Paul's words?

Who takes the command for head coverings as literally binding today? The Amish, plain Mennonites, and a few Brethren denominations, but not most evangelicals or Catholics, Anglicans or Pentecostals.

Head coverings, political issues, women speaking in church, food offered to idols, ownership of slaves...the fact is, our interpretation and application of the Bible's themes and truths *do* change with time.

Let us be honest with ourselves, and bring humility into our perspectives.

Let us obey God's Word, and ask for the insight and wisdom and understanding of his Spirit to enter through the door of our obedience, illuminated into our hearts through the windows of humility and unity.

TOO LITERAL OR NOT LITERAL ENOUGH

Having roundly taken evangelicals to task for their misplaced pride, the opposite error is equally undermining to vigorous faith—not taking the Bible literally *enough*. The average Catholic could learn a valuable lesson from the evangelical's diligent study of the Bible. How can anyone expect to obey Christ's commands when he or she has so little knowledge of what those commands even are? Catholics have to wake up to bold thinking too. How many rank and file Catholics have read the New Testament through on their own? How many liberal Presbyterians and Anglicans are all too comfortable and complacent in their ignorance of the Bible, when its literal commands and instructions have been given to serve as their instruction manual for life?

Orthodoxy, Episcopalianism, and Catholicism often point to the fact that their prayer books and missals are so structured that one hears every passage from the Bible once every three years. This is certainly a worthy objective and a worthwhile result. But what good is this mentally absentee listening if it goes in one ear and out the other, and if those words are not made part of the believer's personal study, diligent application, and moment-by-moment life of intimate obedience?

The same question could be asked of the thousands of mentally absent Protestants who spiritually snooze through sermon after sermon, week after week all their lives, but never incorporate the truths they hear into a moment-by-moment life of prayerful discipleship. It may be that passively hearing so much of God's Word, never asking if there is something contained therein to be obediently *done*, is worse than never hearing it at all.

The emphasis must be made again—to Catholics and evangelicals, Mennonites and Pentecostals, Baptists and Presbyterians, and to myself as well—*What would you have me do?* is the one true basis for faith. Any Protestant minister or Catholic priest who teaches anything other than doing the red letters of the New Testament—the literal as well as the symbolic—is not teaching the true gospel of Jesus Christ.

INERRANCY

Having dismantled the pious illusion of 100% literality, intelligent and mature readers of Scripture recognize that the Bible comes to us as an inhomogeneous, fragmentary, and even contradictory Book. Let us not pretend it to be otherwise. The Bible presents, on the surface of it, a very perplexing and confusing picture of God and his ways.

God is love, the Bible says...but he told the Israelites to slaughter their enemies down to the last woman, child, and goat.

God's nature is to forgive...but there are some according to many orthodoxies that he will never forgive because they have rejected him.

Jesus is a king...but he was executed as a common criminal.

Jesus emphasized the necessity of being born again...yet he never explained with any specificity exactly how it was to be done. Later he said that many of those who called him *Lord* had somehow mistaken the process and would be sent away to aeonian punishment. If such drastic consequences were involved, why was he so intentionally vague about it?

Jesus said we are to know the Father...yet throughout the Old Testament God seemed deliberately to make himself unknowable.

Jesus calls him *Abba*...yet God told Moses that no one could look upon his face. What kind of a "Daddy" is that? It's a contradiction plain and simple in the representation of God.

Everywhere you look the Bible presents us with contradictory information. Anyone who says these things aren't puzzling isn't paying attention. It is *very* puzzling.

Of course, we have been instructed by our theologians how to explain such discrepancies. But on the face of it, they illustrate a very bewildering scriptural account. If the book is inspired at every point and detail, why didn't God *inspire* a greater level of consistency?

Many subtle problems rear their heads when the discussion turns to principles like *inerrant* and *infallible*—claims like *literal* that give rise to an unfounded self-righteousness and causes many to misunderstand the very nature of the Bible itself.

The word *inerrancy* is slippery to define, and is no more capable than literality of providing a Rosetta Stone of hermeneutical reliability.

After all, what *is* "inerrancy"?

Perfection. Without error.

But does inerrancy imply literal *factitude*? Are interpretive and imaginative genres of literature or communication and other modes of expression subject to the same rules of inerrancy? Is there such a thing, for instance, as a perfect poem, a perfect story, a perfect painting, a perfect allegory? Here no *factitude* exists...at least not such as could be defined by the same rules. A painting, a poem, a story...they are not the *real* thing—they are images and likenesses and imaginative representations that remind us of the real thing.

Suddenly, as I say, *inerrancy* has become slippery. When we are talking about *imaginative* modes of expression, what is "perfection?"

What is a perfect, *inerrant* parable? Is the Good Samaritan or the Prodigal Son perfect and *without error* as a parable, as a means of communicating the truths the Lord intended?

But they are not literal. The people Jesus spoke of were *imaginary*. They are fictional stories to help us understand large concepts of truth. But there is no factitude of history present.

This exposes the fallacy of the mantra that the Bible is the "inspired literal inerrant" Word of God. Some of its inspired and inerrant truths are not *literal* at all!

I was reading just today in Mark 3 and noticed something for the first time in my life: *Other seed fell on rocky ground, where it had not much soil, and immediately it sprang up, since it had no depth of soil; and when the sun rose it was scorched, and since it had no root it withered away.*

Wait a minute, I said to myself. No seed I am aware of germinates *immediately*. Germination always takes time. Secondly, in the process of germination, seeds send out two probing shoots—a root and a stalk. There can be no growth upward into the air by the stalk without a corresponding root going down into the soil. Jesus said there was *no* root, even though a stalk had begun to grow—which could not be the case. Thirdly, this statement, as it stands, indicates that by the very next rising of the sun after the seed was sown, a stalk had already begun to grow that withers from the scorching heat. Again, the timing is factually impossible as the parable was spoken.

We have in a single sentence from Jesus, *three* instances of non-literality. He is obviously making a bigger point, not trying to give a factual botany lesson.

Once we recognize that an imaginatively fictional story (the Sower Parable, the Good Samaritan, the Prodigal Son) though not "literal" may yet be an "inerrant" (because perfect) means for communicating truth, why does the biblical literalist argue so vehemently that such could *not* be possible in the case of the account of Adam and Eve? What precludes the possibility that Genesis 3, in the same way, is a perfect and inerrant divinely told "parable" of sin's entry into the world?

INFALLIBILITY

We also have to ask another whole range of questions: Does the Bible contain errors, inconsistencies, and mistakes? Inerrancy now takes on yet more complications when we add the concept of "infallibility." It all depends on what you mean. On what level is "error" defined?

Biblical genealogies don't match. The Lord's own genealogy contains either omissions or outright errors. Historical accounts are occasionally contradictory. Much is contained within Scripture's pages which appears useless to us today, or of interest only in a historical but not a practical sense.

It is universally recognized, for example, that the final passage of the *Gospel of Mark* was not written by Mark himself but was added later, possibly to make up for the fact that the original ending had been lost and to keep the surviving but truncated version of the good news from ending with the rather faithless assertion about Jesus' followers, "they were afraid."

However you look at it, *Mark's* lost and modified ending is unsettling to a belief in inerrancy and infallibility. If Mark was indeed the chosen man whom God miraculously inspired to write the first gospel account, and if he did so infallibly and without error, just as God wanted him to, how did a portion of that perfect and inspired account come to be lost?

This is a strange intermingling of divinely inspired *perfection* with human *error*! Would God not have watched over the document as carefully as he inspired it in the first place?

And if Mark's was such an inerrant and infallible document, all except, for some reason, the ending which somehow was *not* inspired...and if, because of that fact, God saw to the necessity that only that imperfect portion would be lost, torn off at the very word where infallibility ended and fallibility began, and then infallibly inspired some *other* scribe to add the perfect portion that Mark had somehow been unable to produce...what does that imperfection of Mark's say about the *rest* of his gospel?

Was or *wasn't* Mark a "perfectly inerrant and inspired" vessel?

These questions and such a train of reasoning may seem trivial. But follow them out to their end points. *Inerrancy* becomes extremely difficult to support logically. Sometimes it is necessary to think like this in order to follow to their logical conclusions many misconceptions that float about concerning the Bible.

Church people have not been taught to think implicationally. Satisfied to be spoon-fed platitudes from the pulpit, much of their thinking is sloppy. Yet when you try to address the points of their inconsistency, you are usually met with some variation of the absurd argument, "If the King James was good enough for Moses and Paul, it's good enough for me."

Clearly we are not going to unravel the mystery of *Mark's* ending. we only make the point that pride with respect to "inerrancy" and "infallibility" and "inspiration" are no more well placed than is pride in one's *literal* adherence to the Word of God. The leakiness of the scriptural vessel is readily apparent.

Mark's ending was lost—that's all. It is an unfortunate accident of history, just like the tragic burning of the Alexandrian library.

CLOSE-MINDEDNESS…DOUBT…OBJECTIVITY

Several responses are possible to information such as what we are confronted with by the ending of the *Gospel of Mark* or the inconsistent genealogies:

The close-minded response—to deny the historical evidence;

The doubting response—to use the information to deny the veracity of the message altogether;

The mature and objective response—to accept the evidence as indication of the fact that the living water of God's truth comes to us through flawed and leaky human vessels.

The dyed-in-the-wool literalist says, "I don't believe it. The Word of God is perfect. Mark's name is on the book. Therefore, whatever the scholars say, I believe he wrote every word under the direct inspiration of God, and that every word is perfect. Inerrancy requires that the 'added ending' theory be refuted. I reject the evidence as false. If that ending was good enough for Paul, it's good enough for me."

The skeptic says, "There, you see, that just goes to show how fallible the Bible is. You cannot depend on it. Lost endings…fragments…phonied documents bearing false names…there is no way to tell what is authentic and what is not. Jesus' own words were probably incorrectly recorded as well. It is an entirely untrustworthy document."

But he or she who brings a balanced, mature, objective, and knowledgeable reading to the Bible says, "The evidence of the most ancient manuscripts shows all the more clearly God's use of the human drama to transmit his truth. His Word comes to us as no sanitized, test-tube document, but as *history*. The warp and woof of its high themes and eternal truths are woven upon the lives and times and struggles and mistakes of a flawed humanity trying, sometimes unsuccessfully, to understand his ways."

We find the above three differing responses everywhere—closed-minded shallow religiosity, doubting skepticism, and high-truth-seeking objectivity. We find close-minded, doubting, and objective responses to the *Genesis* account, to the dating of the Old Testament genealogies, to explanations of the flood, to the "hard commands" God gave the Israelites, to the figurative passages of prophecy, to the miracles and resurrection, and to a host of biblical difficulties and questions.

We will always have formula thinkers, doubters, skeptics, and agnostics among us. Wouldn't we rather attempt, however, to discover the mind of Christ?

How many Christians have heard of Baruch? Probably not a majority. Yet it may be this brilliant Jewish historian, scribe of the prophet Jeremiah, who actually penned much of the Old Testament. He may also be the one biblical writer who actually knew what happened to the ark of the covenant, and may have had a hand in hiding it.

How many students of the Bible know that three separate Genesis accounts, or fragments, are commonly thought to have originally been written between the 10th and the 4th centuries B.C.—(J) the Yahwist, (E) the Elohist, and (P) the Priestly Code—which were eventually interwoven into the single book produced by Israel's scholars as holy Scripture for their faith,

Such news may be disturbing to those who would rather envision Moses sitting centuries earlier on a mountain with parchment and pen in hand being dictated to word by word from God.

But this is not how the Bible has come to us. Does this information make us *close our minds* to historical evidence, *doubt*, or *seek high truth* in order to obey more diligently?

Likewise, many do not know that for the first 200 years of the Church, 2nd *Peter, Hebrews, Revelation, Philemon,* and 2nd and 3rd *John* were considered spurious and were not included in most lists of canonical texts at all.

No one knows who wrote *Hebrews*.

The apostle Peter did *not* write 2nd *Peter*. It is not even a first century work.

Revelation was considered far too unreliable to be included in the canon.

The authorship of 2nd and 3rd *John* were in doubt.

The letters to the Corinthians are not really *two* letters, but represent a composite of *four* separate letters. If the Bible is inerrant, why didn't these letters come to us as they were written and correctly labeled? As it stands, we have, in a sense, falsified documents that have been altered from Paul's originals and now purport to be something they're not.

Even the *Gospel of John* was for a time held in suspicion. Its inclusion in the canon was a point of great controversy. Early 2nd century scholars doubted its inspiration. Now we revere it as one of the Bible's greatest books.

GOD'S GRAND RAISING UP

What do we do with this information—reject it, use it to discard the validity of the whole Bible, or accept it as part of Scripture's multi-dimensional tapestry of truth?

The gradual accumulation of what we now call the "New Testament" (as had been the Old Testament before it) was a slow and very human process whose divine inspiration is occasionally difficult to discern amid the political and doctrine-driven disputes of the first four centuries of the Church. Simply put, it is hard to see God's hand in some of it. Why was 2nd *Peter* included in the New Testament canon, when the letters of Clement (which date from about 90 AD and are thus contemporary with a number of New Testament books and certainly earlier than 2nd *Peter*) were not?

What do we make of the many—what shall we call them?—foibles, incongruities, humannesses, "mistakes," and "errors" that the Bible contains and that are part of the biblical story? Do they diminish its power, its authenticity, its reliability...its truth?

Many answers may be posed to that question. But the sum of them must clearly be no. The very human origins of the book demonstrate God's use of the natural, the flawed, the growing, the incomplete, the temporal to accomplish his supernatural, divine, perfect, complete, and eternal purposes.

Faith is nowise reduced by such an outlook. In its own way, it makes the Bible bigger, grander, broader, and more precious. It reveals God's adaptability, as it were, to take the human drama and bring to life from it a document with mistakes, lost endings, and errant genealogies, and then raise that document and elevate it to his use by imbuing it with a spiritual power that transcends the level of humanity altogether.

God uses the *imperfections* of humanity to accomplish his *divine* ends.

These foibles, inconsistencies, and humannesses all the more show us that the letter of the Scripture is not to be enthroned as an idol to be worshipped of itself. The *letter* will always kill. It is the *spirit* which God has breathed into his holy instrument, the spirit of his high Logos, this Word, that transmits its *life* to all those who obey it.

C.S. Lewis, in his *Reflections on the Psalms*, speaks of God "meaning more" in Scripture than any individual writer realized during his lifetime, or even perhaps than any one-dimensional analyst is able to uncover. He calls this process a "taking up" of the texts to a higher level than they appear on the surface. He calls it, as I have, a "leaky" process, one we wouldn't have expected, or perhaps even preferred. Yet it is the method God chose to use.

The Bible is an instrument of revelation, but not the only instrument...an incomplete revelation, yet the Perfect Revelation.

To approach the Bible with accurate insight requires that we take our understanding of words such as inerrancy, infallibility, inspiration, immutability, and literal to higher levels. God imbues its foibles and inconsistencies, yes even what to the skeptic may appear as flaws and contradictions, with a higher power, *a deeper magic from before the dawn of time.* He imbues its very humanness and the jerky and uncertain way the Bible came into being, with the Spirit of high Logos truth. In the Bible we have the ultimate example of the whole being greater than the sum of its parts. Any detail, to the skeptic, can be disputed or repudiated. But the high Logos of the whole, through which God himself breathes his own Spirit, remains. Let the skeptic doubt. The heart of the childlike disciple will yet feed on the truth that is hidden from the worldy-wise man's eyes.

The Bible may be errant in the details of the letter, but *Inerrant* at the high level of the Spirit.

It may be fallible in the details of the letter, but *Infallible* at the high level of the Spirit.

It may changeable in the details of the letter, but *Immutable* at the high level of the Spirit.

It may contain mistakes in the details of the letter, but be *Perfect* in every way at the high level of the Spirit.

For when all is said and done, we know that the Bible is *the* Perfect document for the transmission of God's λογος into our hearts.

BALANCE *CAN* BE FOUND...IN A COMMON SENSE APPROACH

Some may think after all this that a correct reading of the Bible seems hopeless, a too high and daunting task. But it is not really so complicated. A wise, objective, intelligent, and true reading is not difficult to attain. It only requires that our hearts remain pure and singlemindedly devoted to *obedience* above analysis.

Obedience to Scripture's commands, as George MacDonald has so succinctly emphasized, is the only path that leads to wisdom.

To the untrue heart, to the lover of doctrine, to the theoretical mind, to the proof-textual one-dimensionalist, to the critic and judge and theologic analyst, the Bible will always be more or less a sealed book. To the true, the humble, the obedient, the child-heart who counts his brother and sister as better than himself, the truth of the Scriptures will open themselves from whatever angle or vantage point that childlikeness makes its approach—from the right or left, from within Orthodoxy, Presbyterianism, the Plymouth Brethren, Catholicism, Calvinism, evangelicalism, or the Society of Friends. Childlike obedience will illuminate the high truth of Scripture along the entire spectrum of faith, revealing the children of God among the Amish and among the Zinzendorf Moravians, and everywhere in between.

There are few more beautifully prophetic and descriptive passages in the Bible than Isaiah 55:3:

> *You will go out in joy and be led forth in peace;*
>   *the mountains and hills will burst into song before you,*
>   *and all the trees of the field will clap their hands.*

Do we read these words and envision an animated Disney cartoon of *literal* fulfillment, with trees suddenly coming to life and big caverns in the mountains opening up to become giant mouths that burst into song?

Of course not. We read them and our hearts grow quietly content at the eternal spiritual realities present. And when we close with the passage—

> *This will be for the Lord's renown,*
>   *for an everlasting sign, which will not be destroyed.*

—we are at peace. God is in all and over all, and will turn all to good in the end.

We have to read the Bible with interpretive common sense.

A correct, balanced, objective, and mature reading of Scripture, though many mysteries remain, therefore, is not so very complicated:

We are to be born again *and* feed the hungry.

We are to anticipate Christ's coming (because we are so commanded) *and* plan to live our entire lives as if we will not see it (for thus are we also commanded.)

We are to study God's Word to show ourselves approved, *and* walk in harmony with our brethren who maintain differing perspectives.

We are to make disciples not converts, pressing no doctrine upon them but teaching them to obey by the example of our own obedience.

We are to show the world that Jesus came from the Father by our love for one another within the great-encompassing family of God.

Does it matter which of us is *right* on matters of debate? Perhaps eternally in some cases it may, though I am not so sure most of our differences will matter then.

Does it matter that we know who is right now?

Categorically not. Where do we find Jesus insisting that his followers resolve their points of doctrinal difference? We are only commanded to obey.

If you love me, you will keep my commands.

Above all, we are to walk in unity and humility toward all men, but especially toward our brothers and sisters.

If you love me, you will keep my commands.

It is not really so very complicated.

C.S. Lewis on Scripture

"I take it that the whole Old Testament consists of the same sort of material as any other literature—chronicle (some of it obviously pretty accurate), poems, moral and political diatribes, romances, and what not; but all taken into the service of God's word. Not all, I suppose, in the same way. There are prophets who write with the clearest awareness that Divine compulsion is upon them. There are chroniclers whose intention may have been merely to record. There are poets like those in the Song of Songs who

probably never dreamed of any but a secular and natural purpose in what they composed...On all of these I suppose a Divine pressure; of which not by any means all need have been conscious.

"The human qualities of the raw materials show through. Naivety, error, contradiction, even (as in the cursing Psalms) wickedness are not removed. The total result is not 'the Word of God' in the sense that every passage, in itself, gives impeccable science or history. It carries the Word of God; and we (under grace, with attention to tradition and to interpreters wiser than ourselves, and with the use of such intelligence and learning as we may have) receive that word from it not by using it as an encyclopedia or an encyclical but by steeping ourselves in its tone or temper and so learning its overall message.

"To a human mind this working-up (in a sense imperfectly), this sublimation (incomplete) of human material, seems, no doubt, an untidy and leaky vehicle. We might have...preferred, an unrefracted light giving us ultimate truth in systematic form—something we could have tabulated and memorized and relied on like the multiplication table. One can respect, and at moments envy, both the Fundamentalist's view of the Bible and the Roman Catholic's view of the Church. But there is one argument which we should beware of using for either position: God must have done what is best, this is best, therefore God has done this. For we are mortals and do not know what is best for us, and it is dangerous to prescribe what God must have done...

"We may observe that the teaching of Our Lord Himself...is not given us in that cut-and-dried, fool-proof, systematic fashion we might have expected or desired. He wrote no book. We have only reported sayings, most of them uttered in answer to questions, shaped in some degree by their context. And when we have collected them all we cannot reduce them to a system. He preaches but He does not lecture. He uses paradox, pro-verb, exaggeration, parable, irony; even (I mean no irreverence) the 'wisecrack.' He utters maxims which, like popular proverbs, if rigorously taken, may seem to contradict one another. His teaching therefore cannot be grasped by the intellect alone...If we try to do that with it, we shall find Him the most elusive of teachers. He hardly ever gave a straight answer to a straight question. He will not be, in the way we want, 'pinned down.' The attempt is (again, I mean no irreverence) like trying to bottle a sunbeam...

"...we find a somewhat similar difficulty with St. Paul. I cannot be the only reader who has wondered why God, having given him so many gifts, withheld from him (what would to us seem so necessary for the first Christian theologian) that of lucidity and orderly exposition...

"It may be that what we should have liked would have been fatal to us if granted. It may be indispensable that Our Lord's teaching, by that elusiveness (to our systematising intellect), should demand a response from the whole man, should make it so clear that there is no question of learning a subject but of steeping ourselves in a Personality, acquiring a new outlook and temper, breathing a new atmosphere...So in St. Paul [the difficulties we encounter] finally let through what matters more than ideas—a whole Christian life in operation...And in the same way, the value of the Old Testament may be dependent on what seems its imperfection...that we may be forced...to find the Word in it...to re-live... the whole Jewish experience of

God's gradual and graded self-revelation, to feel the very contentions between the Word and the human material through which it works. For here again, it is our total response that has to be elicited...

"On almost all levels, that method seems to us precarious or, as I have said, leaky...Scripture can be read as merely human literature. [But] No new discovery, no new method, will ever give a final victory to either interpretation. For what is required, on all these levels alike, is not merely knowledge but a certain kind of insight; getting the focus right.

"If the Old Testament is a literature thus 'taken up,' made the vehicle of what is more than human, we can of course set no limit to the weight or multiplicity of meanings which may have been laid upon it. If any writer may say more than he knows and mean more than he meant, then these writers will be especially likely to do so. And not by accident." [21]

NINE

FAITH OF GIANTS

The Two-Edged Sword of Bold Courage and Humble Trust

"Now πιοτις (faith) is the assurance of things hoped for, the conviction of things not seen. For by it the men of old received divine approval.
By Πιστει (faith) we understand that the world was created by the word of God. By Πιστει Noah....By Πιστει Abraham....By Πιστει Moses....
"Therefore, since we are surrounded by so great a cloud of witnesses, let us also lay aside every weight, and sin which clings so closely,
and let us run with perseverance the race that is set before us."
—Hebrews 11:1, 7, 17, 23; 12:1

πιστις: PISTIS—*Faith*

Clearly a brief word study cannot hope to scratch the surface of a magnificent concept like faith. But in this case we have help to understand this mighty word PISTIS. It comes from the great anonymous writer of the *Letter to the Hebrews*. It is not often in Scripture that we are blessed with *definitions* of spiritual things. The Bible is frustratingly indistinct and vague. Think how much grief would have been avoided had Jesus simply set down in black and white terms what salvation was, and what were the specific entry requirements for heaven and hell. But for reasons that remain as unclear as some of the Bible's truths, God has desired instead for us to have to *search diligently* (EXEREUNAO) to find his truths, which he tends to hide like mysteries for man to discover.

We are, however, most fortunate in two instances. We have John's toweringly simple definition of God's character: *God is love.* And we have the introductory verse to the Bible's "chapter of faith," in which the writer "defines" what is the faith that he will then go on to illuminate with examples from God's historical "gallery of faith." But though it comes in the form of a definition—Faith is...—it does not come to us with the simplicity of 1 John 4:16. Indeed, Hebrews 11:1 must certainly be one of the Bible's deepest and most complex single verses: "Now faith [PISTIS] is the substance [assurance] of things hoped for, the evidence [conviction] of things not seen." (KJV, additions RSV) The writer then goes on to use PISTIS twenty-four times in the examples of the chapter that follows.

PISTIS essentially means exactly what the word implies—trust, being assured of reliability, thus to "believe" in with absolute confidence. Clearly "faith" when applied to the truths of God or the character of God (which are *invisible*) will be faith of a deeper and essentially distinct kind than trust toward *visible* truths and principles. Thus *spiritual* faith always contains the foundational meaning of being able to trust in what is *unseen*. Such is the basis for Hebrews 11:1. We also observe in the Hebrews 11 gallery the faith not only to believe big things of God, but also faith to believe that God and his purposes, and the eternal reach of his love, are more expansive than what men may say about them. It takes faith to believe in a truly infinite God. In part, Abraham's faith was faith to challenge the orthodoxy about God. May we likewise be bold enough to believe big loving things about our Father.

AROUND THE COAST OF NORTHERN SCOTLAND where we live for part of the year, every town and village possesses a harbor originally built to facilitate the fishing industry upon which the livelihood of their communities was based.

Most of these harbors were constructed in the 18th and 19th centuries and are of similar design. Enormous and massively thick concrete bulwarks are set against the sea a hundred or two hundred yards out from the shore. These bulwarks are literally walls of mighty fortresses, up to twenty feet thick and thirty or forty feet high, anchored securely into the bedrock of the sea floor and extending higher than the fiercest winter storm can assault. Occasionally a small red and white lighthouse sits atop it at the seaward-most point. Behind this great protective wall, of varied shape and design, sits the enclosed harbor, bordered inland and to the sea by the shoreline and the bulwark wall, and on the two adjacent sides by concrete walls equally high. Protected by the sea-bulwark, one narrow protected channel between high parallel walls perpendicular to the lay of the harbor, runs to the open sea, just wide enough to allow boats in and out.

If one stands onshore high above such a harbor in the midst of a wintry storm on the North Sea, the effectiveness of the design is remarkable and instantly apparent. Spread out to the horizon as far as the eye can sea, the ocean may be wild and tumultuous, not with mere whitecaps but with huge swells battering the shore, exploding like claps of thunder as they smash against its rocks and crags, sending a frenzy of white spray fifty feet into the air.

Inside the high concrete walls of the harbor, however, the surface of the water remains like glass. Not a breath of wind disturbs it.

Within five miles in both directions of our Scotland home on the Moray coast, sit five such massive gray protective concrete harbors, and all around Scotland they similarly dot the shoreline.

In our particular village, on the bluff above the harbor also stands a solemn gray stone church building that is probably older than the harbor. It rises high, grim, and silent, almost as if standing guard over the harbor below it like an old Calvinist preacher of doom.

DEEP WATERS OF FAITH

This juxtaposition of church and harbor represents a fitting model for what, in many cases, the churches (lower case) of Christendom have become. We even speak of and sing hymns acknowledging Christ and the church as our safe harbor.

But for all the comfort of its imagery when applied to Jesus as our "shelter in time of storm," is the parallel between church and harbor one we ought to be entirely proud of? The harbor is essential for boats that come and go. But for those that never venture past the harbor walls, the harbor becomes an image of stagnation not refuge.

For it strikes me that few graver threats exist to growing faith than *comfortable* spirituality.

Perhaps not to faith itself, for it is possible to believe while not going anywhere. But theological security blankets certainly do much to prevent a deepening, broadening, expanding, *growing* faith.

Do we want to *go* somewhere as Christians? Do we want to progress? Do we want continually to encounter new vistas and experience new depths of faith? Do we want our spiritual muscles stronger five years from now than they are today?

If the answer is *yes*, lounging about in comfortably protected church harbors won't get us there. To accomplish such objectives may require being the kind of Christian the psalmist anticipated when he wrote:

"Some went down to the sea in ships, doing business on the great

waters; they saw the deeds of the Lord, his wondrous works in the deep." (Psalm 107:23-24)

It was only *after* they had gone down to the sea in ships, as the Psalm progresses, that "he brought them to their desired haven. (107:30)

It is a sad fact that most Christians never launch into deep waters of challenging ideas at all. Instead, they live within the safe doctrinal waters of their secure harbors. There they putter round and round in their little dogma-boats, hashing and re-hashing all the same familiar doctrines they have been familiar with from youth up. Nothing ruffles the surface. No whitecaps of question or doubt or deeper meaning are encountered to strengthen and invigorate navigation skills or to test the seaworthiness of their craft.

Along the shoreline are spread many such harbors. But from inside, nothing is visible but the boundaries of our own—enclosed and bordered with high walls to keep storms and rough waters at bay. We never look beyond those walls to the adjacent harbors where other collections of tiny Christian boats of different shape and size and color are paddling around in the placid waters of *their* doctrine-harbors.

Should one of our number venture too close to the narrow outlet to the sea, warnings are shouted out from closer to shore. Not only do we not venture out of our harbors, we're afraid even to *look* out to sea. And when occasionally a craft of spiritual exploration disappears out that opening into the wide waters beyond...the shakes of the head and clicks of the tongue sadly go round the harbor-congregation, accompanied by occasional whispered rumors of backsliding...or worse, *heresy*.

It is time we collectively ask ourselves if this safe-harbor approach is truly representative of our Lord. Is it what he would have of us? Is this the example he set for us? Or are there dangerous waters into which he wants us to launch the vessels of our faith? What might be God's larger purposes out in the vast sea called Christendom beyond the harbor walls?

Such fear did not rule in the lives of the great men of the Bible. They were thinkers, seekers, and questioners. Spiritual daredevils, as it were. Men like Job, who dared confront God, in a sense, eyeball to eyeball, and say, "God, I don't understand!"

God knocked Job out of his comfortable harbor, that's for sure: *How sturdy is this craft called goodness that you have been sitting in comfortably all your life, Job? Is it capable of navigating life's rough waters? It's time you found out.*

As God sent Job out into the wide sea, Job indeed learned some things about the deeds of the Lord and his wondrous works in the deep. Job asked hard questions and thus grew in faith. If comfort zones were God's priority, nothing in the Bible would ever have happened. It was not for love of the status quo, the placid waters, that God told Abraham to go to a distant land, or Moses to confront Pharaoh, or Joshua to march in and conquer Canaan, or Hosea to marry a prostitute, or Nehemiah to rebuild the temple wall...or Jesus to go into the wilderness.

Who are those who apprehend God's larger purposes?

It is they who do business on the great waters.

SPREADSHEET OR REAL PEOPLE?

It might well be said that in one way or another most theological conundrums and the spiritual questions we wrestle with in our prayer lives begin in some way with people.

In my own case, my re-acquaintance with a childhood friend, alongside whose life I could not reconcile the dogma of my belief system, happened to be the catalyst that led to my rejection of the two exclusive humanities view of salvation—one entirely lost, one entirely saved.

Millions still adhere to that exclusive humanities view. I had been steeped in it all my life. Obviously, if one holds to that doctrine, many aspects of belief proceed directly from it. One's approach to evangelism, for instance, becomes not so much a question of discipleship or *living* a Christian life, but an emphasis on getting people across the line and into the saved column. One's view of church, of missions, indeed one's whole theology may proceed out of this doctrine. So also does the nature of the God one believes in. If eternity is decided on the basis of such a rigid line of demarcation, it says much about the Creator who devised the arrangement.

This is one of the reasons I believe so strongly in the imperative of bold thinking Christianity. The doctrines we hold influence our outlook on *everything*. We've got to think through their implications. The two exclusive humanities view turns the human condition into an excel spread sheet. If a flawed doctrine of exclusivity sits squarely in the middle of our belief system, how can we see the people around us as God sees them?

The spreadsheet perspective extends like a cancer to infect our view of the body of Christ. Rather than welcoming our brothers and sisters of differing outlook with the open arms of unity, our emphasis becomes an attempt to *define* doctrines and differences and outlooks so that we can place everyone into their appropriate slot. One's entire perspective of humanity, God's family, the church, doctrine, and the Bible itself becomes a gigantic data matrix.

Jesus did not view the human condition as a spreadsheet. To influence the world, our eyesight toward humanity must get in sync with his. When he looked out upon the crowd, it was not to define and categorize and identify who was saved and who wasn't…he looked upon the people with compassion, because they were like sheep without a shepherd. He wasn't trying to get people from the unsaved column to the saved column, he was trying to get God's love into them.

When my friend walked into my life and began to disrupt that exclusive-humanities perspective, much within my tidy and compact system of formula-belief began to unravel. Without knowing it, he had pulled at a thread in the orthodoxy of my upbringing. Before long that string was tugging at other parts of the fabric. Many aspects of that theology came in for new evaluation and scrutiny. Faith itself did not unravel, only the one-dimensionality of the belief system in which I had been indoctrinated.

Gradually my Christian walk, and the beliefs associated with it, took on wider, deeper, more far-reaching scope. If that line of demarcation between saved and lost was different than I had supposed, *everything* changed. Evangelism changed, the role of the church changed, discipleship changed, the way I read the Scriptures changed, the requirements for understanding heaven and hell changed, how I interacted with people changed.

The spreadsheet mentality shattered.

I began to see the world differently. I believe that I began to see by a few faint glimmers with the eyes of Christ.

WHAT IS GOD LIKE?

What changed most was my outlook on the nature and character of God himself.

If God *hadn't* drawn a big line through the middle of humanity, and if there was *more* to salvation than offered by the formulas of fundamentalism and the predestination of Calvinism, what did that have to say about who God was? It is the big question an insufficient number of Christians ask about their doctrinal beliefs:

What do my beliefs imply about who God is?

Thus began my quest toward what I call the "high Logos" of God's truth.

The doorway into wider truth and a more latitudinarian outlook will be different for everyone who embarks on that journey. In a sense, my progressive journey began with a single observation with regard to my friend's potential salvation, viewed in the context of the two-exclusive humanities line. It was a simple observation, really, yet profound in its own way:

This doesn't appear to make sense.

It's not something the guardians of orthodoxy want you saying. You can never tell where such an observation will lead. Nor is making sense what theologians expect of the orthodoxies they devise. They want people to believe *without* trying to make sense of the specifics.

With the first thoughts about my friend, I began to pray in new ways:

God, what am I to think...my friend doesn't fit the salvation recipe. I don't know where to put him on either side of the line. I know you see more lovingly into the depths of his heart than I. You love him and know him far better than I. A view of salvation that condemns him doesn't seem worthy of you, as the Father of Jesus Christ. There must be more truth to salvation than I am unable to see.

THE DYNAMISM OF DOCTRINAL NEUTRALITY

There will be those to whom such thoughts will only indicate my ignorance of the Bible. Who are *we* to say to the Almighty, "God, this is not worthy of you." God is holy and righteous beyond our capacity to understand him. Mere mortals, we cannot question *him*."

But my probing prayers were honest and sincere. I did not say, "Hey, God, I don't like your arrangement. I don't think I believe it anymore. If you are *that* kind of God...I don't think I can believe in you at all."

As they begin to question the faith of their upbringing, many approach God with this precise arrogance: "Do it *my* way or else. I won't believe in you unless you are exactly what I want you to be."

It is more than a little petulant.

How vividly I recall an intense discussion fifteen years ago in England, in which a number of individuals were doing their best to persuade me toward a belief in universal reconciliation. Despite persistent efforts, I was unable to get them to recognize the validity of my neutrality on the issue. At length one of the women, in a heat of frustration and anger, burst out, "If God dooms so much as one soul to hell forever, I would not believe in him. I *could not* believe in such a God!"

In her face I saw the tantrum of a child stamping her feet if she could not have her own way: God *has* to be like I want him to be, or I *refuse* to believe in him!

That single statement undercut all the arguments that had been marshaled against me in favor of the universalist position.

"I could never say that," I finally replied quietly. "I trust God to *do* right, to *be* right, to do what in his infinite love he knows is right and best and most loving according to his eternal plan. I *trust* him. If hell turns out to be exactly as the Calvinist orthodoxy of eternal punishment maintains, I trust him. He knows best. He is God. He is love. He will carry out his will. I trust God more than I trust my finite capacity to understand and define that will, *whatever* is in his plan for eternity."

But they could neither hear nor understand such a perspective. In their view, doctrinal neutrality was the wimp's way out.

On the contrary, I view doctrinal neutrality on such contentious and ambiguous issues as the most scripturally integritous position—the only perspective of reliability because it is a dynamic doctrinal stance rooted in trust of God rather than intellectual assurance.

Neutrality allows for growth and movement. It is less likely to become obdurate and static and dogmatically inflexible. Neutrality also tends far more to promote unity by making love of the brotherhood a higher priority than doctrinal rigidity. In the discussion with my acquaintances, however, trust in God did not enter the discussion, only the conviction that they were 100% right.

THE OTHER SIDE OF THE SWORD OF INQUIRY—TRUST

However…I am not afraid to go to God with bold questions. Not only am I not afraid, I *love* taking hard, thorny spiritual issues to my Father and saying, "God, help me make sense of this." Such dialog with God comprises one of the most exciting and challenging aspects of my Christian walk.

When I speak of doctrinal neutrality it implies no less interest in getting to the bottom of what beliefs really mean. Nor does it imply that I have no strong beliefs. It only indicates a recognition, when all is said and done, that our hearts and minds need to trust God for *ultimate* answers more than they trust themselves. It is a recognition that our beliefs on points of spiritual doctrine are necessarily our own *opinions* of truth.

I *have* beliefs, I *hold* opinions, I *believe* certain things are true and others are false. I maintain strong and passionate perspectives. Obviously I *think* my viewpoints are true or I wouldn't hold them. But I am not so enamored with my own infallibility as to think that all my doctrinal opinions will in the end turn out to be true. How can we, mere mortals, be so arrogant before God as to think we understand everything about him?

Doctrinal neutrality is simply another way of saying that I am realistic about the limitations and bias of the human heart and mind and intellect.

My response to the universalist highlighted the flip-side of the heart-cry I had added to prayers about my friend years before. I had prayed to understand the mechanics of salvation and God's will for those who didn't fit the orthodoxy. At the same time, I prayed to trust God equally in the opposite direction. The bold-thinking Christian has to remain open-minded from every side.

My prayers were going both directions at the same time—questioning the orthodoxy and asking God to make sense of it for me...*and* expressing trust toward him in the recognition of my own limitation to fully know or completely understand his plans and purposes.

This is this intriguing balance in the life of πιστις. We err when we don't *question* God enough, or when we don't *trust* him enough.

I confess it was fearsome at first when I began to pray after this fashion. I felt like a mousy little boy, cap in hand, timidly approaching the Awful throne of the Magistrate of the universe, saying in a croaking and shaky voice, "Uh...pardon me, God...do you mind if I ask a question?"

I needn't have feared.

He was my Father, not my judge. He was glad to see me come.

GOD'S COURAGEOUS MEN—GETTING IN THE ALMIGHTY'S FACE

In the learning process that followed those first timid questions and prayers, I began to notice a startling and astonishing truth. Some of God's greatest men said remarkably similar things to God as I was now thinking. And not phrased as mere gently inquiring, timid prayers like mine, but as bold challenges. We rarely notice how courageous some of the Bible's men really were. They were not afraid to get straight into God's face and say, "God this doesn't make sense. This is not worthy of you!"

It was with trepidation that I had meekly whispered my prayers.

They walked straight up and said, "Hey, what's going on here!"

How bold were the men who walked with God!

I'm afraid I wasn't so bold of faith. If I had been meek before God with my initial questions, I quickly learned to keep my mouth completely shut around my friends, and especially when in the hearing of the leadership at church. They did not want ripples of inquiry disturbing the waters of the harbor. If one person raised whitecaps, it might set all the other boats to rocking.

I innocently tried to explain some of my thoughts early on to our pastor, with whom I was very close. I thought he would be excited. I was totally unprepared for the icy blast of his angry response that sent me home, tail between my legs, literally in tears that did not stop for an hour.

It took me a long time to recover. When I began again cautiously looking out to sea, I did so with a healthy reluctance to share my thoughts openly . Instead I turned for guidance and insight to God's giants of faith who had gone before.

The bold men of the Bible were not merely *thinkers*, bold enough to ask hard questions, they were bold enough to challenge God himself. "No, God," they were not afraid to say, "something's not right here—you can't do that!"

In today's churches, Abraham, Moses, David, Peter, and Paul would all be heretics!

Contemporary theology is afraid to offend the divine Holiness. We mustn't question the Almighty's methods and plans. His ways are perfect and beyond knowing. If we do not fully understand the creation account, suffering, the trinity, the basis for salvation, hell, the condemnation of good unbelievers, evolution, the inconsistencies of the Old Testament, we learn to keep our questions to ourselves, just like I did after the humiliating interview with my pastor. We must beware of inadvertently committing the unpardonable sin. God might wag a stern finger and send *us* to hell for crossing into the dreaded heresy called doubt.

Not so God's great men. They *knew* God. So they were bold in his presence. If something seemed to their sensibilities to go against the nature of what they instinctively knew of God, they went straight to him with their objections.

"Hey, God," they weren't afraid to say, "hold on a minute! I've got some questions. I want some answers...and they'd better make sense!"

CONSIDER MOSES

Time and again we are told that God became so angry with the Israelites that he vowed to destroy them. Yet every time Moses boldly voiced his objection: "No, God, you can't do this—it is not worthy of you!"

We are further told that Moses was the most humble man on the face of the earth. What an extraordinary thing to say of a man, Might it be that humility is a *required* ingredient for the boldness God expects of us in knowing him? There was Moses with the courage to get into God's face, telling God what he could and could not do.

In Moses we see nothing of the arrogance that lacks humility to trust God: "If you don't do it my way, I'll walk!" Rather we observe the wonderful balance between *boldness* and *humility*, between righteous *anger* and childlike *trust*.

Moses wielded the two-edged sword of bold and humble faith.

Ultimately as we know God destroyed Korah and Dathan and Abiram and more than 250 others (Numbers 16). Not only did Moses at this point trust God to do right, it was at Moses' voice that the earth opened and swallowed them. Moses' trust was so great that he was willing to be God's agent in the carrying out of a portion of God's will that went *against* his own. This is an amazing detail in the chronicle of Moses' life—he was willing to carry out God's will contrary to his own.

We might draw a thought-provoking parallel:

Could a universalist—discovering aspects of God's will in the next life to be different than he had supposed—trust God enough to be the agent for sending sinners to hell?

Or a could a Calvinist—similarly discovering more to God's will than *he* had imagined—trust God enough to escort repentant sinners from hell into heaven once hell has done its purifying work?

Do we trust God enough to be wrong? Does the universalist trust God enough to admit to the possibility of eternal damnation of the unrepentant? Does the Calvinist trust God enough to admit to the possibility of eventual salvation for all?

Do we trust God enough to carry out his will though it turns out to be different than we had imagined?

Moses was *bold* in due season, and he was *trusting* in due season. He said, "God, please don't destroy them...but *if* you do, I trust you. And I will obey whatever you ask me to do." This is faith indeed.

CONSIDER ABRAHAM

Think what boldness Abraham displayed in his walk with God. The Scriptures indicate that God purposed to destroy Sodom, as Genesis 18:20 says, "because their sin was grievous." What follows in verses 22-33, must surely represent one of the most astonishing stories in the Bible.

When he learned of God's intent, Abraham's brain, his intellect, his heart all sensed something wrong.

Abraham said, "Lord, what you propose contradicts your character of love and justice. I know you have said you will destroy the city. But I cannot believe such to be consistent with who you are. How is your justice served by destroying it? There must be a better way."

He went straight to God, got in his face, and said, "God, this cannot be worthy of you."

His actual words were, *Far be it from you to do such a thing*. He boldly challenged God's judgment.

It was unbelievably courageous. What if God struck him down with lightning bolts for his impudence? And when he began to reason with God on behalf of what few righteous men and women might live in Sodom, Abraham did not flinch from God's penetrating stare.

He *knew* God. He was not afraid.

The text in full is simply astounding:

> *Abraham remained standing before the LORD.*
> *Then Abraham approached him and said: "Will you sweep away the righteous with the wicked? What if there are fifty righteous people in the city? Will you really sweep it away and not spare the place for the sake of the fifty righteous people in it? Far be it from you to do such a thing—to kill the righteous with the wicked, treating the righteous and the wicked alike. Far be it from you! Will not the Judge of all the earth do right?"*
> *The LORD said, "If I find fifty righteous people in the city of Sodom, I will spare the whole place for their sake."*
> *Then Abraham spoke up again: "Now that I have been so bold as to speak to the Lord, though I am nothing but dust and ashes, what if the number of the righteous is five less than fifty? Will you destroy the whole city because of five people?"*
> *If I find forty-five there," he said, "I will not destroy it."*
> *Once again he spoke to him, "What if only forty are found there?"*
> *He said, "For the sake of forty, I will not do it."*
> *Then he said, "May the Lord not be angry, but let me speak.*

What if only thirty can be found there?"
He answered, "I will not do it if I find thirty there."
Abraham said, "Now that I have been so bold as to speak to the Lord, what if only twenty can be found there?"
He said, "For the sake of twenty, I will not destroy it."
Then he said, "May the Lord not be angry, but let me speak just once more. What if only ten can be found there?"
He answered, "For the sake of ten, I will not destroy it."
When the LORD had finished speaking with Abraham, he left, and Abraham returned home. (Gen. 18:22-33, NIV)

What a remarkable exchange! Is Abraham conning God, playing a game of logic, feigning timidity but refusing to back down? How would you like Abraham to negotiate your next contract or pay hike!

Did God slay Abraham on the spot for his insolence? No. Abraham's determined yet trusting "argument" with God reveals none of the rebellion and self-exaltation at root in Satan's defiance of God's purposes (Genesis 3:4). Because it was born in trust and humility, God *honored* Abraham's courageous plea.

Thus, throughout the rest of Scripture, Abraham is considered one of history's great men of faith.

Notice how different is Abraham's response just four chapters later when God tells him to sacrifice his son Isaac.

Not a word of objection now. Just raw obedience. It is another of those powerful *So Abram went* moments (Genesis 12:4) of *pure faith* that we see over and over from Scripture's giants.

Abraham was skilled in wielding the two-edged sword of faith. He knew when to step forward with *bold courage*. He knew when to lift the empty hands of *humble trust*. He knew when to object and when to obey. He knew when to say, *This doesn't make sense,* and when to say, *Be it unto me according to your word.*

He knew when to speak and when to be silent.

COURAGE TO PROBE THE DIVINE CHARACTER

God honored Abraham for something else than faith on that day when they argued over Sodom's fate than merely his concern for the city's people.

God honored Abraham for being willing to probe the Divine character sufficiently in his mind and heart to say, *God this isn't worthy of you! I believe you are more compassionate than this.* He honored Abraham for being bold to ask hard questions about his own

Creator's being.

He honored Abraham, if *we* may be so bold as to phrase it thus, for challenging the orthodoxy of his time about God's nature.

Can we grasp that truth?

God *honored* Abraham for challenging *what was wrongly believed about God.*

God called it, not "doubt," but *faith!* Indeed, is it not our duty to reject low teachings of God that are unworthy of his nature? Because such bold courageous faith is undergirded by humble trust. God honors the two edged sword of faith.

Contradictory as the two character qualities seem on the surface, *bold humility* is the sword of giants in the spiritual realm.

In the end, though Abraham in a sense bested God in the argument, God *did* destroy Sodom and Gomorrah. Abraham won the battle but lost the war.

What did Abraham do then? Did he say, "God, if you destroy those sinners I won't believe in you."

No, he stepped forward and laid down his weapon of argument. He wielded the sword of giants now in humble trust and obedience. He had made his case. God listened and even, apparently, temporarily changed his mind. Then God acted. At this point Abraham lifted the empty hands of faith with implicit trust.

The inquiry into the purpose of scriptural conundrums is an honorable quest. God *honors* the sincere, humble, courageous, questioning, *trusting* heart.

God, give us faith like Abraham's! Give us faith **not** *to believe what is unworthy of you. Give us boldness of faith to say that you must be more loving and forgiving and compassionate than the doubters say. Give us bold courage and humble trust—to walk before you and with you in confidence and obedience, confident in who you are, trusting you whatever you do, obedient whatever you ask us to do.*

This stupendous truth is found all through the Bible: Men of faith in the spiritual realm were men who used their intellects!

When the Bible's great men engaged in honest and humble debate with their Maker over aspects of his being or purpose that didn't make sense, it was considered bold *faith.*

When we engage God in dialogue, therefore, about aspects in his Word that don't make sense, we are exercising a prerogative he *wants* us to exercise.

The mental tools and spiritual weapons being handed out in many of today's churches are made of rubber not steel. They are lightweight pretend tools, not tools of true faith. Attend a forty day seminar and what are you left with—a tool kit for children not warriors.

The powerful example of the giants of faith, however, holding a sword of hardened spiritual steel whose two blades are sharpened by bold courage and humble trust, enables us to raise hard questions to the throne of an infinitely loving Fatherhood.

We are following in the tradition of biblical giants!

COMFORT ZONES CAN BE HAZARDOUS TO YOUR HEALTH

Some time ago I was in Israel to research and write on the final portions of one of my books. In awe I traveled through the Judean desert reflecting on those forty days our Lord spent there in temptation, the final strengthening preparation for his ministry. It is a place whose stark desolation words are not adequate to describe.

Again it impressed upon me that Jesus was no comfort zone Savior. His life on earth was no comfortable harbor life. He faced questions and uncertainties the likes of which we cannot fathom. As I stood in Gethsemane, with a sense of reverent prayer I pondered just how deep into our Lord's marrow of humanity probed his own agonizing perplexities of faith. But he faced them unafraid with his heavenly Father, because he knew who his Father was.

Likewise, I stood at Peter's house in Capernaum where a few weeks after the temptations Jesus jolted the people of Galilee out of their comfort zones by beginning his healing ministry. I was at Joppa on the Mediterranean where, years later, God said to Peter in the dream of the descending sheet, "Get out of your comfort zone! You misunderstand and limit my salvation. You draw boundaries around whom you think I will save and whom you think I will condemn. You think I am only the God of the Jews. Wrong, Peter. Your vision needs expanding. Your dogma is too narrow and limited. My salvation is far more embracing than you imagine. I want you to go to the Gentiles."

What a liberal message *that* was for the time! To the placid waters of evangelicalism, nothing short of heresy with a capital H. Imagine—salvation to include those thought to be unclean and therefore lost. And the startling announcement came straight from God's mouth! How could Peter respond but, "Wow, God...is your salvation truly that embracing!"

By then Peter was used to it. Jesus had been jolting him out of his comfort zones from the day he said "Leave your nets. I will make you a fisher of men." Though fear did its best to entrap him, Peter was not ruled by fear. And even in Peter's early failures in the gospel account, we see a giant of faith in the making, a man learning to turn the bold and courageous side of his sword of faith (which no one ever doubted from Peter) into humble trust.

From that same shoreline at Joppa I gazed out upon a stormy sea, reflecting on Paul's hazardous travels throughout the Roman empire spreading the gospel. The great apostle certainly lived no safe existence of luxury and ease.

Paul knew what it was to go out to the sea in ships and do business in the great waters!

Jesus brought to the world no untroubled, prosperous, tranquil religion. He came shattering the image of the first century Jews toward their expected Messiah. Everywhere he went Jesus challenged men and women out of their comfort zones. He continually tried to get his disciples to think in *new* ways. How often, when he was with them, do we see Jesus simply asking questions. Original and revolutionary *thinking* was an important element in his training of the twelve.

He was trying to teach them to walk with the faith of the giants who had come before.

God is still trying to teach us the same thing—to walk with the bold faith of the great men and women of his kingdom.

Comfort zones do not breed warriors.

Laying Aside Fear—Bold Faith for Big Things

There are things, say in learning to swim or to climb, which look dangerous and aren't. Your instructor tells you it's safe. You have good reason from past experience to trust him. Perhaps you can even see for yourself, by your own reason, that it is safe. But the crucial question is, will you be able to go on believing this when you actually see the cliff edge below you or actually feel yourself unsupported in the water? You will have no *rational* grounds for disbelieving. It is your senses and your imagination that are going to attack belief. Here, as in the New Testament, the conflict is not between faith and reason but between faith and sight. We can face things which we *know* to be dangerous if they don't look or sound too dangerous; our real trouble is often with things we *know* to be safe but which look dreadful. Our faith in Christ wavers not so much when real arguments come against it as when it *looks* improbable—when the whole world takes on the desolate *look* which really tells us much more about the state of our passions and even our digestion than about reality.

TEN

EIGHT PRINCIPLES OF SPIRITUAL TRUTH

A Deepening Personal Revelation Toward Obedient Childship

> "The αληθεια (truth) is in Jesus."
> —Ephesians 4:21

αληθεια: ALETHEIA —*Truth*

Like "faith, *truth* is clearly a word and concept whose depths we can hardly hope to plumb with a brief word study. The phrase in Ephesians 4:21 represents another of those biblically succinct moments where an enormous truth is captured in a few words: *"The ALETHEIA (truth) is in Jesus."* [22]

The Greek ALETHEIA literally means "nonconcealment." At first glance this may seem like a weak definition, using a negative—what truth isn't—instead of a positive—what truth *is*. But the more one ponders the implications, the more powerful *nonconcealment* actually becomes. Think how many things in life and the world are hidden, mysterious, veiled from our understanding—concealed. We know so little about the universe, about its origins, about ourselves. God, of course, is the greatest mystery of all—invisible, beyond our sight, existing outside the reach of our understanding. And in the world of relationships, what stupendous energy is devoted to *hiding* our true selves from the outside world. Yet here is ALETHEIA speaking against all that is hidden, to what IS—things as they really are, without falsehood, without dishonesty, without duplicity, without uncertainty...authentic, genuinely real. *Nonconcealment* is light, revelation, understanding, wisdom spread abroad throughout the universe, penetrating everywhere...the eradication of darkness. "And God said, 'Let there be light.' *And there was light!*" Truth had come to drive out all that was concealed.

From such etymological origins, ALETHEIA obviously stands in direct contrast to what is "concealed." What is a lie but an attempt to conceal and hide? To *tell the truth* is to reveal everything and conceal nothing. When Jesus uses expressions such as, "I tell you the truth," he is solemnly introducing a statement of important revelation—in which things that were perhaps hidden and obscure before are concealed no longer. Paul's statement in Ephesians 4:21, "The truth is in Jesus," can be thus read along with Hebrews 1:1—What has been hidden till now, is concealed no longer. Truth has come!

OUR EMPHASIS HAS NOT BEEN to specify a new list of so-called bold thinking doctrines to replace those dogmas from our traditional and personal orthodoxies that have grown stagnant from the infiltration of untruth. We are attempting to fill in no doctrinal matrix to please the legalizing mind of the old man. We are trying rather to learn to *think* with God courageously.

It would be futile, therefore, to expend great effort attempting to resolve the dispute over free will between Armenianism and Calvinism...or whether salvation is primarily a spiritual experience *(you must be born again)* or doing good *(feed the hungry, give drink to the thirsty)*...or to resolve the old-earth/young-earth debate...or weigh in on the various pre, mid, and post second coming theologies...or speak to the universal salvation vs. eternal punishment controversy...or attempt to determine whether speaking in tongues is intended for everyone...or dogmatize whether the Eucharist is literal or symbolic.

It is not chiefly for the purpose of resolving such debate-quandaries that we must learn to think boldly, but so that we might know who God is...and know him aright.

I do not therefore lose much sleep worrying about such issues. Of course I work hard to interpret the Bible and the world around me correctly so that I *will* understand truth (both macro and micro) as accurately as possible. The above point implies neither laziness nor nonchalance about truth.

Yet resolving the pre, mid, or post prophetic puzzle could not be of less interest to me. I only care with all my heart that I know God accurately—that I know his character and intrinsic being, that I have placed myself in a lifelong relationship with him, and that I am engaged in the daily growth process of learning to properly and obediently relate myself to him as my Father.

With this priority in place, then, there are certain underlying priorities upon which the broader range of ideas, doctrines, and beliefs of our faith must be built. We can identify the following principles by which God established and ordained his creation to function, and through which Christianity's more specific truths will be revealed. With these truth-foundations established, the specifics begin to fall into line.

The eight principles are: *Universal Fatherhood, Command and obedience, Free will, Rebellion and independence, Jesus our elder brother, Relinquishment of self-rule, Other-worldly citizenship, Discipleship of Christlikeness.*

PRINCIPLE ONE: *UNIVERSAL FATHERHOOD*

God is the Creator and therefore Father of the universe and everything in it. He is a good and loving Father. He created every human being in his image, with the intent that they would by free volition grow into his mature sons and daughters.

God is a personal being, not an abstract entity. He thinks, he makes choices, he has goals, he feels emotions. He is in all ways *personal.* His intrinsic life has existed forever. His essential nature is goodness and love. Everything in his eternal Will proceeds out of that goodness and love. He created because he loves. He created mankind because he loves. He created you because he loves. He created me because he loves.

Though we came into being in our mothers' wombs, before that conception we were each individually envisioned in the divine idea of God's heart. He *created* us, both in the potential and in the reality, then our fathers and mothers gave that creation birth into the physical world.

God is not merely the abstract Father of mankind, he is *your* personal Father. He loves you and wants good for you—the very best life has to offer in every way. He created you and me to live in loving relationship between perfect Father and created child.

He created mankind as good, made in his very own image, so that we would enter into that wonderful relationship of sonship and daughterhood. As a child is like his father because he is his offspring, God created you and me to be *like* him in the way we think and grow and feel and learn and understand and respond to people, situations, choices, the world around us...and all of life.

PRINCIPLE TWO: *COMMAND AND OBEDIENCE*

God established the universe to function according to the interrelated harmony of authority and submission, lived out through command and obedience.

For most of the world's history, the institutions of man functioned according to authority and submission, command and obedience. This principle in God's economy has thus been generally understood because authority was one of the self-evident truths of the universe. Many of those living *under* authority may not have been fond of it, but most accepted the principle of authority as intrinsic to life. They were therefore able to grasp the truth that God created the universe from a foundation in which he is the *ultimate* sovereign and authority.

In modern times, however, the world has come to hate the principle of authority and to resent the suggestion that an obligation of obedience applies to *any* people, group, or individual. The very word *submission* has become vile to modern men and women. Society, culture, education, and government are seeking to strike it from the practical vocabulary of life in favor of equality and tolerance and independence.

This major historic shift in outlook has made it more difficult now in the third millennium A.D. than at any time in history for men to understand the nature of God's intended order, both in the universe and in daily life.

This single deterioration of an important cornerstone of truth has done more than nearly anything to erode the world's capacity to hear and understand the Christian message. It is the root and cause of the present era of secular relativism in which western culture is rapidly sinking. At no time in history has the prophetic wisdom of the first chapter of Paul's letter to the Romans been more in evidence. Truly, as the great apostle foresaw, modern men and women "became futile in their thinking and their senseless minds were darkened. Claiming to be wise, they became fools."

Absolute truth *qua* "truth" has become a non-existent non-entity in the deluded mind of modernism. The long-term consequences of this titanic shift in outlook are impossible to predict with certainty, but they will undeniably be dire unless the slide is halted.

PRINCIPLE THREE: *FREE WILL*

In order to enrich the interconnection between created and Creator, and to give authority and submission reality and growing substance, God gave to his highest creature a priceless gift found nowhere else in creation—the gift of free will. He gave man power to choose, to make decisions that carry consequences. He gave you and me the opportunity to order our lives and make of them what we will. His intent was that we use the gift to live in harmony and obedience to his will as his growing sons and daughters.

God desired no race ruled by coerced submission, but a race of men created in his image that lived by *chosen* obedience to his good and loving Fatherhood. He therefore designed the gift of free will as the mechanism by which command and obedience would function. By freely *choosing* to fall in with his created order, free will was to be the life-giving, joy-producing vehicle through which God's children would grow into the fullness and destiny of their personhood through an ever deepening relationship with him as their good and loving Father. It was intended to act as the means through which we would eventually become his mature sons and daughters.

God established the lower animal kingdom to function without determinative power of choice, ruled by the instinct he placed inside each creature-species. Animals can be no other than what they are. But in man he placed the capacity and opportunity to *become*, to *grow*, to *enlarge* as beings. Man could only do so fully by the wise exercise of volition: free will.

Thus, in his own creative act, God allowed a great risk into his own creation. By giving man the opportunity to decide for himself *whether or not* to live according to his will, at the same time he gave man the power to reject it. This divine risk, and its consequences, can be seen as the characterizing foundation for all human history.

PRINCIPLE FOUR: *REBELLION AND INDEPENDENCE—SIN*

> *Man has fully exercised the prerogative God gave him, but has done so in rebellion against God's design. Instead of obediently using the gift of free will to fall in with God's intended order, man has used his power of choice as a self-centered child. In his vanity and pride he has assumed himself capable of living independent from his Father's authority. He has turned his back on God, , rejected submission, and has reaped the consequences.*

Taking the gift, mankind quickly forgot its origin. From the beginning of his history man has lived as if he needs no Father. He has used the power and creativity of his essential being to advance to the heights. In so doing, however, he has plunged to the very depths of cruelty, self-centeredness, depravity, envy, arrogance, immorality, greed, loneliness, poverty, and despair.

Not "mankind" alone is guilty, every man, woman, and child is guilty. You and I are guilty. *We* have disobeyed God's laws. *We* have disregarded the inner voice of conscience. *We* have misused the gift of free will to live selfishly, sinfully, and pridefully against God's established order. We and all mankind—every one of us—have corrupted this precious gift by using it for our own ends, attempting to fulfill ourselves rather than asking if we have a Father who has a claim to our obedience. We have rejected submission as the imperative ruling dictum of life.

We have, in a word, *sinned*. Moreover, we are as a result sinners, having disengaged ourselves from our Creator.

This is not to say that we are *totally* evil. The goodness of our createdness remains. There is great *good* within mankind, but with it are mingled innumerable evidences of sin. Some are sinners guilty of murder. Others are guilty of envy, anger, deceit, jealousy, judgment, bitterness, and unforgiveness. Among us are tyrants like Nero and Hitler. Among us are those who silently and invisibly don masks of respectability to the outside world while hiding a corruption of self-centeredness in their hearts. But in spite of the manifest goodness that remains as an internal image-fingerprint from our Creator, we are all sinners of the rebellion together.

There is no escaping the reality of it—you and I are *sinners*. Some may be "good sinners." But we remain sinners.

In our lust for independence, we have separated ourselves from our Father and Creator. We are willful children. We have gained our independence, for he created us with that power. But in so doing we have cut ourselves off from everything that can fulfill the human soul at the depths of being.

For all its seeming success in creative and technological advancement, humanity is therefore a failed species. Mankind has failed in its singlemost important calling—to reflect, fulfill, and grow into the potential for which we were created. We have failed to become the sons and daughters of God we were meant to be.

PRINCIPLE FIVE: *JESUS, OUR ELDER BROTHER*

In spite of our independence, God remains a good and loving Father to his rebellious children. He sent One to earth to help us learn to become children of obedience. He sent his son Jesus, our own elder brother, himself a part of God's own being, to show us how to lay down the instrument of our waywardness, which is self-will, and to lead us back into the presence of the Father whose presence and Fatherhood we abandoned.

Jesus shows us how to live the life of submitted childness. His teachings and example in the four gospels of the Bible reveal the life of *childness* in relationship to our Creator-Father.

The prayer that characterized every moment of his life—*Not my will, but your will be done*—and his death on the cross, reveal his ultimate willingness to die to motives of self so that he might live in obedience to another—his Father.

In following the example of Jesus, taking his death into

ourselves—by embracing its *example* as well as appropriating the life-changing *miracle* of its living reality into the depths of our being—and thus dying to independence of motive as he did, we can become again God's good and obedient children. Doing so is no different than a wayward young person who has left home in rebellion, deciding to return home and repentantly make amends with his or her parents.

The historicity of Jesus' resurrection from the grave following his crucifixion forever distinguishes Jesus from all other spiritual teachers before and since. His resurrection authenticates Jesus as the one Son of God capable of bringing salvation to the world. There is much other valuable, though partial, truth in the world. But Christianity, by the resurrection, is uniquely validated as the *full* revelation of truth given to man. No other religion or worldview can make the historic claim of having conquered death before eyewitnesses. If the resurrection did not take place as a historic fact, then Christianity is a fraud from beginning to end. If it *did* take place as historic fact—if on a certain day at a certain time, a man verifiably dead for two days walked out of his tomb suddenly alive—then all other religions must recognize Christianity's preeminence as a revelation of Truth, and must recognize their subservience to that miraculous Truth. Those who are uncertain about the historicity of the resurrection do well to study the historical documents and evidences, not draw their conclusions from the opinions of others. There are many such historic documents that have been accumulated and printed in many books on the subject.

Through his resurrection, Jesus brought to the world a new form of Spirit-life. By invitation, that same Spirit—the Spirit of God brought to the world in the form of the Spirit of Christ—can dwell in the human heart. You and I can invite the same Spirit of Christ that conquered death to abide in *our* hearts, energizing and stimulating our own childness toward obedience to the Father's will.

Contrary to much misplaced hellfire preaching through the centuries, Jesus did not come to save us *from* God and his wrath. He came to take us *to* the Father as children returning home. Then the Father will himself save us from the sin inside us that we allowed to corrupt our hearts with self-centeredness. He will make us clean again, as we were when he first created us.

Holding Jesus' hand, we can return to the Father and tell him we are at last ready to be the children he created us to be. When we go to him, his loving forgiveness will swallow us in an embrace of Fatherly love.

PRINCIPLE SIX: *RELINQUISHMENT OF SELF-RULE*

The mechanism for renewed childship is the same mechanism by which mankind rebelled against the universal Fatherhood in the first place—free will. Now, however, we can use it to arise and return to our Father. By an act of the will, we can now look him in the eye and, by free choice, willingly relinquish self-rule to become again his children. Jesus used the term "born again" to describe this second birth into the new and higher childship with God.

Many names, many descriptions, many formulas have been used to explain and describe the process of this surrender, this laying down of arms, this relinquishment of the right to rule our lives...this homegoing. But none of them *is* the process. Its reality, you and I and each man and each woman must uniquely discover on our own. It is a completely individual process.

The single word that most aptly describes this surrender is *repentance*—the recognition of being heedless of God's Fatherhood and the principles of that Fatherhood in our lives.

The whole world is full of self-contented satisfied people who imagine that they have no need of God. That they are not conscious of it makes that need no less. They are children disconnected from their inborn Father-life. They are thus separated from the vital Source upon which all integration of personhood is built. They may consider themselves happy. They may think their lives fulfilled. But they are not fully integrated men and women who are in harmony with life's origin and destiny. Many people indeed *are* happy and content. They need God none the less. Turning to God is not based on felt "need," it is based on *truth*—a recognition of the ordained created structure of the universe.

One's waywardness may not be huge in the world's eyes. It may even be evidenced by much that the upside-down world of modernism actually admires, and would scoff at as being lumped in with "sin"—selfish attitudes, conceit, self-satisfaction, and independence from God. But the man or woman whose heart has turned homeward knows better. He or she knows what such traits say about them. They recognize within their hearts a complex mix of good and bad. They now come to recognize as well, in spite of what may be good elements of their character, the fundamental disconnectedness with the root of their Origins.

They want to be disconnected no longer. Such a homeward-bound child wants at last able humbly to submit, by an act of the will, to the good and loving sovereignty of God's Fatherhood.

This is humanity's deepest need—to arise and return to our Father. The story of the Prodigal Son in Luke 15 characterizes the human condition, with God eagerly awaiting our return with open arms.

He is not the scowling vengeful tyrant of dour old theologies, but the *Abba-daddy* of Jesus Christ!

The words of the prodigal perfectly express the heart's attitude of humble return: *Father, I have sinned against heaven and against you. I am no longer worthy to be called your son.*

We need to return to our Father not because of what he will do for us, or because he will make us happier or fill our lives with blessing, nor because of heaven or hell—whether getting into the one or staying out of the other...but because he is our Father.

It is *right* that we return to him.

Truth requires our return to him.

It is our *duty* as human beings created in his image to return to him.

Not only is it right and true, and is it our duty and obligation, it is our priceless *privilege and joy* to make ourselves again God's children. By so doing, we rise up into the fulfillment of our humanity.

Relinquishment of the right to self-rule may or may not be accompanied by an emotional release or a lifting of guilt, purposelessness, sadness, or aloneness. It may be accomplished by a mere few words in the quietness of one's own heart—"God, I am sorry. Please forgive me for allowing the sin-virus to make me think I had the right to live without you. I acknowledge what I failed to see, or perhaps refused to see for so long—that you are my Father. I know that I need a Father. More than that, I now *want* you as my Father. I am ready to be taught by Jesus to be your son, your daughter. I am ready to relinquish the right to rule my own life. I give that right to you. I want to be your child again. I *choose* to be your child again. I want your Spirit to live in my heart. I ask you and invite you to live within me, and to help me be the son or daughter you want me to be. Take me where I am, the good along with the selfish, and help me learn what childship means."

No two people surrender self-will in exactly the same way. God cares for no specific words. There is no formula, no magic wand of salvation. God cares only for a humble and contrite heart. Contrary to many such simplistic prescriptions, there is no "plan of salvation" in the Bible. There are *principles* that the biblical writers make clear, but no ironclad recipe that all must follow in precisely the same manner. There is a progressive *path* to salvation. With God's help and Jesus as our Guide, we each walk that path for ourselves.

Three things this repentant relinquishment are not are—*persuasion of belief, emotional experience,* nor *promise of blessing.* Through the years much Christian evangelism has erroneously focused on these three false premises—attempting to *persuade* its listeners to accept Christ on the basis of belief in the ideas and truths of Christianity; urging its listeners toward a life-changing *experience* of salvation; and promising its listeners future rewards from their belief, including happiness, joy, peace, blessing, and eternal life.

None of these is the foundation of salvation as Jesus taught it. The world's churches are full of "believers" who have never laid self-will on the altar. The Bible says that even demons believe and tremble. Likewise, bars, rescue missions, and prisons are full of men and women who have had spiritual "experiences" at various times in their lives, the reality of which has faded because self remained on the throne of will. The seeming realities of persuasion, emotion, and experience can be fleeting and deceptive.

Relinquishment of *self-rule* into *Father-rule* by an act of volition is the sole defining foundation of what it means to be born again—whatever the circumstances, and whatever the words and heart murmurings by which we make ourselves children again. When Jesus spoke of being born again, he was talking about *choices* to live as God's child, not being sprinkled with salvationary pixie dust.

Being born again into the second and higher childship may bring new joys, and will certainly bring peace through the years. But the lives of God's men and women are not always filled with worldly blessing. Many suffer for their faith. Life as God's children is not necessarily accompanied by earthly reward. God is our Father and Jesus is our Brother-Savior regardless of life's circumstances.

PRINCIPLE SEVEN: *OTHER-WORLDLY CITIZENSHIP*

In submitting to his Fatherhood by relinquishing the right to self-rule, one becomes a citizen of a new and other-worldly kingdom—a spiritual kingdom, which is a spiritual family. The parameters of citizenship and priorities of childship change all of life from what we have been accustomed to. Henceforth, we put aside our own goals and ideas and perspectives. They no longer exist at the center of life. God is our Father and we are his children. He is also our King and we are his subjects. Our purpose in life is to live in his will. His will becomes our will. One important aspect of that will is to be witnesses of his goodness, by our lives and by unity with our fellows.

When self-rule is laid on the altar to be consumed by the flames of God's love, and God's will is taken for one's own, at last have we taken the first steps into life indeed. A second childhood has begun.

Now we are children by choice not physical necessity. We now *want* and *choose* to live in obedience to our Father. Whereas in our earthly childhood, enforced obedience was burdensome, now in the second childhood of our maturity it becomes a chosen obedience, enforced only by our own volition. We are now "spiritual" children, not mere physical offspring. With that second birth begins a process of growth into mature sonship and mature daughterhood. It is a long slow process of learning, of forming new habits...a process of obedience. Henceforth life is no longer our own. We no longer determine and dictate our *own* attitudes, perspectives, thoughts, or decisions. Having handed rule over to God, he now truly becomes a *Father*. We dedicate ourselves to walk and behave and think and respond as his children, as *he* behaves and thinks and responds.

With Jesus, in all things we say, *Not my will, but your will be done.* With these words, the daily light of our lives becomes the unceasing prayer, *Father, what would you have me do?*

The maturity of the sons and daughters of God gradually grows within us, not by belief nor by learning Christian ideas and doctrines, but by the daily denial of self will into the Father will. We now model our lives after he who is both the Savior and Lord of men, Jesus our brother. The world and its ways—its values, its attitudes, its perspectives, its priorities, its ways of looking at things, its entire value and attitude structure—becomes nothing to us. It may continue to pull in many directions on our outer man. But in the deeps, we recognize that we are no longer effected by the surging of its temporal ebbs and flows. Thus we gradually purge the effects of thoughts and habit patterns caused by our former lives of independence. We have chosen to make ourselves citizens of a different kind of spiritual kingdom. We are henceforth out of step with the culture and values and outlook of the world, because we *want* to be out of step with them.

Free will is once again the powerful instrument of this gradual transformation into the radiant sons and daughters of God. By the determinative power of choice we daily reaffirm the death of self-rule. Daily and in all circumstances we learn to say, "Father, I take *your* will for my own. What do *you* want me to think, say, or do? How do *you* want me to respond? I no longer listen to the voice of self interest. I want only what *you* want for me. In all ways, in all things, I choose to be *your* child. I choose to obey you in all things. My independent will I lay at your feet, and I lay it down again this day, and every day."

Making such a commitment, however, does not prevent motives and attitudes of self, from years of past habits, to continue to exert themselves. Patterns from past years in the rebellion of independence persist. The battle is now against these old ways that sin has ingrained in us—the new man fighting the old man for supremacy. But now the Spirit of God himself lives inside us, as the spirit of all fathers dwells in the hearts of their sons. That indwelling Spirit helps us vanquish the habits and tendencies of the old man by daily obedience to God's outlook and priorities.

One of the hallmarks of this new kingdom citizenship is a responsibility to demonstrate actively to the rest of the world, by our living of kingdom principles, the validity of God's truth. The world is supposed to come to know God by its observation of the lives of those dwelling across the invisible boundary of that other-worldly kingdom of Fatherhood. This is the witness of Christianity to the truth.

This imperative component of the Christian faith has been grievously mistaken over the centuries to be a witness of preaching, persuasion, argumentation, and, in the instances evidenced of the darkest episodes of our history, even coercion. But persuasive preaching is no more capable than the Crusades or the mass baptisms in tenth century Russia of producing belief or kingdom life. All such false representations of Christianity suffer from a mistaken notion of how God's truth is transmitted.

Jesus made clear that our witness to the world will be effective and successful in the transmission of his life *only* when it is comprised of the two fundamental realities he commanded of those who call themselves his followers and disciples:

The visibly distinct loving and sacrificial lives of separation from the world's values and attitudes, and;

The visibly distinct sacrificial love for and unity with the brothers and sisters within the expansive body of Christian belief.

Without these two truths palpably and demonstrably causing the world to stand up and take notice, saying as it did in the first century, *Behold how these Christians love one another!* all of Christianity's persuasions and programs, sermons and ministries, buildings and assets, books and groups and music and tracts and television programs will amount to mere stubble and straw, blown away like a few wisps of smoke and lost to memory in the winds of eternity.

PRINCIPLE EIGHT: *DISCIPLESHIP OF CHRISTLIKENESS*

> *By becoming his disciple, a Christian (literally, "follower of Christ") makes Jesus Lord and Master. It is a discipleship not of theology or doctrine, but of obedience. A "Christian" is not one who believes certain things, but one who has made himself a follower, a disciple, of Christ—doing what he did, obeying what he tells him to do. Thus slowly he becomes more and more like Jesus himself.*

The discipleship of God's children to Christ his Son is a discipleship in which the highest objective is to become, over a lifetime, as much like Jesus as the fallen humanity allows. This is the primary and *only* objective of true Christianity. All its lesser components and objectives flow out of this high purpose. It is intended to be achieved by the modeling of life after his, and by obedience to his teaching and commands.

To obey Jesus requires study of his life and teachings. We must know his commands so that we can obey them. His will is our will. He is our Lord, we are his disciples. Our desire is to do what he says, and thus learn to see like him, think like him, love like him, respond like him, deny ourselves like him. This "obedience" is not external and superficial—donning robes, eschewing earthly possessions, and walking the countryside as itinerant preachers. It is Christlikeness of outlook, priority, attitude. It is relating ourselves to God as Father as Jesus related to God as Father. It is an *internal* Christlikeness.

The worldwide institutional religion called "Christendom" is not in general actively engaged in promoting such forms of radical discipleship. It has become a doctrinal and political entity. Childship obedience is neither its focus nor outlook. Thus it is not truly "Christian" at all, though it still goes by that name. Among the thousands of so-called Christian churches worldwide, misplaced priorities dominate the agenda: Social activities, the ritual of worship in diverse forms, and an obsession with doctrinal correctness. Most churches, like Christianity as a religion, give but scant emphasis to the true discipleship of obedience. There are, however, some occasional fellowships where this focus is discovered. A "disciple" of Jesus, therefore, may or may not be what is called a good "churchman." *Christian* and *churchman* are two entirely different labels that may have a great deal, or next to nothing, in common.

Discipleship is not a process of learning Christian doctrine, nor of engaging in Christian activities. Church involvement may in some cases promote the obedience of Christlikeness, but may also inhibit it. Discipleship, rather, exists in following the Master's steps—thinking as he thought, responding as he responded. One studies and learns of him, neither to gain knowledge nor sharpen the spiritual intellect, but to more effectively obey the principles by which he lived. Thus the power of Christ's life and death gradually come alive within us. In corresponding proportion as grows our obedience to the red letters of the New Testament, our spiritual eyes become open to truth in many realms.

The simple prayer, *Make me like Jesus,* is the underlying heart-cry of life for those who by relinquishment of self-will have made themselves Christ's disciples.

Enemy-Occupied Territory

"Enemy-occupied territory—that is what this world is. Christianity is the story of how the rightful king has landed, you might say landed in disguise, and is calling us all to take part in a great campaign of sabotage...

"God created things which had free will. That means creatures which can go either wrong or right. Some people think they can imagine a creature which was free but had no possibility of going wrong; I cannot. If a thing is free to be good it is also free to be bad. And free will is what has made evil possible. Why, then, did God give them free will? Because free will, though it makes evil possible, is also the only thing that makes possible any love or goodness or joy worth having. A world of automata—of creatures that worked like machines—would hardly be worth creating...

"Of course God knew what would happen if they used their freedom the wrong way: apparently he thought it worth the risk...The moment you have a self at all, there is a possibility of putting yourself first...wanting to be God. That was the sin of Satan; and that was the sin he taught the human race...What Satan put into the heads of our remote ancestors was the idea that they could 'be like gods'...be their own masters....And out of that hopeless attempt has come nearly all that we call human history...the long terrible story of man trying to find something other that God which will make him happy.

"The reason why it can never succeed is this. God made us: invented us as a man invents an engine...Now God designed the human machine to run on Himself. He Himself is the fuel our spirits were designed to burn, or the food our spirits were designed to feed on. There is no other...God cannot give us happiness and peace apart from Himself, because it is not there. There is no such thing.

"That is the key to history...

"And what did God do? First of all He left us conscience, the sense of right and wrong...Secondly, He sent the human race...those queer stories about a god who dies and comes to life again and, by his death, has somehow given new life to men. Thirdly, He selected one particular people and spent several centuries hammering into their heads the sort of God He was...

"Then comes the real shock. Among these Jews there suddenly turns up a man who goes about talking as if He was God. He claims to forgive sins. He says he has always existed...And when you have grasped that, you will wee that what this man said was, quite simply, the most shocking thing that has ever been uttered by human lips....

"The central Christian belief is that Christ's death has somehow put us right with God and given us a fresh start." [23]

Part 3

The Continual Quest

The individual journey of faith is a lifetime pilgrimage of growth into deepening truth, and toward higher regions in the understanding of God's nature.

Key Scriptural Concepts:

GROWTH, HUMILITY, DISCERN

Eleven

THE DEVELOPMENT OF THE IDEAS OF CHRISTIANITY

Truth Grows and Expands

> "In many and various ways God spoke of old to our fathers...
> but only God...gives the αυξανων (growth)."
> —Hebrews 1:1; 1 Corinthians 3:7

αυξανω: AUXANO —*Growth*

Growth in the Bible is nearly always associated, either directly or by implication, with the plant world. God clearly created the universe to grow, increase, and multiply. AUXANO is used in the Old Testament to mean "to become fruitful." The entire purpose of growth is for a plant to fulfill itself by bearing fruit and thus reproduce itself. The animal world parallels the plant world. Animals grow and mature. As human beings, we are intended to fulfill ourselves, to grow into full fruit-bearing maturity. Obviously the spiritual parallels the physical in the same way. The maturity toward which growth points is not mere physical maturity, but the fulfillment of our complete *being-ness* as sons and daughters of God. Jesus' numerous parables about seeds and plants and vines all point to this growth into maturity summed up in John 15:5: "I am the vine, you are the branches. He who abides in me, and I in him, he it is that bears much fruit..."

The concept of "growth" as a process of maturing, increasing, fulfilling, and bearing fruit, extends outward into every sphere of life. The plant world provides the clear illustration all about us every day. Growth extends to the living world of beings, and extends to all phases of life. We are not merely to grow physically but in all ways—emotionally, relationally, psychologically, and spiritually. In all ways we are to increase, mature, bear fruit, and *fulfill* that for which God intended us. But it is larger than individual growth. The church, Christ's body, is to grow and mature in the same way, as indeed is all of mankind. Obviously, however, neither the church nor the human species have matured and fulfilled themselves with the perfection of growth that was to be the intended flowering of its being. Much of the *growth* that God intends yet lies in the future.

CHRISTIANS CUSTOMARILY READ THE FIRST VERSE OF *HEBREWS* and other New Testament statements concerning the growth of faith as indicating progressivity *up to* a certain point…and then stopping.

We read accurately in Hebrews 1:1 that truth—previously shadowy and incomplete—emerged in its full expression in Jesus. But in doing so we restrict our outlook about how the ideas of faith develop over time. In satisfying ourselves with *only* that reading, we neglect the high principle that God's revelation of truth—*complete* in Jesus but not in every respect yet fully *revealed* nor fully *understood*—is an ongoing and continually expanding revelation of what God has "spoken to us by his Son."

We recognize this principle of continued growth at work early in the first few centuries of the church. We accept it without question. But when it comes to increasing revelation *in our own time*, we are reluctant even to the point of paranoia to bring the high principle of Hebrews 1:1—an *ongoing* revelation of what God has spoken—to bear upon doctrines that need to be continually expanded and deepened.

DOES LONGEVITY PRODUCE TRUTH?

For most of my life I have been fascinated with the diversity of ideas within Christianity.

Not only are the doctrines and beliefs held by those who consider themselves Christians diverse almost beyond imagining, they are also fluid and changeable. We tend to think that our beliefs came straight from the Lord's mouth, or, failing that, from the Apostles themselves. But in fact, the ideas of our belief systems emerged slowly over centuries of time. Most of its doctrines were actually developed by men far removed from those early years.

We talk wistfully about getting back to the reality of the first century church. But doctrinally, to do so would change everything. We might not recognize the result.

The question about this that we have already considered is whether tradition in every case validates *truth*. On the contrary. It indicates longevity. But as Islam demonstrates clearly enough, *longevity* of tradition is as susceptible to falsehood as to truth. We cannot be so pompous as to assume Christianity immune to the same principle. *All* systems of belief are invisibly infiltrated by error over time.

We are naïve to equate longevity with truth. When a particular view has been held for a long time...it *may* be true. However, it may *not* be true. The duration of its hold upon minds says nothing either way. To continue the perpetuation of long held errors that have infiltrated our doctrinal systems simply because they are a revered part of our tradition, is to deny the very truth Jesus came to reveal. Jesus brought newly deepening and expanding truth. If we learn anything from his life, surely it is that revelation of truth *grows*.

THE HISTORIC FLOW OF IDEAS

Church history, in all the diverse branches of inquiry it affords, is one of the sadly neglected disciplines within evangelicalism in particular. Orthodoxy and Catholicism, for whom tradition is pivotal and sacred, emphasize their histories usually more than does Protestantism. What is normally studied, however, are the roots of one's *own* particular belief system, and only those trends of thought that bolster and support its doctrines and traditions. Protestants (when they study it at all) and Catholics alike are guilty of this compartmentalized outlook on church history. Catholics can quote the Popes, but how much do they know about Menno Simons or the Wesleys? Protestants study the ideas of Calvin, but how much do they know of Augustine?

Our knowledge and awareness of how Christianity *as a whole* has come to believe what it does—in all its great diversity—is superficial. In many cases it is also historically inaccurate.

To study the entire scope of Christian thought and tradition is not only enlightening, but humbling. No matter where we happen to find ourselves at any moment of time, all present expressions of the Christian faith represent but tiny slices out of an enormous historic flow and gradual development of ideas, beliefs, doctrines, practice, and tradition.

DEEP OR SHALLOW SOIL

A study of church history in this larger more encompassing sense is more than a mere intellectual exercise, it represents a vital component in understanding what it really means to be a bold-thinking Christian. The *roots* of faith are an imperative requirement in the process of growth. Without roots there can be no growth. Roots pull nutrients up into the living organism to produce the growth that bears fruit. Jesus emphasized that without roots, spiritual plants wither and die.

What gives soil its life-producing power? The dead past, made alive through the miracle of organic decay to feed the new growth of the present in a never ending cycle of life. The *past* makes possible the *present*. Fruit cannot mature when roots have but an inch of soil. Growth is fed by the *past* to produce *present* fruit.

Throughout my own spiritual life, therefore, I have made a study of the past an intrinsic part of my intellectual diet in order to keep myself aware of the spiritual soil out of which I as a Christian living in the twentieth and twenty-first centuries have emerged. I have especially tried to familiarize myself with the fascinating development of Christian *thought* and the emergence of the *ideas* which gradually came to be considered acceptable and orthodox within Christian belief. Viewing Christianity solely through the lens of the present, I recognize that my perspectives will necessarily be one-dimensional. A study of the past acts as a protective and balancing influence against the futility of hoping to bear fruit as a Christian while giving one's roots no soil to grow in.

Out of an understanding of our historic roots—both good traditions and erroneous ones, both positive developments in church history and detrimental ones—we become capable of discerning broad and eternal truth for our own time. The old saying is as true for Christians as for political movements: Those who do not learn from history are destined to repeat it.

Knowledge of history is not the objective. *Truth* is the objective. Balanced truth emerges out of an awareness of how and why we got to where we are, and how God wants us to move forward.

The example we have alluded to before of what it means to "be a Christian" remains enormously illuminating of this principle. Is it as simple as evangelicals present it—praying a prayer to "invite Christ into one's heart?" Is it as simple, as Catholic and Orthodox teaching present it—being baptized, confirmed, and then being faithful to "the church" and its "tradition?"

History reveals that both prescriptions, and all other such formulas, are too simplistic. They may represent *part* of what being a Christian entails. But a thorough study of the New Testament, as well as historic Christianity, reveals how much broader and deeper a thing it is to be born again into true *belief*, and more importantly into the childness of Christlike discipleship that accompanies it. In attempting to understand the full scope of what "salvation" means, we've got to give our roots more soil.

THE EXPERIMENTAL CHURCH

To an extent, all expressions that the Church at large, and perhaps millions of churches individually, have given to the corporate Christ-life among us are experimental.

The first "church meeting" in the upper room recounted in the opening chapters of *Acts* was experimental. Peter and the other disciples had no idea what to do. They hadn't a clue what was in store for them. They had no plan. They were totally winging it! Jesus left no instruction manual. His followers had to figure it out as they went, in matters of both belief and practice.

The enormous diversity of movements and sects and debates and councils and denominations that have gone to make up the church since those first days in 30 A.D., reveals just how experimental the whole enterprise was and still is. Jesus never came within a mile of giving clear indication of what he intended a "church service" to look like, or even whether such formal and structured services, and elaborate buildings to contain them, and professional clergy to oversee them, were supposed to be components of discipleship. There are some who believe that "church" buildings and organizations and programs and denominations were never intended by Jesus at all. These are not wacko fringe Christians but serious men and women who have studied the gospels carefully. They see no hint in Jesus' teachings pointing in such directions.

Obviously no one is suggesting abolishing churches. But the fact of this diversity of viewpoint on the church soberly reminds us that Jesus did not spell these things out with precision. He left his followers pretty much in the dark about most of the specifics of how they were to organize themselves.

So Christ's followers have had to figure it out as they went. In so doing, they have come up with *many* different perspectives on how things ought to be done, and what constitutes accurate belief.

No wonder it is confusing (and, sadly, inconsistent) to the outside world.

This leads to a conclusion I have long puzzled over—that in some mystical way I still do not completely grasp, Jesus must have *intended* this fluid and dynamic uncertainty. Had he wanted the worship and doctrine and practice of his followers rigidly to adhere to strict standards, surely he would have said so.

That he did *not* specify a rigidity of practice seems to indicate that the "Follow me," discipleship to which he called the twelve, and to which he likewise calls us, is not a discipleship of structure, worship, church organization, doctrine, or practice, but something else entirely. It is rather a discipleship of obedience, heart attitude, humility, and childness before the Fatherhood of God.

THREE DIRECTIONS OF INQUIRY

With all this in mind, then, it seems that in our quest for truth in any specific area of uncertainty, question, or study we would do well to follow a three-pronged interrelated inquiry:

1) *Where have we come from:*

How has Christianity progressed (both toward truth and away from it) in its thinking and practice through the centuries with regard to various doctrines, beliefs, or practices (salvation, the Eucharist, baptism, universal salvation, the second coming, the Trinity, etc)? How did the many ideas representing Christendom as a whole develop and change over time? How accurate were those changes in reflecting God's leading and truth? Are those changes true to the gospel and the words of Jesus, or do they take interpretive liberties, possibly in directions unintended by the Lord?

2) *Where are we now:*

What is current belief and practice throughout the broad spectrum of Christianity and the church? What are the roots of those ideas? Were they God-inspired or man-devised? Again, to what extent are the gospel and the words of Jesus represented? And to what extent have we added to his teachings and overlaid them with our own biases, preconceptions, personal preferences, and opinions?

3) *Where does God want us to go from here:*

How is God leading now? What *new* revelations might he be attempting to infuse into the church at large in *our* time? Have our doctrines, beliefs, and practices reached the apex and pinnacle in God's plan, or have some of them grown stagnant and their roots crimped and shallow? Where might current revelation still be incomplete? How does God expect eternal truth within our doctrinal beliefs to *continue* developing into greater harmony with his eternal Will and purpose?

I have used this method to search into a deeper understanding in the areas of salvation, prophecy, obedience, the work of the Holy Spirit, worship, the nature of God and man, the role of experience in the walk of faith, in my understanding of the Bible, as well as many other components of my life and faith. The method I employ is not so cut and dried as sitting down and listing scriptures or historical facts or movements within the church in an attempt to fill in an informational matrix. Such rigidity of study would only lead to dogmatic and formularistic conclusions. I would but replace the stagnation of old formulas with a list of new ones that would itself in time become equally stagnant. Rather I am continually looking for dynamic, *growing, living reality* within the beliefs of my Christian faith.

Though these three progressive elements can be identified (past, present, future), the quest for truth is fluid and dynamic—energized by obedience to the truth we know.

All these areas of inquiry occur simultaneously in my heart and brain. They occupy my prayers and study of Scripture and other reading in a threefold unity. Undergirding the process is the constant prayer: *God, guide me into **your** truth. Illuminate my heart and mind with **your** perspectives, with the mind of Christ. Help me to see and understand **your** Will and eternal purposes for myself, for your people, and for the universe.*

PROGRESSIVE DEVELOPMENT OF THE DOCTRINE OF THE TRINITY

As one example to illustrate this process at work, I have studied in some depth the doctrine of the Trinity in an attempt to understand its complexities more fully. The role of past, present, and future, and the *development* of the ideas of belief, is easy to see.

Whatever the subject under my scrutiny, I always go first to the gospels. It is there I discover the two all important foundation stones of any scriptural quest:

What did Jesus say *about* the subject?

What did Jesus command that I *do* in response?

In this particular case, Jesus said *nothing* specifically about the doctrine we call the Trinity. His only words that relate to the doctrine that later developed were: *I and the Father are one.* But he went into no detail about what he actually *meant*. Therefore, we must carry the inquiry further. As we do, we observe that he gave his disciples a very specific *do* with regard to his relationship to the Father—the "do" of following his example. He said: *I do nothing but what the Father tells me to do.*

Here we find the doctrine (the Trinity, as it were...his oneness with the Father) transformed out of the theoretical into the realm of obedience. Suddenly the high doctrine has become practical. Jesus has given us something to *do*—what the Father tells us. Any attempt to analyze the doctrine apart from this obedience, therefore, will end in futility. In the gospels the two are always one.

Next we turn to the writings of Paul. Like his Lord, Paul does not specifically discuss, still less does he doctrinalize, the Trinity as such. He wrestles with the depth and complexity of Jesus' relationship with the Father with wonderful insight (*Ephesians* and *Colossians*) and in a manner which establishes a scriptural foundation for all future Trinitarian studies. Yet all serious biblical scholars must admit that in many respects Paul's writings make the mystical Father-Son relationship all the more difficult to grasp.

So we must progress further.

We come next to the gospel of the beloved disciple John, written c.95-100 A.D. The first chapter of John's gospel represents one of the towering mountain peaks in all Christian writing, in which, furthering Paul's theology of the Father-Son relationship, John confronts the essential question: *Who is Jesus?*

However...John's definition of the man he walked beside as the *Logos*, the Word, in one sense obscures the matter still further. John places into definite and unmistakable language his conviction that the Son existed "in the beginning," and was not merely *with* God...he *was* God.

By the end of the first century, then, we find in place a threefold foundation for the development of what would later become the doctrine of the Trinity—the words of *Jesus* concerning his relationship with the Father, the writings of *Paul* about that relationship, and the first chapter of *John's* gospel. Neither the full doctrine, however, nor the use of the word "Trinity," yet exist anywhere on the historic horizon.

As the second century progressed and the Apostolic Age receded into memory, Christian thinkers and writers concerned themselves more and more with this all important pivotal question, "Who was Jesus?" and where did he stand in relation to the Father?

In the process, Christianity was gradually becoming increasingly *doctrinal* with regard to many of its beliefs. Perhaps this was a change born out of *necessity* as Christianity found itself combating the philosophic influence of Greek and Roman culture. Perhaps it was a change to the *detriment* of true gospel Christianity. That debate will have to remain for a future inquiry. In any event, the second, third, and fourth centuries were ones in which *doctrines* coalesced into hardened form and the church gradually assumed an increasingly rigid structure.

Eyewitnesses to the Apostolic era died. Second and third generations of believers also passed from the scene. Whereas at first the church had depended on eyewitness accounts of the events, facts, teachings, parables, principles, sayings, and commands of Jesus and his disciples, over time it became the *doctrines* of belief that were relied on as the cornerstone of faith.

Traditions became established. Theologies were set in place that solidified over coming centuries.

Certainly the passage of years makes change inevitable. Yet as the church progressed from events, facts, principles, and commands to *doctrines* and *creeds* as the primary vehicles for the teaching and promulgation of its essential truths...much of the reality of the original gospel was lost in translation.

Scholars convincingly argue that this shifting emphasis toward doctrine was necessary to combat the Hellenistic and Gnostic influences prevalent in the Mediterranean world. With the death of early generations of believers, and as Greek and Roman culture infiltrated Christianity, certain ideas gained widespread appeal that were completely alien to gospel foundations. As early 120-130 A.D., Gnostic Docetism arose maintaining that Jesus had never been an actual flesh and blood human being at all. Rather he was a phantasm, an illusion.

Many such Gnostic ideas sprang up in the centuries following the Apostolic Age, necessitating vigorous rebuttal by "true doctrine," in this case, the historic factual manhood of Jesus. We see clearly, by the example of the heresy of Docetism, the value and necessity of true "doctrine" in the growth of the Christian church. Our quest as bold thinking Christians is not to eliminate doctrine, but to rightly divide between those doctrines that are rooted in the Gospels, that have stood the test of time, and that are eternally true, and those that have been produced by the temporal needs and perspectives of passing historical eras that may not be.

As Christian theology coalesced into a generally recognized set of doctrines, many of the disputes of ideas revolved around the person and nature of Jesus Christ. How did his life, example, teaching, death, and resurrection bring salvation to a fallen humanity? The *Trinity* and the *atonement* were therefore pivotal. Still today, these arguably represent the two most central and debated doctrines within Christendom.

Yet orthodoxy in both areas was slow to develop. Certain ideas were put forth that were closer to the final doctrine than others. Some were recognized as completely spurious. Even those suggestions that were later discarded, however, contributed in a long process of trial and error and debate and discussion toward a slow focusing and eventual synthesis of ideas that would come to be considered acceptable and "orthodox."

We must not lose sight of the organic, growing, fluid nature of this process. Fallible men were involved. No telegrams from heaven, no tablets of stone, were delivered to early believers with "orthodoxy" written on them.

As this process continued, by the end of the second century, we find hints of Trinitarian doctrine present in various Christian writings. Then the word "Trinity" appears in the third century. By the fourth century creeds were being established to set various "beliefs" into easily understood forms. By early in the fifth century, the writings of Augustine set the doctrine of the Trinity into the concrete of tradition, where it has remained ever since. We will have occasion to examine this fascinating and important historical process in more depth later on, as a way to further exercise our gray cells in bold thinking.

By this point in the history of the church, another trend had entered the mix. In every succeeding generation this new factor had the potential to kill increasing revelation.

That was simply this: *doctrinal self-perpetuation.*

Doctrines *themselves* gradually replaced the realities to which they had originally pointed.

LOOKING BACK...LOOKING FORWARD—GROWTH AND DOCTRINAL DRIFT

Throughout a process such as this, notwithstanding the example of Docetism, it is healthy to remind ourselves of the question: Did Jesus want us developing the tenets of our discipleship into doctrinalized formula?

It is a matter of going back through time, sifting through the historical developments of belief, and arriving again at the touchstone and foundation of our faith—Jesus himself. If *he* did not doctrinalize his teaching, are we right in attempting to do so?

He said, "Follow me." That ought to be enough.

Then he said, "I and the Father are one." Perhaps that too ought to be enough.

Yet Hebrews 1:1 speaks of two important yet occasionally contradictory principles—truth is to be found in Jesus, and God's revelation is *ongoing.*

We are left to ask whether the Trinity offers an example where the revelation was complete in Jesus' statement, *I and the Father are one,* or whether God intended us to probe and delve more deeply into the meaning of those five words, and *grow* it into greater and expanded revelation. If so, did that growing revelation stop with Augustine? Or is it supposed to continue…even now?

Such questions have no easy answers. We must in humility, and with some fear and trembling, both return to the solid gospel rock of *I and the Father are one,* and say, "Perhaps this is the revelation God intends," while also asking, "What *more* does God have to reveal to his people about the Father/Son relationship?"

While looking back to the gospels for truth, we also look forward and pray for *more* truth.

HARDENED CONCRETE OR INCREASING REVELATION

This has been but a cursory glance at how Christian doctrine has *grown* through history. The Trinity is but one example of many. We might similarly trace developments in how Christians view numerous points of differing outlook.

The flow of Christian thought has not produced complete truth in every area of perspective and practice. Many would say that the traditional orthodoxies concerning the justice of God, sanctification, predestination, grace, election, the role of the priesthood and clergy, and the limited atonement are ones that want more looking into.

This is why any inquiry must examine historical developments and make intelligent, unbiased, and non-opinionated determinations—pro and con—and then carry those conclusions forward to an examination and evaluation—pro and con—of current and contemporary views, practices, and beliefs.

In the matter of the Trinity, there have been few significant developments of mainstream Christian thought since the time of Augustine. Once the doctrine hardened, those who deviated from the accepted view, or even who attempted to continue the process of prayerful inquiry into yet unexplored regions of its mystery, were branded as heretics and excommunicated. I do not imply that we *should* question the doctrine. I only observe (except for the secularized "historical Jesus" tangent by liberal scholars) that there has been little original thought within Catholic and Protestant mainstream theologies regarding this central element of our faith.

So it is with most doctrines. The concrete hardens. But are we better or worse off in our understanding of the nature and character of God?

Has the doctrine of hell changed appreciably from Dante's time?

Has the doctrine of election and predestination changed appreciably from Calvin's time?

Do we really believe that these men possessed such fullness of revelation that we are prohibited from subjecting their ideas to the scrutiny of Jesus' own words?

WHAT DOES HISTORY TELL US?

The conclusions of history tell us nothing for certain about one specific doctrine or another. The process of the church's development, however—with its ups and downs, its failures and successes—ought to make us more capable of discerning truth ourselves.

Looking at the dearth of progressive illumination concerning most doctrines during the centuries, and recognizing that the orthodoxies of the third through fifth centuries, or the sixteenth, were often reached after significant *deviations* from the words of Jesus, Paul, and John, I am forced to conclude that God indeed has more truth to reveal than that presented by the hardened concrete of much traditional Christian belief.

In this process of evaluating our history, we must be ever on the lookout for a genius with uncommon wisdom—men like the Apostle Paul and George MacDonald, and perhaps Augustine, as well as countless humble men and women around us who never write a word or preach a sermon or lead a Bible study. It is such as these, though often the fact is not fully recognized by those nearest them, who strike deep into the rich veins of eternal truth.

Then we must synthesize all the grand sweeps of past thought into a representative unity built on current insights that reflects *true* truth as God would have it revealed and lived in our time and in our lives.

The Experimental Growth of Theology and Doctrine

Though C.S. Lewis perhaps tends to revere the theology of tradition to a greater extent than does his mentor George MacDonald, he yet recognizes the growth process and experimental nature of theology as it has developed. He writes:

"That is how Theology started. People already knew about God in a vague way. Then came a man who claimed to be God; and yet he was not the sort of man you could dismiss as a lunatic. He made them believe Him. They met Him again after they had seen Him killed. And then, after they had been formed into a little society or community, they found God somehow inside them as well: directing them, making them able to do things they could not do before. And when they worked it all out they found they had arrived at the Christian definition of the three-personal God.

"This definition is not something we have made up; Theology is, in a sense, experimental knowledge...

"The instrument through which you see God is your whole self. And if a man's self is not kept clean and bright, his glimpse of God will be blurred...

"God can show Himself as He really is only to real men....Consequently, the one really adequate instrument for learning about God, is the whole Christian community....Christian brotherhood is, so to speak, the technical equipment for this science—the laboratory outfit." [24]

Twelve

The Open-Minded Spiritual Quest

Unity, Openness, and the Role of Spiritual Quest in Understanding God's Eternal Purpose

> "Truly, I say to you, unless you turn and become like children,
> you will never enter the kingdom of heaven.
> Whoever ταπεινωσει (humbles) himself like this child,
> he is the greatest in the kingdom of heaven."
> —Matthew 18:3-4

ταπεινοφροσυνη: TAPEINOPHROSUNE—*Humility*

TAPEINOPHROSUNE comes from TAPEINOS, low-lying, and means lowliness of mind, the opposite of pride and arrogance. In other words, "lowness" in personal outlook (in a good and positive sense), taking the low position, meek but not necessarily servile or lacking in confidence.

M y work with George MacDonald through the years has resulted in many individuals seeking me out in hopes that I will be able to shed light on and clarify various difficult scriptural subjects that MacDonald explores in his writings.

Bold Thinking Christianity

George MacDonald was a bold thinker who was not afraid to delve into the most controversial subjects in his quest to know God more intimately. Some of those areas of inquiry remain controversial today. Others seem more humorous than troublesome by today's broader and more tolerant sensibilities.

For example, one of the chief arguments against MacDonald's theology that contributed to his ouster from his first pulpit was his expressed belief that animals will share in the afterlife. This was not the only charge of unorthodoxy against him, but it does illustrate to what an extent the heresies and unorthodoxies of the church through the years (such as the "heresy" proposed by Galileo that the earth revolved around the sun) have been shown by the passage of time not to be as serious as was once thought.

In any event, MacDonald roused controversy, in his own time and in our own. I have for years been on the receiving end both of that controversy and of mail from readers hoping that I will be able to enlighten them concerning MacDonald's views and perspectives on various areas of uncertainty.

Some of the issues raised are difficult to get to the bottom of. I haven't known how to weigh and sift and sort the scriptural evidence in every case either. MacDonald's writings on the atonement, on the trinity, on the doctrine of "adoption," on God's justice, on the Fatherhood of God, and other topics, are weighty and dense. I hesitate to put too many words of my own interpretation into his mouth unless I am very sure I know what he was attempting to communicate.

The following titles of some of MacDonald's well known written treatises, which he mostly titled "unspoken sermons," indicate the range and extent of his theological writings: *Salvation From Sin, Truth, Righteousness, The Fear of God, Self-Denial, Life, God's Family, Justice, The Truth in Jesus, Opinion and Truth, The Knowing of the Son, Abba Father, The Higher Faith.*

From this brief list of a handful of his addresses, realizing that MacDonald wrote during a contentious and doctrinally debative era within the British church, it is hardly surprising that controversy resulted.

Long ago I came to the conclusion that the best good I could provide those who contacted me was to maintain as much as possible a position of doctrinal neutrality, then try to point them to clarifying passages in MacDonald's own writing and toward what other sources I felt might be helpful, including the Bible. My intent was always that they read what others have had to say, especially the biblical writers, and decide for themselves what conclusions to draw. How could I speak knowledgeably on an issue such as whether animals will be in heaven? I have no idea! Doctrinal neutrality is the most reasonable position for me to take. So it has been with many other aspects of MacDonald's theology.

In many cases I haven't known what to make of MacDonald's points of view. I have been a seeker along the same road as most of those who contact me. What I am comfortable saying with absolute certainty is this:

I believe that the love, goodness, forgiveness, and trustworthiness of the Father of Jesus Christ are infinite. Therefore, I trust Him completely. Though he slay me, yet will I trust him, and so may all creation likewise trust him. He is a good Father, so all he does **must** *be good and can only be good. His essential nature is love, so everything that proceeds out of his divine being must reflect that love. It is in his heart to forgive infinitely. Jesus told us so. Therefore...we may trust him, and trusting him, may trust him for all things, for all men, for all possibilities. What is in the heart of God the Father to do will be full of love, full of goodness, and full of forgiveness. And in those foundational truths of his essential nature and character I rest. In those foundational truths of his essential nature and character are all my questions swallowed up. I am at peace...for I trust Him.*

Beyond that, I care not to go. For many years I have been fascinated and intrigued in my explorations beyond the boundaries of traditional thought concerning what might be in God's heart to accomplish. But I find no need within myself to formulate a systematic theology, as it were, of his reconciliatory purposes. I trust *God* far more than I trust in *my* capacity to understand the infinity of his loving purpose.

In my view the key reason why those on both sides of most controversial issues struggle so hard to systematize their personal theologies (and err in the process) is that they don't trust *God* enough. They feel they must put together systems of belief constructed out of their incomplete intellects in which they *can* trust, limiting God to such an extent that they are then able—in their own minds—to explain everything about him.

Something about it seems backwards to me. I would far rather trust God for biblical uncertainties, than to convince myself that I am certain of his will on every thorny issue as many seem to consider it their duty to do. Being wrong does not frighten me nearly so much as being unable to trust God to do what is right and good...though my fallible human intellect will be unable to discern *how* he will accomplish that in every instance.

It may seem simplistic to phrase it thus, but I think the basic problem is one of ταπεινοφροσυνη, *humility*. We think too highly of ourselves. We make too much of our intellects. *We* must be right...everyone else is wrong.

I *do* believe there are great truths hidden deep in many of these doctrines (mysteries hidden far beyond the formula-explanations offered of them.) I also believe that God desires us to lay hold of them. But not so that we may formulate ironclad belief systems which we grow to worship more than the God they describe, but *so that we will know who God is and be able to trust him more deeply.*

We will only lay hold of them by approaching them with a *humble* heart.

TRUTH NOT DEBATE

I have no desire to argue on behalf of or against any doctrine. Scriptural viewpoints on contested subjects are interesting to me because I relish in the exchange of *ideas*. But they are not things of the first rank. I would rather expend my energies seeking more deeply to understand the character of God, than attempting to determine rightness or wrongness about every debated issue where the Bible leaves room for varying interpretation. Doctrinal "ideas" are something like a hobby to me. They do not form the foundation for my life.

The endless jot-and-tittle debate between Christians, it seems to me, has done more to impede the coming of the kingdom of God with power than all the unbelief in the history of the world. There are many high matters to be discussed with our Father in heaven, to the center of whose heart all questions and controversies and unanswerables must lead in the end. But most of them do *not* need to be debated between the brethren.

Prayers, heart-cries, even tears, may accompany the wrestling through of such ideas. But it is always a grief to our Father when brothers and sisters line up on opposite sides of various doctrinal fences and toss viewpoints and proof-texts back and forth. Jesus did not offer himself on the cross so that we could be at each other's throats over who is or is not included in the atonement or whether animals will go to heaven, or whether God is the Father of all mankind or only the elect, but that the world might be saved.

Such argumentativeness cannot exist in an atmosphere where the humility of Christlikeness rules. But where humility toward our brothers and sisters is absent, contention is almost inevitable.

On all matters doctrinal, my own points of view are still forming. I became intrigued by possibilities outside certain aspects of the orthodox belief system of my upbringing long before discovering George MacDonald's writing. MacDonald furthered the process by forcing wide within me new doorways into the inexhaustibility of God's goodness. Yet MacDonald himself persistently refused to articulate firm positions on many very controversial issues. Yet when one reads his works, one cannot help being stretched into wondrously enlarging realms in the understanding of God's character. While not addressing the controversies themselves, MacDonald constantly urges his readers "upward and onward" in their capacity to trust in the infinite goodness of God's Fatherhood.

I find the idea by no means fearsome that God might have more in mind to ultimately accomplish than is commonly taught, but rather an exciting one to prayerfully consider. To my astonishment, however, I have gradually learned, as do most who explore the less-traveled pathways through the spiritual yellow wood, that those *not* inclined similarly to inquire how expansive might be the love of the God, do not find this quest into God's heart exciting, but rather heretical.

For me these are no mere doctrinal matters. They sit at the very core of the Christian belief system—to what extent are God's love, goodness, and forgiveness infinite? Will the victory of God's love in the universe be complete...absolute...total? These are significant questions. Who *is* the God we worship and seek to obey? Is the universe a great dualism, where the two sides of Good and Evil each lay *eternal* claim to the souls in their camp?

The implications make such inquiries as these of the utmost importance with regard to the nature of the Christianity we present to the world. Nor do I think, as George MacDonald's pastoral mentor F.D. Maurice pointed out, that the world has much reason to listen to the gospel until we truly apprehend the character of the God that gospel is purported to be about. Is it truly *good* news we proclaim to the world, while at the same time we speak of the eternal retribution of God against a huge portion of his created universe?

Though I say that I am at peace trusting in the infinite trustworthiness of the Father without resolving an ironclad answer to that question, I yet believe this is a matter we need to explore. And I have explored it in some depth and am the richer in my walk with the Lord for it.

Those who would not wade into such theological waters often

dismiss difficult questions with a light and subtly pietistic air: "Ah, but brother...you're adding to the Word of God...you must just take the inspired Word for what it says."

Unfortunately, it's not that easy. Much in the Word of God doesn't support the orthodox positions to the extent their proponents assume. It was precisely the desire to take the Word of God for what it says that first led me down this road less traveled, I know this is the case for many thousands like me.

And while we mustn't add to the Word of God, nether must we subtract from it.

TOO GOOD?

For reasons which have puzzled me as long as I can remember, it seems that the multitude of evangelical Christians don't want God to be *too* good. They are inexplicably threatened by the thought that God might be *more* loving and *more* forgiving than they. This remains a baffling mystery. Nor is it a challenge most people want to face. They simply do not want to think about it.

But as God's people, we *must* think about it.

Do we want to know who God is? Or are we content with an image of him that has been passed down to us which *may* not be based on Scripture?

It is a vital query, upon which the future effectiveness of our evangelism depends. If we don't know whether God's love and forgiveness are *really* infinite, what then is the good news we proclaim to the world? That with his right hand of love he rescues us from his left hand of vengeance? That the loving Son protects us from the wrathful Father?

That may be news. I'm not sure whether it's very *good* news.

The people in today's world are more sophisticated than we give them credit for being. This doctrine which puts something like a divine schizophrenia at the heart of the Godhead sounds less than ridiculous to them. Is it any wonder the large percentage of thinking men and women aren't listening with much attentiveness to this thing that we continue to insist is *good news*?

Might it not be time we realistically face how the God that we insist loves them actually appears to a large percentage of people? We have to be pragmatic about that fact. We flatter ourselves with minuscule pockets of revival, but the stark fact is for the most part, the world isn't heeding the gospel message. I think it is largely because *we* are confused about who God is and what is his intrinsic character.

To do so is not, as some would mistakenly argue, changing the gospel to accommodate unbelief. In fact it is just the opposite. It represents an attempt to *eradicate* unbelief from our orthodoxy so that at last we might present the sophisticated modern world with the *true* and glorious gospel that Jesus himself proclaimed.

Much of the unbelief we rail against actually exists in the doctrines of our orthodoxy, not in the world. Will the church be able to handle such a statement? Much *unbelief* exists within *Christianity's* orthodoxies.

Though it is not recognized in most Christian circles today, scriptural evidence exists on both sides of even the most controversial of doctrines. Once a man or woman begins opening his or her eyes to the broader view to which many scriptures point, he or she often becomes astounded at what they suddenly begin seeing on almost every page of the Bible.

It's not as easy a matter as saying, "I just take the Bible at literal face value." The words themselves (the "words" given us by the translators) sometimes point in opposite directions, as Matthew 25:46 and Philippians 2:10 clearly evidence. Here sit the most obvious proof-texts for the two opposing viewpoints on one particular controversial doctrine, the eternal destiny of sinners—the one, as commonly translated, speaking of "eternal punishment," the other declaring that "every knee" will ultimately bow, by choice, in reverential honor and profession of faith. Those who explain away the force of the latter with talk of sinners being *compelled* to bend the knee do not grasp the universality of veneration Paul's Greek actual implies.

Such contradictory scriptural evidence can be cited on both sides of nearly *all* debatable doctrines, as can the reasons justifying the ignoring of one side of the evidence or the other.

The searching and humble heart must come to all scriptural conundrums with an open and prayerful mind. The Scriptures simply aren't as clear on most matters as we might wish. But when we are thinking too highly of ourselves, that obvious truth escapes us altogether. The reason is simple: without humility, we think we have all the answers.

THE QUEST

The following observation might also be worthy of consideration as we ponder the means by which we come to truth.

Often *opinion* and a *pre-formed viewpoint* lead the way on the part of those advocating what perhaps would be called the orthodox position on most matters. Writings in support of any widely-held orthodoxy generally reflect a desire to maintain the established position. Rarely do you find accounts of humble-hearted personal search leading the way into increasingly deeper understanding of some Catholic or evangelical or Pentecostal or Anglican orthodoxy. In my own experience, I have not encountered the writings of the individuals holding tight to every cherished orthodoxy as reflecting a hungering for *more* of God's truth, looking for a *deeper* reach of God's love, crying out to discover a *wider* extent of God's salvation. Usually the writings in support of a long-established perspective or methodology exhibit none of the aspects of *quest*, only proof-textual proofs and reasonings and non-original analysis.

This is a *most* significant point.

In general, Scripture indicates that humble hunger and a search for truth lead to wisdom and understanding, while an adherence to the traditions of men, without a heart-hunger accompanying it, can lead to spiritual stagnation.

A hundred biblical passages could be brought in to support this principle, that *understanding and wisdom come as a result of an intense search for truth* with one's whole heart. The entire book of *Proverbs* and most of Jesus' teachings and Paul's epistles resound with the cry to leave no stone unturned...to search, knock, dig, seek, pray. Personal *hunger* offers a necessary searchlight into constantly new and deeper dimensions of faith.

"If you *call out* for insight and *cry aloud* for understanding, and if you *look for it* as for silver and *search for it* as for hidden treasure, then you will understand...and find the knowledge of God." (Proverbs 2: 3-5)

How do we imagine that Jesus grew into such confidence and boldness that he walked through the grain fields on the Sabbath, breaking the law in plain view of the Pharisees? How else other than by challenging the orthodoxy of his day in just this seeking, searching, praying manner. What was he doing in the temple among the teachers and elders when he was twelve—*questioning* the stale orthodoxy of the day.

The related principle is equally supported scripturally: Steadfastly adhering to a spiritual orthodoxy (*any* spiritual orthodoxy), calling those who disagree heretics, and directing one's study and energies exclusively to the bolstering of that orthodoxy with greater strength than toward the discovery of new and deeper truths...such is a potential pathway toward spiritual stagnation and eventual error. Such does not *always* occur, but the danger is always there.

These two factors, on the face of them, recommend the conclusions of those who have labored in prayer and study over some matter to a greater extent than the conclusions of those whose views are set in concrete on the basis of traditions which often they have not wrestled through for themselves.

Opinion and *tradition* come more into the various arguments in support of so-called orthodoxy, while *prayer* enters more into the personal accounts of those seeking for truth no matter where the search might lead. And prayer, if it comes from the heart of a sincerely God-hungry individual, must yield a harvest of truth in the end. Its compass is pointed in only one direction—toward God. The compass of opinion and tradition, however, can point to any of the 360 degrees of a circle—*toward* truth or *away* from it.

Why are orthodox doctrines (be they Baptist, Mennonite, Methodist, Anglican, Assembly, or Calvinist) always supported and bolstered and written and preached about *without* this level of personal hunger and search?

This tells nothing *for certain.* A searching individual *may* just as well wind up following a pathway toward error, to which the growth of the cults attests. The perennial seeker who makes little headway in life, may be a spiritual nomad without much of a clue to what's going on about anything. On the other side of it, many traditional doctrines and opinions *are* indeed true, and become widely held just because they are *accurate* interpretations of the Bible.

We have to make some determinations concerning the character and spiritual integrity of those whose words we read.

Hannah Hurnard, for example, recounts her personal and prayerful search in detail. George MacDonald's struggle to find truth in the midst of the prevailing traditions of his times is well documented. William Barclay spent a lifetime of Scriptural study, gradually developing a view of the afterlife that he did not make public until three years before his death. C.S. Lewis's writings are all full of reminders of his quest for truth that led him out of atheism and to Christianity.

Are Hannah Hurnard's and George MacDonald's "searches" prompted by hearts truly listening to God, or are these individuals desert nomads whose experience really doesn't tell us much? In the case of the words you happen to be reading at this moment, does *my* admission that "I have been a seeker along the same road myself" and that "my own points of view are still forming" recommend *me* as reliable witness to these matters, or as a kook who has been out in the desert too long and has had too much sun? These are questions you have to determine on the basis of what you know about anyone you listen to and whose perspective you choose to heed.

OPENNESS

As I have observed this principle at work, there is another factor that reveals itself very differently on the two sides of the doctrinal fence—*open-mindedness.* I witness what seems a deeper humility toward Scripture on the part of those hungry searching individuals than I have seen from those, many renowned theologians among them, whose aim is to prop up and support the orthodox traditions which have been passed down to them.

Now humble open-mindedness is not in and of itself necessarily always a virtue. Yet it *is* often a requisite to clear thinking. If Peter had not been open-minded on the rooftop in Joppa, where would we be now? If Paul had not been open-minded on the road to Damascus, where would we be now? God had to jolt both Peter and Paul out of their comfortable, existing orthodoxies.

So open-mindedness is a vital doorway into truth when God speaks something new to his people.

The difference between the reliance on tradition, orthodoxy, and opinion on the one side, and personal, open-minded search, led by hunger, humility, and prayer, on the other tends toward the following result—that orthodox-tradition driven studies are more proof-text oriented, while search-and-prayer inquiries probe more persistently into the long-range, general, and more overarching purposes of Scripture.

Proof-text spirituality was precisely the pit into which the Pharisees had fallen. This, therefore, concerns me about the many studies I have read and the countless sermons I have heard in support of orthodox traditions. Opinion and proof-text motivated treatises simply do not, in my experience, yield the quality of ore as do those penned by men and women who have struggled, prayed, and searched their way deeply into the mine-shafts of God's Word, led by hunger after God's heart rather than a desire to bolster existing theologies. It therefore becomes a matter of the most serious import in our research that we ask to whom we are listening.

My own pursuit has involved a great deal of reading on both sides of many doctrinal fences. I have read today's leading evangelical theologians, searching for truth just as avidly in their writings as I have in MacDonald and others. I have read Catholics, Protestants, Anglicans, Quakers, scientists, and the devotional writings of the old saints. I have genuinely, and I hope humbly, sought to be open-minded and to examine evidence presented by Christian thinkers across the spectrum. When fundamentalist theologians engage in discussion, however, I find their analyses more often than not attempts merely to argue on behalf of the orthodox status quo with automatic knee-jerk scriptural interpretations. I do not find them upturning new scriptural soil, wide-eyed and enthusiastic to see what they might discover. Passages that might be interpreted differently are dismissed with a wave of the hand. I do not say such personal quests do not exist in hardened evangelical and Catholic orthodoxies, only that I have rarely found them. The scarcity of such seems to be a result of the fact that many preachers, teachers, and would-be theologians do not set themselves to prayerfully study the scriptural possibilities, so much as they set themselves simply to expound upon what has been expounded and re-expounded by thousands before them.

Dr. Loyal Hurley, before his personal quest for truth began, describes such a mentality. "Like Saul of old," he writes, "I had thought that I ought to do many things against this heretical teaching—everything but to study it!" [25]

WHO ARE WE LISTENING TO?

Sadly as a result, through the centuries a great deal of superficiality has come to pass for sound doctrine. Anyone may expound on any passage of Scripture he likes. If he is a clever and logical and humorous writer, he can easily make his expositions and proof-texts and opinions *sound* as if they occupy a level of stature equal to that from the pen of one who has studied and prayed the same matter through for fifty years. But the difference in weight, integrity, and erudition is enormous.

A few years ago I perused the shelves of our own Christian bookstore to see what current teachings on the subject of hell were being published. One was written by a former sports figure, a well known and popular author and speaker, full of attempted humor, cute witticisms, and a general tone which made light of a very serious matter. Grievously, the following kind of thing passes for sound teaching in today's church. I quote from his so-called "commentary" on Luke 16:19-31. Lazarus is renamed Larry:

> "There was a rich kid who dressed well. Clean! Slick! Very together...He lived it up daily. In other words, he was a total party animal...
>
> Bill had it all...The best CD and DAT recorder...a forty-two inch tube TV...Of course he was great looking and was one of those unusual teenagers who didn't have any zits...a standout jock; the star quarterback...the top track guy...The luscious lover was great in the girl department...What can I say? The guy was a stallion, Sir Studly....
>
> The son of the gardener was named Larry. He lived by the entry to the estate in the gatekeeper's cottage down below the rich kid's house. Larry had a pretty tough life. He had some terrible zits and was covered with sores. We're not just talking simple pimples here. Larry had acne vulgarus. His was a severe case...The medical plan for Larry was obviously deficient, because instead of a prescription for his face...they got a dog to lick his zits...How gross! Poor Larry. (Remember, I didn't write this stuff. You'll have to take this one up with God.)...
>
> It came about that this poor, pitiful, and pathetic person died and went to heaven. I think the doctor diagnosed Larry's cause of death as a case of infected zits.
>
> The very next day Dollar Bill was driving his 'vette, wrapped it around a tree, was killed, and went to Hades. Looking up, the rich kid saw Larry in the penthouse." [26]

It is pointless to continue. And painful, to see the important things of God written about in such a careless, juvenile manner. However, this is the sad state to which much current evangelical teaching has degenerated. Many books of this caliber find their way onto the best-seller lists every month.

It isn't merely the frivolous treatment about holy things that concerns me. Where is the *humility*?

Most worrisome is that by such lighthearted foolishness are God's people being taught. Believe it or not, the above-quoted book received rave reviews. Its back cover and front matter proclaimed endorsements and recommendations by twenty-two pastors and ministry presidents and directors, many of whose names you would instantly recognize. Christian leaders are encouraging their people to form their spiritual perspectives by listening to this kind of immature scriptural analysis.

This same author's deep and studied advice concerning the subject of hell was quick and easy, "It's a kinda' double-whammy retribution reunion, lasting forever. We're talkin' bad berries...Stay out of hell. You don't want to go there. It's the pits—literally."

Has he studied the matter, prayed and wrestled with God over it, searched the Scriptures to see what the biblical writers might have to say beyond his proof-texts? The pat answers are given with little more than opinions and superficial anecdotes. The heartbreaking fact is, Christians are *listening* to this. It is such shallow, populist, pseudo-theology that fills the books and pulpits by which evangelicalism is forming its perspectives.

At the same time, the prayer-driven searches of people like Hannah Hurnard, and scriptural studies of depth and scholarship of men like William Barclay, and the wisdom and insight of men like Andrew Jukes, William Law, Thomas Allin, George MacDonald, and A.R. Symonds are dispensed with in a few words of warning. Nor is this new. Francois Fenelon was denounced in the seventeenth century by the pope for teaching people to love God too much.

It matters very much who we listen to. It matters how they have arrived at their conclusions, and what is the Scriptural basis for the words they speak. Have their ideas and writings stood the test of time?

Several of William Law's books are viewed as classics three centuries after his death. George MacDonald and Andrew Jukes are still read more than a century after their words were written. William Barclay and Hannah Hurnard's books have been in the forefront of influence within Christendom for the past fifty years. The mine tunnels of such writings—as I have prayerfully chipped and probed and picked away—are ones where I have discovered much to enlighten, invigorate, and challenge me, and send me ever more deeply into the Father's heart of infinite goodness and love.

PHARASAISM EXISTS EVERYWHERE

I would add but one further warning of my own.

Neither personal search nor great scholarship, nor studying every Greek lexicon for every original meaning and nuance of every applicable word and phrase, will protect anyone from stagnant Pharisaism either. I know a number of individuals who consider themselves completely enlightened in matters of wider and more expansive views, yet sadly who are no more open-minded, forgiving, and committed to obedience to the Scriptures than those of more traditional viewpoint they so hastily condemn.

Obsession always leads to imbalance and away from truth.

On the other hand, some of the most Christlike men and women it is our privilege to call dear friends are lifelong believers in every orthodox doctrine in the book. They have never given so much as a moment's thought to any of these bold principles I write about. Most have no idea that I write about them. We love these individuals and they love us. Our differences never arise. Our love for one another completely transcends doctrinal issues. Our interest in probing distinct areas of faith pales into insignificance alongside the value of those relationships. If we had a difficulty to resolve, it is to such individuals (on *both* sides of the many fences of doctrinal difference) whose overall lives represent balance and a priority of Christlikeness to whom we would go. Similar outlook on doctrine matters far less in such relationships than similarity of life-purpose—*Christlikeness*.

Lewis on Humility

"Do not imagine that if you meet a really humble man he will be what most people call 'humble' nowadays...Probably all you will think about him is that he seemed a cheerful, intelligent chap who took real interest in what you said to him...He will not be thinking about humility: he will not be thinking about himself at all.

"If anyone would like to acquire humility, I can, I think, tell him the first step. The first step is to realize that one is proud. And a biggish step, too." [27]

THIRTEEN

THE PENDULUM OF PERSONAL BIAS

Understanding the Soil Out of Which Emerge our Ideas, Choices, and Conclusions Regarding Truth

> "When I was a child, I spoke like a child, I thought like a child, I reasoned like a child; when I became a man, I gave up childish ways. For now we see in a mirror dimly, but then face to face. Now I know in part; then I shall understand fully, even as I επεγνωσθην (have been fully understood)."
> —1 Corinthians 13:11-12

επιγινωσκω: EPIGINOSKO—*Discern*

The interesting and complex Greek word EPIGINOSKO is technically translated "know." But it conveys far more than mere knowledge of facts, and denotes observation, full attentiveness and perception, deep and personal understanding...ie—*discernment*. It is obviously related to GINOSKO, which implies more knowing in the abstract—taking in knowledge and understanding it. Thus in 1 Corinthians 13:12, both elements of knowing and self-knowing are brought into unity: "Now I know in part (GINOSKO); but then I shall know (EPIGNOSOMAI) even as also I have been fully known (EPEGNOSTHEN.)"

The root word GNOSIS (knowledge) from which was derived second century Gnosticism, originally noted man's knowledge of himself, which strikes to the heart of the self-discernment that is the subject of this chapter—what is man's true nature and how can his existence in the world be thoroughly explained. Of this GNOSIS, Clement of Alexandria wrote that it is the knowledge of "who we were, what we have become, where we were, into what have we been cast, where are we going, from what are we delivered, what is birth, what is rebirth."

Applied to the awareness and discernment of our growth out of the soil of parental influences into the maturity of childship in God, Clement's words take on very practical significance.

WE HAVE EMPHASIZED MANY TIMES the fundamental requirement of bold thinking faith—the direction of one's bold thinking and prayerful humility inward. The *mirror of personal inquiry* and *humble self-examination* will always be the bold thinker's most valuable assets in his lifetime pilgrimage toward maturity.

In a sense this imperative boils down to the old saying *Know thyself.*

We have to be capable of prayerful and discerning self-introspection and self-analysis—in order to know *how* we think and *why* we think as we do. We need to maintain a keen working understanding of our own built-in and predetermined leanings, biases, strengths, and weaknesses. Otherwise most of our thought will be ill-considered, subjective, and far too reliant on that treasonous imposter of counterfeit wisdom—*personal opinion.*

We know that we are commanded to rightly divide the word of truth. But are we capable of rightly dividing *ourselves*? That requires bold thinking at a high level. But without it, the objectivity that leads to true wisdom is impossible.

Objectivity requires brutally honest self-knowledge, and a keen awareness of how one's personal background and biases are always working overtime to skew objectivity.

It is called *discernment*...επιγινωσκω into ourselves.

To illustrate this need in the only human laboratory I have available, my *own*, I will again diverge into the personal, in hopes that it will encourage you also to look into your own personal mirrors.

A TWO-EDGED SWORD

Thinking boldly about matters of faith is a two-edged sword. Those of us who take it up need to wield it carefully...and in both directions.

It is easy to play the critic. There is a lot wrong in the world. There is a lot wrong with every human institution, with governments, with schools, with churches. It's not difficult to see what *isn't* working as well as it might.

It is far more difficult to see what is wrong within *ourselves*.

That's where special eyesight is required.

When G.K. Chesterton was asked to contribute along with other writers his thoughts to an essay by the *London Times* in the early twentieth century by responding to the question, "What's wrong with the world?" his succinct reply took the editors off guard.

Dear sirs, he wrote back,
I am.
Sincerely,
G.K. Chesterton.

Few possess either Chesterton's wit or insight into the human condition. He was a man who properly *discerned* himself.

The twin curses with which the church is afflicted—self-satisfaction and self-righteousness—stymie its progress toward the Christlikeness of a worthy bride at almost every possible point. That's why God sends prophets, teachers, and critics among us—to awaken and arouse, goad and urge and exhort toward our high calling.

But those who point to higher things must take care to bring an even more rigid scrutiny to bear upon themselves lest they lapse into the self-motivated role of mere critic rather than the God-led role of helpful guide. Bold thinking is risky business. The prophet, critic, priest, author, and counselor has to know himself or herself, and how he or she fits into the milieu of ideas and circumstances they are responding to.

None of us is as objective in assessing truth as we like to think. We are filled with biases, experiences, personality kinks and attributes, and background influences that color and sway and influence our responses, choices, and our approaches to everything life throws at us. He or she who would point others toward what he considers truth must know himself or herself well, and be more acquainted with his own weaknesses, flaws, and immaturities than everyone else's. He should have a pretty clear sense of the nature of his own blind spots (seemingly oxymoronic as that statement will be.) The bold thinker needs the speck and beam images of Matthew 7:3-5 ever in the forefront as a self-correcting screen to his observations.

In this light, it seems perhaps time in this quest to pause for self reflection...to look inward to see what we are made of, to see where and how and under what conditions we entered life's flow. This will help us see from what directions we approach truth, and thus discover how we respond to ideas.

Obviously I am speaking to myself. I hope some of my own self-discerning reflections may prove helpful to you whom I consider my companions in this inquiry upon which we have embarked together.

INBORN INFLUENCES

Now that both my parents are gone, I find myself prayerfully reflective of their lives in new ways. Of course there are many things I wish I had been more aware of, things I wish I had said, many questions I now want to ask. But perhaps their deaths are intrinsic to the process of my own self-knowing.

The pendulum of personal bias is in constant motion. The older I grow the more aware I am both how *like* my parents I am, yet how *different* I am.

Isn't this exactly the reality we always discover? We grow either *mirroring* our upbringing and spiritual training, or *rebelling* against them and coming to reflect the opposite of that upbringing and its values.

In most cases it is a mixture of the two—the rebellion against early values and training rising to the surface in the teens and 20s, with often the 30s and 40s bringing a gradual return swing of the pendulum back in the direction of one's roots.

We see numerous examples of this process at work around us. Two Christian families with whom we are intimately connected, with eight children between them ranging in ages from about ten to over thirty, haven't a rebel in the lot. Every young person appears an exact duplication of his and her parents down to the parroting back of the tiniest doctrinal details. More often, however, is the opposite true. We grieve with numerous other families, in spite of loving and consistent spiritual training, in which the young people have turned their backs on their parents and the Lord. Never, it seems, has Satan's assault against the institution of the Christian family been so tumultuous and violent.

A unique and fascinating corollary to this development is seen, too, by the increasing number of Christian young people who turn their backs on their parents...but not on God. How can this spiritualized form of rebellion be explained other than by the fact that the church tolerates it, in the same way that it tolerates divorce and remarriage? Even within the Christian church, the family is crumbling.

We all enter life somewhere. God imbues us with characteristics that effect our responses. We receive training and teaching as we grow that comes from one slant or another. We respond to aspects of personality and temperament. Other factors and influences come to bear on us. Slowly our own choices shape the men and women we become.

Thus, we all come at truth differently. An introverted Quaker, a liberal atheist, an orphan Episcopalian, and an extroverted Southern Baptist will each react inwardly with a dozen responses to the same passage of Scripture. All will think they understand "truth." But how do they separate out their inbred biases of perspective, training, and personality to get at the real bedrock of meaning God intends. No easy task!

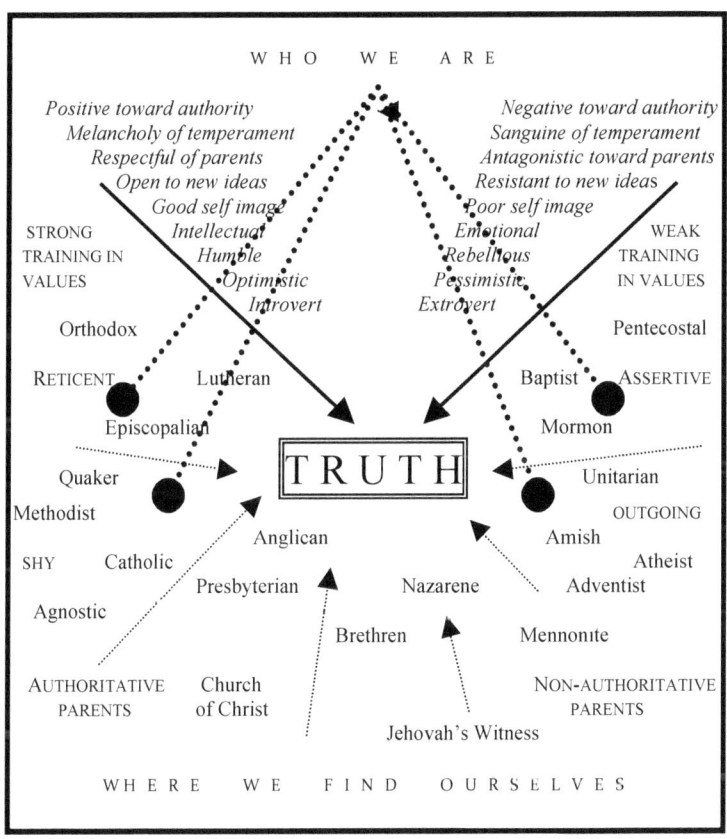

In the end we are each accountable for our own use of these multitude of influences (good and bad) to discover and live truth. Though the pendulum of our own bias has been set in motion by dozens of hands other than our own, *we* are responsible for how it swings and where it comes to rest.

One has but to circle a few of the labels shown in this diagram to see what mixed and complex factors we bring into our lives. The arrows all point different directions! No wonder we have such a hard time communicating. We are perceiving and speaking and listening from hundreds of individual points of view!

In the diagram of a pendulum oscillating back and forth on all sides of "truth," observe that it is not truth as such that is revealed, but rather *the direction from which we are coming at truth.*

There will continually be an ongoing push against and pull toward those influences in our lives that have shaped us. We respond in the *same* direction as some of the training that has been ingrained into us, in the *opposite* direction from other things, or in a complex combination of both. In the midst of this *conscious* process, many parallel influences become part of our personalities and characters in *unconscious* ways. Even our parents' weaknesses and foibles...lo and behold those same tendencies rise up to manifest themselves in us! We look in the mirror, and—whether physical or psychological—there stands our father or mother!

TRUTH'S COMPLEX EQUATION

The direction of our individual collection of arrows determines everything about how we perceive truth.

Truth is never analyzed in a vacuum. We are trying to get at it *from* someplace. We are looking at it from a particular angle. That *perspective of the observer* is as great a factor in the end result as raw truth itself.

Truth is thus comprised of multiple factors.

In physics, the concept of *momentum* is made up of two elements. Momentum is not mere raw speed—it indicates the *directionality* of speed. Raw speed is called velocity. But momentum is comprised of both *velocity* and the *direction* in which that velocity is moving. The game of golf is obviously based on more than how *fast* one can make a golf ball travel through the air. Far more important is the carefully-controlled *directionality* of speed the skilled golfer is able to harness.

Similarly, truth is also a more complex equation than raw factual analysis. It's even more complex than momentum.

I might propose the following equation. You may have other components you would add.

Truth = (knowledge) + (understanding) + (objectivity) - (personal subjectivity) ± (directionality of observer) + (discernment) + (wisdom)

A PERPLEXING FAMILIAL MILIEU

Now that several years have gone by since my mother's passing, I find myself trying to place her life and influence into a long range perspective. In the immediate aftermath of death, of course, one is dealing with loss on the heart level. Laudatory words are easy to find. Praising my mother's many strengths is a natural thing. Her influence in so many lives in tireless and compassionate service to church and community was widespread. Even now, over a decade after my dad's passing, his influence, too, is still being felt.

Both my parents, each in their own way, were great people in the true sense of that word—giving, humble, compassionate, caring. They were a man and woman of *character*. They were *good* people, who spread that goodness about them. I believe that they are now in a place of high honor in God's presence. Just two days ago, which happened to be Father's Day, Judy read me aloud my own tribute to my father in the dedication to *Rift in Time* as a reminder that the day was about our honoring our two fathers not about being honored ourselves. It was a poignant and happy reminder of the man I loved.

My mother and father spent their whole married life building into lives around them. What a legacy to pass on to me and my two sisters! The honor, respect, and appreciation I will always have for them in my heart is profound. I am so grateful for the many influences that came from them to make me the man I am today. The example of their lives is with me every moment. Indeed, one of the favorites of my own books is a tiny pamphlet of less than forty pages I prepared to give away at my dad's memorial service about my father and how his life had influenced so many. It is simply called *A Tribute*. In the years since, my father has only grown greater in my memory. In the same way, the positive influences of my mother's life are too numerous to mention.

But in the matter of bold thinking faith, my mother's influence was a two-sided coin. Her example of being unafraid to challenge status-quo thinking is one whose positive effects in my own life I am eternally grateful for. In her own way, more by example than direct input, she encouraged me to *think*. What a wonderful gift to give a son.

Yet that coin has a flip side, which now the passage of time is gradually allowing me to investigate with enough loving honesty to evaluate its equal impact. I dearly love, and loved, my mom, foibles and all. Indeed, the soul-searching that accompanies the recognition of some of the difficulties associated with those positive influences brings a unique anguish to the memory. I want to retain in the forefront of my mind the honor I feel. Yet my own growth compels that I bring honesty, both toward myself and toward her, into that process along with a son's endearing fondness and love.

My mother grew up in a fundamentalist Baptist environment. She was always uneasy with it, I think, but did not make a change until the age of 48 when she became an Episcopalian. In the following years her liberalism as she aged came to border on the extreme. For the rest of her life, as I observed it through the lenses of my own perceptions, she seemed to grow more ardently antagonistic toward the evangelicalism of her spiritual foundations. I admired her courage to question, to grow, and to free herself from, as she saw it, a too-narrow perspective. No doubt some of her courage rubbed off on me. Those of you who know something of my own pilgrimage will recognize the similarities between mother and son. At the same time I determined in my own spiritual development to avoid what I felt was an overreaction on her part. Admire her as I did, it was my perception that her pendulum had swung *too* far in the opposite direction. She was often *reacting* to something, rather than coming at situations and issues with objectivity. Hers was a rapidly swaying pendulum of response and counter-response, strong opinion, social tolerance but spiritual intolerance. (And what a common blind spot *that* is in today's liberalism! Bigotry wears many masks...some of them very respectable and progressive.) It will remain for the light of eternity to judge whether I have been able to avoid some of the pitfalls of the oscillating pendulum of overreaction.

And yet...who am I to speak objectively about my own mother? I am her son, after all—a fact which some might say precludes objectivity on my part altogether.

Are any of us able to probe with clarity these foundational relationships of parent and son or daughter where we ourselves are involved? Only God knows.

My mother and I, as alike as we were in so many ways and as similar as were our spiritual journeys, enjoyed what I would call an emotionally tumultuous relationship. For reasons that remain perplexing to me, there was a tension between us through my adult life because I did not go so far as she in a repudiation of spiritual roots which I still value and treasure. She was thus unable to come to terms with my outlook, my priorities, or my writing. In her opinion (though I am guessing here) I too much reflected the Baptist tradition she had grown up in. She could not be at peace with the spiritual being I became. Was it because I did not allow my pendulum to swing so distantly from my Baptist roots as she?

Some regularly call me unorthodox in my perspectives. To my mother, however, I was a fundamentalist through and through. She didn't like it. It was almost as if she felt she had failed in her duty because I did not become as progressive and liberal as she.

These are difficult questions for a son to consider. They probe the marrow of my fundamental personhood. After all, with whom do we share closer physical bonds than with our mothers and fathers? Thus it brings a certain quiet melancholy to my heart to know that she wasn't interested in my spirituality except in a curiously disconcerted way. She died with but one book of mine on her bookshelf. I think my writing embarrassed her. She considered me ultra-conservative, and thus an embarrassment to her extreme late-life liberalism.

My father was similarly complex. A wonderful man, honored and respected by all who knew him and whom I love and miss every day, he was yet singularly unexpressive about such things. Neither was my spiritual journey of much interest to him. I later found a book I had signed and dedicated to him, unread, in a stack of giveaway books. These are deep personal and emotional waters.

DISCOVERING THE VITAL CENTER WHERE BIASES GIVE WAY TO OBJECTIVITY

My reason for drifting into these self-reflections is this: *How* we come at truth is often as significant as our conclusions.

In what ways does my relationship with my mother color my responses? Does it fill me with biases and prejudices of which I am unaware? From which direction am I approaching the high questions I ask of God? Are my conclusions reliable?

These are difficult questions to pose. Even harder to answer with objectivity.

The underlying fact is: My pendulum is in motion too. I did not arrive into the midst of the landscape of my life out of a vacuum, but out of a cultural, spiritual, and emotional milieu which effects everything about me.

So did George MacDonald. So did C.S. Lewis. So do you.

By the overpowering strength of who she was, my dear mother is the dominant personality in my life. In my own quest for truth, *my* roots of personhood extend deep into the soil of *her* character and temperament. The oscillation of her pendulum will continue to influence me until she and I meet again where all earthly encumbrances will be gone.

And gradually along the eternal timeline come my own sons, who are now responding to *me* and all the influences, training, strengths, and weaknesses that my strong personality has brought to bear in *their* lives. How will their pendulums swing in response? What spiritual soil have I provided them in which to grow toward Christlikeness? Am I as attentive to their spiritual development as I ought to be and have tried to be? Sometimes one never knows how one is perceived by those closest to the heart?

Each of us, then, wherever we find ourselves, all our lives are engaged in a constant process of responding uniquely to dozens of factors. Some do not care whether they respond objectively. But those who *are* trying to discover objective truth must recognize the "directionality" of the influences pushing and pulling at them.

I have placed my somewhat confusing relationship with my mother into the test tube of my observation, because I am convinced it is this process that enables bold thinkers to divide their own biases from objective truth. We must understand the forces—internal and external—pushing and pulling us in varying directions. Bias and opinion do not always point toward truth. We have to recognize these urgings for what they are. Otherwise we will never apprehend with clarity the vital center where biases cease, opinion stills, liberal and conservative values lay down their stridency and harmonize into a unity of wisdom, and all responses come to rest in quiet and focused objectivity. This is something age and experience, as attentiveness to God's voice guides growth and development, should bring about. Reactionary opinions and prejudices gradually fall away as we mature.

The pendulum slows.

Our responses come to rest about a dynamic center of wisdom and truth.

For too many, steeped in traditions and one-sided teaching, and interpreting all ideas through the single-dimensional lens of experience, their own opinions *are* truth. How different are the responses of those who discover the vital resting place where the oscillation of personal bias loses its influence in the overpowering solidity of TRUTH itself.

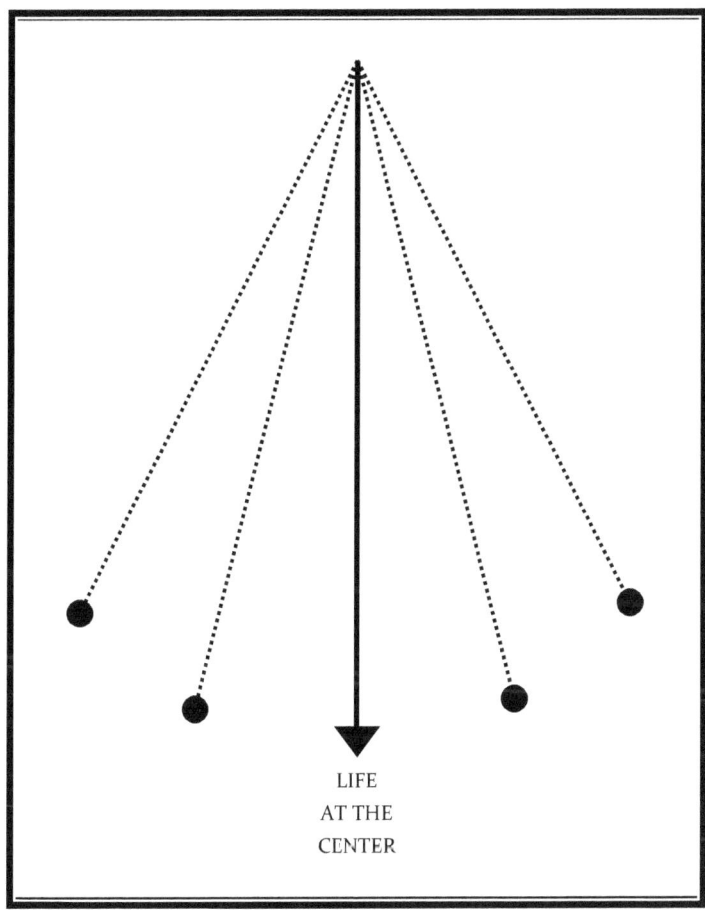

It is not a question many consider. But because I desire to know myself, and because I desire to know *true* truth, *balanced* truth, *objective* truth, I am not afraid to ask: *How accurate are my own perceptions? Is my self-discernment operating at a high level?* I think any honest truth seeker must ask these questions. And then be scrupulously humble in his or her answers.

To think boldly about things of faith must be more than opinion, more than a liberal or conservative perspective, more than opinionated response and counter-response to ideas.

Objectivity, rather, originates out of a maturing and slowing of the pendulum. Wisdom comes as by degrees it gradually comes to rest in the vital Center where Jesus lived every moment—where the only Voice influencing thought and action and response is that of God himself.

Lewis on Self-Discernment

"'If our heart condemn us, God is greater than our heart.' And equally, if our heart flatter us, God is greater than our heart. I sometimes pray not for self-knowledge in general but for just so much self-knowledge at the moment as I can bear and use at the moment; the little daily dose.

"Have we any reason to suppose that total self-knowledge, if it were given us, would be for our good? Children and fools, we are told, should never look at a half-done work; and we are not yet, I trust, even half-done." [28]

Part 4

Doctrinal Stepping Stones

Christian doctrine and theology are not intellectual destination points, but living stepping stones toward obedient discipleship.

Key Scriptural Concepts:

Obedience, Diligence, Maturity

FOURTEEN

THE TRINITY: A TRIAD OF RULE, OBEDIENCE, AND REVELATION

An Exercise In Bold Thinking Applied to Christianity's Most Widely Held Doctrine

> "...as they are knit together in love, to have all the riches of assured understanding and the knowledge of God's mystery, of Christ, in whom are hid all the treasures of wisdom and knowledge...For in him the whole fullness of deity dwells bodily.... Although he was a Son, he learned υπακοην (obedience)... and being made perfect he became the source of eternal salvation to all who υπακουουσιν (are obeying) him."
> —Colossians 2: 2-3, 9; Hebrews 5:8-9

υπακοη: HUPAKOE—*Obedience*

The Trinity is founded in rule, obedience, and revelation. But whereas it may be that Fatherness is its originating foundation, it is the Son's *obedience* that gives the Godhead its vital creative life-energy. In one of his masterpieces of insight, George MacDonald, in his sermon entitled "The Creation in Christ," from *Unspoken Sermons, Third Series*, posits that a misplaced period in most translations of John 1:3-4 has given an erroneous impression of what actually was the "creative" work of God's Word, his λογος. The familiar text reads: "All things were made through him, and without him was not anything made that was made. In him was life, and the life was the light of men." MacDonald says that the period between *made* and *In* should perhaps come three words earlier, yielding a much more sensible and powerful reading: *All things were made through him, and without him was not anything made. That which was made in him was life, and the life was the light of men.* This *life*,

MacDonald goes on, made through him, was the life of obedience, "created in Christ" toward the Father. It is this obedience that gives the Godhead its pulsating life, outflowing and correspondent, between Father and Son.

MANY FUNDAMENTAL PRINCIPLES OF THE CHRISTIAN FAITH are not merely hard to understand, they are *impossible* to understand. They come to us in Scripture as vague mysteries because *only* as mysteries can such high-dimensioned truths approach the one-dimensionality of our limited capacity to understand.

Well meaning men throughout history, however, anxious to reduce high truth to the single dimension of their cramped intellects, have sought to codify and define God's being and methods by smaller definitions than God intends. Believers then take their one-dimensional definitions as truth, rather than as faint reflections of unknowable mysteries. In the end, sight of the high mysteries themselves gradually fades and becomes even more blurred than it was in the first place.

No example of this truth-shrinking process is more clear than in the case of the Trinity. We have come to the point within some Christian circles where even to confess that one is *thinking* about what the Trinity might mean in a greater way is viewed with suspicion. To suggest that there might be *more* involved than a "three persons in one" cliché reveals something seriously amiss in one's faith.

HERESY IN THE DETAILS

Several years ago a prominent Christian writer suddenly found herself in hot water by the ever vigilant guardians of truth at her publishing house. A relatively simple statement—"The Bible does not use the word *trinity*, and our feeling is that the word *trinity* implies equality in leadership, or shared Lordship. It is clear that the scriptures teach that Jesus is the Son of God...God is clearly the Head."—caused the company to withdraw her books from print. An active campaign to discredit her was begun by cultwatch groups on the internet, saying that she had "denied" the deity of Christ and was teaching "false doctrine." They called her dangerous.

This is not my only acquaintance with such a mentality. I encounter it regularly in working with certain publishing houses where a constant pressure exists to sanitize all spiritual content toward the cliché-doctrine.

A few years ago I began a series of novels with high hopes. After two books, however, the project was halted and those two titles withdrawn from print. There were many contributing factors, among them that one of the company's key men, in reading a certain passage in the manuscript, became concerned that my doctrinal orthodoxy on the Trinity might be suspect. The words came in a Christmas prayer from one of the characters:

Our loving heavenly Father...we give you thanks...for this season of giving and remembering, and for your great gift most of all. Thank you for this very precious and special day when you sent to earth your Son for the express purpose that man might know you as he had not known you before, know of that most fundamental aspect of your nature...thank you, God our creator, whom we now know to call by that cherished and wonderful name—Father...Let us dare, on this day especially—for Fatherhood is the message of Christmas, as your own Fatherhood is your greatest gift to us—as Jesus told us we should, to approach you in intimacy, and call you, as he did, our Abba...our very own daddy.

Before the book went to print, "Fatherhood is *the* message of Christmas" was changed to "Fatherhood is *a* message of Christmas." And, "Fatherhood is your *greatest* gift to us," was edited to read, "Fatherhood is *such a great* and wondrous gift to us."

Now the point isn't that these are such huge changes. Maybe they are changes for the better. I'll let you decide.

But are we really so afraid that we have to protect God's dignity from the slightest misstatement. The editorial process with most books I have written is riddled with such doctrinal sanitizations. I have no way of knowing how many hundreds of minor changes like this have been slipped into my printed works. Authors are not generally consulted about these things. Nor in most cases do they have a vote. I happen to remember this particular example because the above words caused such a fuss, as if I was denying the Trinity altogether, and a year or two later led to events which resulted in the cancellation of the series.

It is hardly a secret that I speak outside the cliché-box. I consider it healthy to do so. Maybe it is outside the formula box to suggest that God's Fatherhood is his greatest gift to us. But is it not exactly and precisely what Jesus taught about the Godhead—that *Fatherhood* exists at its core?

Whether that assessment is correct is not so important as this intense fear that infects evangelicalism, such that its leaders feel they must protect the Christian public from being exposed to the idea that God's Fatherhood might be the originating power and love within the Godhead. In a double standard that mystifies me, my peers write "edgy" sexual and ethical themes into their Christian fiction and their editors consider it fine, their books win awards, and publishers flatter themselves that such edginess is meeting the world where it lives. But write of thought-provoking doctrinal themes, and the Orthodoxy Patrol swoops down like a hawk. Nothing must violate the accepted doctrine. Sexual and ethical edginess in Christian fiction has become the norm. But *doctrinal* edginess is forbidden.

The greatest threat, in my view, to bold thinking Christianity comes from this pseudo-intelligentsia of fundamentalism that has taken it upon itself to act as the Doctrine Police of truth. This intelligentsia has come to occupy most of the key positions of leadership, power, and influence throughout evangelicalism. This leadership drills formulas of belief into the Christian masses, anesthetizing them to the need to think with energy and vigor about the principles of faith. Yet *sexually* the mores in Christian fiction (and I cannot but conclude this trend emblematic of Christianity as a whole) are looser than ever. Push the ethical boundaries...fine. But so much as *look* at the doctrinal boundaries...strictly verboten! If someone can explain this double standard to me, I would be extremely appreciative. Thus the system perpetuates and protects itself year after year, generation after generation.

In truth, we don't really know what the "Trinity" means, nor does our understanding of the workings of the Godhead penetrate very far into its most intimate regions. For reasons he alone knows, God has not chosen to reveal to us a great deal about the inner Godhead relationship. He has revealed *enough*. We certainly have more information than those of Old Testament times. But our information remains sketchy. Nor did Jesus or Paul ever mention the "Trinity" as such. We don't know whether they believed in the sort of three-sided equilateral triangle that the Trinity more or less became three hundred years later. Certainly neither Jesus nor Paul urged such a belief upon their listeners.

As I read Jesus' words about the being he calls "God," I do not get a three-equal-persons view. Jesus relegates his own role to an utterly subservient one, an idea completely inconsistent with the contemporary elevation of the Son's status to equality with, if not (practically speaking) *superiority* to, the Father's. As for Paul, he more often seems to speak of a sort of *dual* functioning Godhead—Father *and* Son—with the Holy Spirit being the spirit of both. Paul's perspective I would instead call a "Duality" not a trinity. A strong case could be made for the view that the "Trinity" as commonly taught (three *equal* divine Beings or "personalities" in one) is actually difficult to find spelled out with clarity in the New Testament.

A BRIEF HISTORY—ORIGINS

It was not until about a hundred years after the apostolic age that the doctrine of the *Trinity* as we know it began to form within the church. (Even my computer's secular spell check doesn't like me writing "trinity" in the lower case, and automatically changes it to *Trinity*, one more indication, even from unbelieving Microsoft, that the revered doctrine is sacrosanct in the *upper* case...and not to be tinkered with.)

During the fifty years from approximately 175 to 225, many church fathers grappled with the nature of God's revelation in Jesus Christ as implied by Paul's writings. They wrestled with it but failed to arrive at any more succinct conclusion than Paul had.

This uncertainty was not limited to later generations. The Lord's own disciples, the first gospel writers, and church leaders in the years immediately following the Lord's life on earth—men like Paul and Luke, and even the disciples who had known Jesus personally—didn't quite know what to make of that remarkable life. Indeed, the discussion and controversy over the fundamental question of just who Jesus was and what was the nature of his work, prompted extremely diverse opinion in the early church.

If *they* were uncertain, and debated the matter, why do we in our time condemn uncertainty and discussion? Those who condemn inquiry, it seems to me, do not understand the fluid nature of the church's doctrinal development. Would all the apostles be banned today for not being "orthodox" on the Trinity?

Mark, the first gospel writer, as well as Matthew and Luke whose gospels came a few years later, all used terms and titles to describe Jesus which tradition leads most Christians to assume indicate Jesus' divinity. But this may be an inaccurate assumption. The word *Messiah* and the term *Son of Man*, two of the most obvious such titles, throughout the Old Testament, and thus to the mind of first century believers, actually designated *human* roles. The Messiah was to be a *human* king, and "son of man" was a term that simply meant *man*.

Biblical textual scholar Elaine Pagels writes: "The Christians who translated these titles into English fifteen centuries later believed they showed Jesus was uniquely related to God, and so they capitalized them—a linguistic convention that does not occur in Greek. But Mark's contemporaries would most likely have seen Jesus as a *man*—although one gifted, as Mark says, with the power of the holy spirit, and divinely appointed to rule in the coming kingdom of God." [29]

Though most assume that only four accounts of Jesus' life were written, it may be, following the first three synoptic gospels, that *two* gospels were written in the final decade of the first century not just one, both bearing the names of original disciples—Thomas and John. Though we have had John's writings for 1900 years, those of Thomas have only recently been discovered. Their two portrayals of Christ are very different, the *Gospel of Thomas* emphasizing his humanity, the *Gospel of John* emphasizing his divinity. In a sense, they characterize the nature of the debate in the church at the end of the first century. Mrs. Pagels suggests that one of the motives behind John's writing was to denounce Thomas's teaching and assert Jesus' divinity. Apparently the disputes between the Twelve, which we see in the gospels, continued long after Jesus' death. This fact may account for John's inaccuracies of chronology and lengthy discourses.

In John's gospel, then, do we have our first glimpse of Christianity's Orthodoxy Patrol attempting to squelch spiritual inquiry? Like many such attempts throughout history, the attack against Thomas's "heresy" (as John viewed Thomas's very different, even "Gnostic" portrayal of Jesus) was successful. Thomas's gospel was eventually lost to the world until 1945.

Elaine Pagels continues: "Why had the church decided that these texts [Thomas's gospel] were 'heretical' and that only the canonical gospels were 'orthodox'? Who made those decisions, and under what conditions...how [did] certain Christian leaders from the second century through the fourth [come] to reject many other sources of revelation and construct instead the New Testament gospel canon of Matthew, Mark, Luke, and John along with the 'canon of truth' which became the nucleus of the later creeds that have defined Christianity to this day...

"John's gospel was written in the heat of controversy, to defend certain views of Jesus and to oppose others...although John's gospel is written with great simplicity and power, its meaning is by no means obvious. Even its first generation of readers (c. 90 to 130 C.E.) disagreed about whether John was a true gospel or a false one—and whether it should be part of the New Testament. John's defenders among early Christians revered it as the 'logos gospel'...Its detractors, by contrast, were quick to point out that John's narrative differs significantly from those of Matthew, Mark, and Luke...

"John's gospel differs from Matthew, Mark, and Luke in a second—and far more significant—way, for John suggests that Jesus is not merely God's human servant but God himself revealed in human form...In one of the earliest commentaries on John (c. 240 C.E.) Origen makes a point of saying that while the other gospels describe Jesus as *human*, 'none of them clearly spoke of his *divinity*, as John does.'..

"Yet...after the gospels of Mark, Matthew, and Luke were joined with John's gospel and Paul's letters to become the 'New Testament'—a process that took... two hundred years (c. 160 to 360 C.E.)— most Christians came to read these earlier gospels through John's lens, and thus to find in all of them evidence of John's conviction that Jesus is 'Lord and God.' The gospels discovered in 1945 in Upper Egypt, however, offer different perspectives. For if Matthew, Mark, and Luke had been joined with the Gospel of Thomas instead of with John, for example, or had *both* John and Thomas been included in the New Testament canon, Christians probably would have read the first three gospels quite differently. The gospels of Thomas and John speak for different groups of Jesus' followers engaged in discussion, even argument, toward the end of the first century. What they debated is this: Who is Jesus, and what is the 'good news'...about him?" [30]

It is true that the authenticity of the gospel purported to have come from Thomas remains an open and debated question. We may find it not to be from Thomas's hand at all. That uncertainty, however, does not tell us anything one way or another. Many biblical texts are subject to uncertainties of authorship, as well as to the mystery why they were included in the canon at all. Does anyone really know why *Philemon* is in the Bible when many so-called "apocryphal" works were rejected? We must not forget the lesson of Ezra and Nehemiah. The entire Law of Moses was lost, passing out of sight for generations, only to be rediscovered anew when God's people returned to Jerusalem. The temporary obscuring of ancient texts does not necessarily invalidate them.

Therefore, I have always been intrigued by the question whether certain manuscripts, now lost, *should* have been included in the Bible and may in fact have contained more truth than others that *were* included for various political reasons on the parts of those making such determinations at the time. Do *Philemon* or the thirteen verses of *2 and 3 John* really contain more insight into the nature and character of God and his work than any other writings from the first or second century that might have been included? For all these reasons, until the question of authenticity should be determined more categorically by those more knowledgeable than myself, the issues raised by the discovery of the *Gospel of Thomas* remain intriguing.

A BRIEF HISTORY CONTINUED

The point in looking at the historical origins of the debate over Jesus' identity is not to *resolve* that debate, or to "take sides" in the John-Thomas gospel controversy, but simply to recognize that there *was* a debate.

That fact is hugely significant. The discussion of Jesus' nature was not in itself a heresy. *Everyone* was discussing it. Publishers and evangelical leaders in our time have made the inquiry *itself* a no-no, deviating blatantly from the first century example of our bold-thinking forebears.

How has it come to this...that it is a "sin" to ask the *very same questions* those in the early church were asking!

When the Apostles' Creed arose, it was not Trinitarian in emphasis. "God" was specified as *the Father Almighty, creator*. "Jesus Christ" was specified as *His only Son, our Lord*. But "the Holy Spirit" was included with other matters of belief along with the Church, the Communion of Saints, etc., and not raised to the level of divinity. As I read it, the Apostles' Creed is distinctly *not* Trinitarian, but also, like the writings of Paul, points to a *Duality*.

The word *triad* was first used by Theophilus about 180 A.D. He wrote, "The three days which were before the luminaries are types of the Triad of God, His Word, and His Wisdom."

A careful analysis of that sentence reveals a differentiation between *God*...and his Word and his Wisdom. There is no three-way equality at all.

Athenagoras, Iranaeus, and Clement of Alexandria also wrote in similar veins. But it was Tertullian (c. 160-225) of Carthage whose extensive writings on the relationship between the Father, Son, and Holy Spirit at last led to the codification of a *triune* Godhead into accepted doctrine.

"For the very church itself is," he wrote in 212 A.D., "—properly and principally—the Spirit Himself, in whom is the Trinity of the One Divinity: Father, Son, and Holy Spirit."

Tertullian's extensive writings did not put the matter to rest or settle all doctrinal disputes about what his new term "Trinity" meant. The church continued trying to rigidly define the relationship. Perhaps in this very effort we observe the beginnings of error. If Jesus himself did not make these matters completely clear, does God want *us* to create rigid and defining restrictions of belief? Will not those definitions always and inevitably be subject to error?

In any event, a series of councils and debates were held through the years at which the matter was discussed. Early in the fourth century a fierce controversy was raging in Alexandria. Now it was not two of the original twelve disciples promoting differing perspectives, but a church leader and the Emperor himself. At the center of the debate stood a presbyter of the church in Alexandria by the name of Arius. He suggested that the Son, though also creator of the rest of creation, was himself created and therefore could not be originally divine to the same extent as was the Father. Arius believed that the Father alone was truly *God*, and that the Son was in essence different from the Father in that he did not exist before he was begotten by the Father. Looking at his perspective objectively, it seems perfectly consistent with Jesus' own word in the gospel. I don't see heresy in Arius's proposal. Perhaps you do.

Roman Emperor Constantine called the first general council of the whole church at Nicaea in 325 to settle the dispute prompted by the Arian controversy. Constantine himself suggested the Greek term *homoousios* ("of one essence") as a definition to clarify the Son's relationship with the Father. A statement of orthodoxy was produced which, after later revisions, became the Nicene Creed. Arius refused to accept the council's definition and was subsequently excommunicated as a heretic. Thus in the end, a *higher* truth than any doctrine (unity in the body of Christ) was set aside for the sake of the *lower*—a fact which in itself may render the conclusions of those defenders of the faith suspect. Whenever lower truth supplants higher truth, error cannot be far away.

The controversy over the relationship between Father and Son raged on even after both Arius's and Constantine's deaths, leading ultimately to the Council of Constantinople in 381. At that time a further revision of the Nicene Creed was adopted, producing the definitive statement (actually not so very far from that of Arius after all) which would form the basis for the orthodox view ever after:

We believe in one God the Father All sovereign, maker of heaven and earth...

And in one Lord Jesus Christ, the only-begotten Son of God, Begotten of the Father before all ages, Light of Light, true God of true

God, begotten not made, of one substance with the Father, through whom all things were made......

And in the Holy Spirit, the Lord and Life-giver, that proceeds from the Father, who with Father and Son is worshipped together and glorified together....

In the decades following Constantinople, in his major theological work entitled *On the Trinity*, Augustine (354-430) at last took Trinitarian studies to their completion.

And thus has come down to us one of the highest of all doctrines, in the eyes of nearly all mainstream Christian denominations, that must be adhered to in order to be considered an orthodox Christian.

ETERNAL MYSTERY OR RIGID DOCTRINE?

Perhaps the question that might now be raised is this: How important is the Trinity in defining and living out true faith in Christ? Is it of such paramount significance, as it was to those church leaders of the fourth century, that failure to comply with a precise statement of uniform agreement constitutes heresy and is means for excommunication? Or is further scriptural inquiry allowed?

One major contemporary book on Christian theology concludes its treatise on the Trinity with these words:

Try to explain it, and you'll lose your mind;
But try to deny it, and you'll lose your soul.

Where do ideas like that come from? Nowhere in the New Testament is a doctrinally correct belief in the Trinity made a condition of salvation. Is this author actually suggesting that incorrect belief on the Trinity will result in an eternity in hell!

Some of the unbelievable foolishness by which today's Christians are being taught is simply beyond comprehension! But if you're famous enough, publishers will publish *anything*, and people will eat it up. Yet how ill-prepared today's tidal wave of superficiality has made Christendom to combat the world's slide into secularist oblivion. If comfort zones do not breed warriors, neither does that sort of shallow thinking.

Such unscripturality as represented by the above statements is just what many Christians believe today, ignoring the fact that some of the best minds throughout history have wrestled with the mystery of the Trinity and come to varying conclusions.

To reemphasize because it is such an important point—Paul described the relationship between Jesus and his Father in many interesting ways that *cannot* be stuffed into the box of contemporary jargon.

Consider the book of *Colossians*. Paul says that Jesus was the "firstborn over creation," that he is "the image of God." To my ears, this sounds very much like what Arius proposed. Consider also Philippians 2:6, in which Paul states that Jesus did not "count equality with God something to be grasped." Did Paul mean that Jesus *was* equal with God, but did not grasp at it, or that he was *not* equal with God? If ever Paul set up an opportunity to clarify exactly that *Jesus Christ was God himself*, it was in these mysterious passages of Col. 1: 15-20; 2: 9-12 and Phil. 2: 5-11. But he stops short of such a declaration, calling him, not "God" but rather "the *image*" of God. What does Paul mean by "in Christ all the fullness of God lives in bodily form"? He clearly speaks as if a distinction exists between "God" and "Christ," adding that "God" *exalted* him to the highest places and *gave* him the name that is above every name. Those sound very much like after-the-fact, cause-and-effect results of Christ's obedience. What does *in the form* of God (Phil. 2:6) imply?

Mysteries upon mysteries!

I realize of course that God cannot be bound in time, nor held to human conventions of what we mean by cause and effect. I raise these points simply to illustrate the scriptural difficulties we are up against. One simply *cannot* find doctrinal rigidity about the Trinity in the writings of Paul.

If our present doctrinal inflexibility did not originate in the gospels or the epistles, on what basis do we make such a fuss when honest thinking people explore spiritual themes in creatively prayerful ways...exactly as Paul did?

It might be asked further whether the terms *Father* and *Son* when applied to the Godhead imply that the Holy Spirit is feminine in nature, and functions as our divine mother. There are those who believe that the relationship between Father and Son could not exist unless the corresponding role of motherhood also enters the eternal equation. Why else, they say, would God take such pains to use familial terms unless a creative, even procreative, threefold unity were implied?

Do you find this an intriguing idea...or a new heresy? Is this a modernist notion, or perhaps one that probes to the essence of a fundamental truth? I don't know what to make of it. But neither can I escape its common sense.

REVELATION IS ONGOING

Thought, prayer, and revelation of truth is *ongoing*, not static. God may have revealed truth on certain levels to our forefathers about many things. But revelation does not stop. Paul himself did not possess *full* truth about everything. He helped orient the new church in the right direction so that it would have a framework upon which to build *further* revelations of God and his purposes. Neither did those who followed Paul and wrote in the 100s and 200s and 300s possess full truth. Nor did those in the centuries to follow who codified their ideas into the doctrines and creeds upon which the Catholic Church was built.

Revelation is *ongoing*. We should not fear that process. Yet many *are* afraid. The church through the years has made an idol of orthodoxy itself, worshipping doctrinal correctness more than it worships the God that orthodoxy is supposed to reveal.

It is intriguing to note that many of our most revered orthodoxies originated during periods of history when knowledgeable scholars would agree that the church was not particularly reflective of the character of its Founder. The church of the fourth century was not one whose leadership was altogether motivated by the selfless prayer of Christlikeness. It was a period of political dispute between the churches of the East and West, a time when the futures of the Roman Empire and the Catholic Church were hotly contested. *Political* significance carried more weight toward correct doctrine than did the requirements of lifestyle and obedience.

We must merely ask: Is that a wise foundation for the discovery of truth?

Do we really want to base our outlook about God's revelation on the conclusions of men in the fourth century for whom a governmentally enforced and regulated religion was the paramount objective? Do we want to codify the orthodoxy by which we interpret truth according to the conclusions of Roman Emperors, bishops, cardinals, and popes who lived 1,500 years ago, whose motives in many cases were more political and self-serving than spiritual?

More present day doctrinal correctness comes from Constantine, Augustine, and the highly politicized Catholic hierarchy of their era than many realize. Is that a reliable foundation upon which to base our lives as followers and disciples of Jesus Christ? Surely God has revealed truth to men of all generations. I ask only if we are wise to base the largest portion of what we believe about God on the conclusions of a handful of men who were active in Catholic Church and Roman Empire politics in the fourth century A.D.

The Reformation added fresh new thought in some directions, but did not really change the underlying orthodoxy all that much. The Reformation modified church structure more than orthodoxy itself. And about the Reformation, I think we must ask the same question: Do we want to codify our interpretations of truth according to the ideas of men like John Calvin and John Knox, men who were perfectly content to see those who disagreed with them thrown into prison, beheaded, or burned at the stake? I find Christlikeness difficult to discern within the characters of these two men as the accounts of them have come down through history.

We cannot maintain that one's own era produces more truth and necessarily better truth than all previous eras. We are subject to the same limitations of vision as are the men and women of all times. That said, however, the ongoing nature of revelation insures that there will be aspects of spirituality that the sensibilities of later times will be more capable of grasping than the men and women of previous generations. Notwithstanding the courage such men as Constantine, Augustine, Luther, Calvin, and Knox displayed in taking stands new for their times, it seems short sighted to pedastalize these pillars of past orthodoxy. In many respects they were self-motivated, ambitious, and politically driven men. We can respect them as brothers for what they accomplished. But to worship the orthodoxies that grew, in many cases, out of the political small-mindedness of certain contentious times in the history of the church strikes me as giving the ideas of fallible men far too much credit. If I am going to revere another's ideas and his perspectives of God, I want first of all to know if that man knew God intimately, whether he walked with him in obedience, and whether he was trying to please God or the political powers of his day. Only then do his ideas rise to significance in light of eternity, and take on the higher validity of perhaps having been revealed to him by the God with whom he walked in close and daily companionship.

For this reason, I place a higher credibility, for instance, on the words of one of whom C.S. Lewis said, "I know of hardly any other writer who seems to be closer, or more continually close, to the Spirit of Christ Himself," than I do a man, say, such as John Knox, about whom, to my knowledge, that particular claim is rarely made.

Christlikeness of character may be a greater validation of revelationary truth than the lower-case church of Jesus Christ—in its relentless pursuit of doctrinal correctness—has any idea.

WHAT IF...?

With revelation ongoing, therefore, and with all the ambiguity associated with the nature of the Godhead, one wonders what the Orthodoxy Patrol is afraid of? Do they actually want to discourage Christians from following Paul's example and thinking boldly about the relationship between the Father and the Son? Are they fearful that perhaps more light might be shed on God's nature?

What if, for example, after the sketchy and incomplete revelation of God's Fatherhood presented in the Old Testament, and following the new covenant revelation of Sonship given the world when Jesus came, and following Paul's preliminarily sketchy attempts to grapple with how these two emerging revelations intermingled...what if God desires *further* prayerful inquiry into his character as revealed in both Fatherhood and Sonship?

What if there are *additional* depths of God's nature to be explored?

What if these new and additional revelations God wants to give are *necessary* to the expanding, growing, and deepening revelation God desires in order to ready his upper-case Church for Christ's coming?

Do we honestly think that revelation about every doctrine *stopped* at some moment in history? In the case of the Trinity, that would probably be in the year 381, and with the publication of Augustine's *On the Trinity*. In the case of other doctrines, we might identify different dates at which certain ideas were codified into a correctness from which various segments of the church have not deviated since.

Paul was one of history's boldest thinkers. We are called to follow his example. The revelation God gave him was intended to example to us how to approach the inquiry after truth—with common sense, prayer, intelligence, scriptural integrity, wisdom, selflessness, and daily practicality...with bold thinking!

We have the priceless opportunity—which we must believe God not only endorses but has set before us to step into—to *continue* that process of prayerful revelationary investigation into realms into which even Paul himself did not see.

Instead, the Orthodoxy Patrol of every era has taken it upon itself to *prevent* that flow of inquiry and revelation, declaring that all truth is to be rigidly formulated into the doctrines of its approval. One of the overriding motivations of the Orthodoxy Patrol controlling the

Council of Constantinople in 381 was to categorically defeat Arianism. Though we revere the creed that came out of it, we have to recognize that the motives of those men was to *discourage* free and honest thought.

What kind of foundation is that for the discovery of truth! If the *squelching* of ideas is the paramount motivation, how trustworthy will be the revelation?

TRUSTING GOD ABOVE DOCTRINE

Raised in the tradition of conservative evangelicalism, for most of my life I have taken the Trinity as it has come to me. Yet it does not frighten me to consider deeper and wider implications raised by the incarnation. My own perspectives remain growing. I find no need within myself to formulate a "systematic theology," as it were, of God's nature. I trust *God* far more than I trust in *my* capacity to understand the infinity of his multi-faceted being.

I have said before that I would far rather trust God for biblical uncertainties, even uncertainties about how the Godhead functions, than to convince myself that I am certain of truth on this difficult issue. Being wrong does not frighten me so much as being unable to trust God because he himself is true.

The Godhead must mean more than three persons sitting together as many envision it—a stern old man with a long beard, an earthly Jesus of 30-35 years, and a white glowing radiance without human body—each dispensing their distinct portions of truth to humanity: The Father scowling at man's sinfulness, determined to protect his holiness with judgment and justice, insisting that all sin deserves to be eternally punished; the Son saying quietly, "Don't worry, I'll talk to him for you. I'll take the punishment in your place if you believe certain things about me. Then he'll let you into heaven even if you don't deserve it;" and the Spirit filling people with joy and causing them to dance and speak in tongues.

From such simplistic caricatures may the Spirit of Truth deliver us.

I believe that Jesus was the human expression of our Father-God. He called himself God's Son not to elevate himself to the level of the Father but to clarify how much *greater* the Father was than himself. The character of Fatherhood is preeminent within the divine nature because Jesus told us so. God became a man (in Jesus) to tell us that we were created by a good, loving, forgiving, compassionate, embracing Abba-Father who is his Father and our Father, his God and our God.

If the incarnation means anything, it surely means this.

Therefore, following both Jesus' words and his example, we are not to worship the Trinity...we are to worship *God*, who is our *Father*. In that worship and intrinsic to it and thus validating it, we are to obey the commands and instructions of Jesus, who is an obedient *Son*. Jesus never laid claim to our worship, though he is certainly worthy of our honor and veneration. He laid claim only to our *obedience*, to the following of his example.

Perhaps that means he is worthy of our worship as well. These are great mysteries into which I see only as through a glass darkly. I only say that Jesus himself did not insist upon or even suggest that we worship him *as* God. It simply isn't in the gospels unless one reads into his words the flawed orthodoxies of a later time.

A TRINITY OF RULE, OBEDIENCE, AND REVELATION

From the beginning of time, God's purpose in his creation has been to reveal himself. For men to know him as he is, to grasp his being and character and will, would mean to obey him and be one with him. To truly know God would be an end to strife, self-will, and all disharmony in the world. All God's actions and commands, throughout both Old and New Testaments, point toward this single end—that men know him as he truly is. Jesus came to further this process of revelation.

Anxious, however, to legalize high truth into limited precepts, Pharisees in all times and from every branch and denomination and sect have *reduced* this revelation rather than sought to explore its full extent. And thus, within a few short generations of his death, his followers were attempting to define and codify exactly *who* Jesus was rather than to do what he told them. It is out of this misplaced priority that the doctrine of the Trinity, however true elements of it may be, originated.

If his disciples in all ages had simply set themselves to practice and live the principles embodied in Matthew 5-7 and John 13-17, we would probably not be discussing the Trinity at all. I'm not sure the term and its accompanying doctrine would ever have been invented as a pillar of Christ's church. Through the years the church has been more intent upon analyzing and studying Jesus and dissecting his words intellectually than in following and practicing them.

About this we may be sure. Jesus continually taught *against* what might be called an equity in his relationship with the Father. Any serious lover of the Bible, then, must to some degree or another find himself constrained by a perspective of the Godhead that reduces God's being to a committee of three equal members, Any careful reading of the gospel indicates that God's being and nature are far higher and more eternal—of perhaps even *more* than three dimensions—than human understanding can apprehend.

These multiple expressions of God's being are no more equal than they are separate. His love and his wrath are both true expressions of God's being and work. But they are not equal. His love is always *higher* than his wrath and is more intrinsic to his being. It *is* his essential nature, whereas wrath reveals only one aspect of it. Wrath *subserves* love, not the other way around. His mercy and justice both reveal aspects of his nature. But mercy is higher than justice, and he who would worship God's justice alone will invariably worship a false god.

In like manner, Fatherhood and Sonship *both* represent the divine heart, the divine nature. *Both* are expressions of who God is. They are not, however, *equal* expressions, as Scripture plainly tells us...as Jesus himself plainly tells us. The Fatherness of God is greater than the Sonness of God.

The Father is greater than I.

Sonness *subserves* Fatherhood.

God's Fatherness is his originating, self-willing, self-creating life. His Fatherness creates and loves, and creates that he might love the more. His Sonness responds to that love, responds by returning that love in joyful obedience.

The two are one because the outflowing love of Fatherness and the responsive love of Sonness beat as a single heart-pulse of harmonious purpose. Though not equal, they are *one*.

The Holy Spirit, likewise, is no separate entity, no third distinct "person." The Holy Spirit is just the living, breathing, spirit of this divine heart-pulse of life and love that exists in the interactive energy between the Fatherness and Sonness of God's being. The Holy Spirit is God's personality, his voice, his soul, the spirit that reflects both and all other aspects of his nature. The Holy Spirit is simply *God's* spirit itself, emanating *from within* the heart of man *to* the heart of man messages of the divine Fatherness and Sonness.

These thoughts take us straight back to the Nicene Creed. In this case, those men at Constantinople, political motives and all, may have gotten it just right.

One God the Father...

This simple assertion clearly establishes the Father's preeminence and dismisses the idea of a committee of three equal members. When we speak of "God," according to the Nicene Creed, we first of all mean the Father.

And in one Lord Jesus Christ...

Then, when we speak of *the Lord*, we are speaking of the Son, a reflection of the Father, of the same nature as the Father, but not the same as the Father—the Lord to whom we owe unconditional obedience because he gave unconditional obedience to the Father— though what follows remains full of mystery..."Begotten of the Father...true God of true God."

And in the Holy Spirit...that proceeds from the Father...

This seems to draw the distinction as clearly, though with mystery, as we could have it:

The Father is supreme, all sovereign, the creator, whose role in the Godhead is *rule*.

Jesus Christ is the Lord, the image of the Father in the flesh, not the same as the Father but rather his Son, whose role in the Godhead is not rule but *obedience*.

The Spirit, who, again, is not equal to, but proceeds from the Father, and whose role is *revelation*.

Thus we end where we began, with the conclusion that it is a glorious mystery. I pray that our thoughts will be stimulated to fresh prayer, and toward wonder and thankfulness for the greatness of his being that is God himself.

Lewis and MacDonald on the Trinity

"We must remind ourselves that Christian theology does not believe God to be a person. It believes Him to be such that in Him a trinity of persons is consistent with a unity of Deity. In that sense it believes Him to be something very different from a person, just as a cube, in which six squares are consistent with unity of the body, is different from a square. (Flatlanders, attempting to imagine a cube, would either imagine the six squares coinciding, and thus destroy their distinctness, or else imagine them set out side by side, and thus destroy the unity. Our difficulties about the Trinity are of much the same kind.)" [31]

George MacDonald was certainly one who did not limit himself to the revelation of the past, but who always sought more and deeper truth. He wrote:

"I believe, then, that Jesus Christ is the eternal son of the eternal father. I *believe that from the first beginnings of all things Jesus is the son, because God is the father. This statement is imperfect and unfit because it is an attempt of human thought to represent that which it cannot grasp, yet which it believes so strongly that it must try to utter it even in speech that cannot be right.*

"I believe therefore that the Father is the greater, and that if the Father had not been, the Son could not have been...

"I worship the Son as the human God, the divine, the only perfect Man. He derives his being and power from the Father, and is equal with him as a son is both the equal and at the same time the subject of his father. Yet he makes himself the equal of his father only in what is most precious in the Godhead, namely Love...It is a higher thing than the making of the worlds and the things in them, which making he did by the power of the Father not by a self-existent power in himself. For this reason, the apostle, to whom the Lord must have said things he did not say to the rest, or who was better able to receive what he said to them all—says, 'All things were made' not by, but 'through him.'" [32]

FIFTEEN
GUARD AGAINST SUPERFICIALITY
Counterfeit Parameters of Spirituality

> "For this reason, σπουδην (with diligence) supplement your faith with virtue,
> and virtue with knowledge, and knowledge with self-control,
> and self-control with steadfastness, and steadfastness with godliness..."
> 2 Peter 1:5-6

σπουδη: SPOUDE —*Diligence*

Though the concept of "diligence" in Scripture is most often associated with work and business, reflected in *Proverbs* as well as through the New Testament, it is also a quality that we are commanded to bring into our beliefs and our lives of faith. SPOUDE indicates earnestness and zeal. We must not only work diligently at our daily work and responsibilities, we must also work diligently to *believe* correctly and then live that belief with practical zeal and earnestness. The progression of 2 Peter 1:5-7 is beautiful in revealing the depth of growth and maturity such diligence is supposed to produce in the life of the believer: virtue, knowledge, self-control, steadfastness, and love...in short the *godliness* of Christian maturity.

The next verses, 2 Peter 1:8-9, as we now look back over almost 2000 years of church history, read as a poignantly prophetic warning of what has been the result of the failure to heed Peter's words: "For if these things are yours and abound, they keep you from being ineffective or unfruitful in the knowledge of our Lord Jesus Christ. For whoever lacks these things is blind and shortsighted and has forgotten that he was cleansed from his old sins." Alas, the many counterfeits that the church has produced has indeed resulted in just such blindness, shortsightedness, ineffectiveness, and unfruitfulness.

MY WIFE JUDY AND I ARE REACHING THE AGE when life's rapid passage is vividly being brought home to us with increasing regularity. In the past two years, almost two dozen individuals of our acquaintance have died. Every such death makes one thoughtful and reflective. Most of these people were Christians, and with each passing I find myself prayerfully wondering how prepared each was for the end and beginning signified by the final days of life's earthly sojourn. What had they made of themselves during their time here...or more properly, what had they allowed God to make of them throughout the years of their lives?

Where were they on the continuum of spiritual *growth* at the point when their earthly lives came to an end? How far had they progressed toward that mature and humble childship which must be the goal of every Christian?

Two of these sixteen included dear men whom I considered among my closest friends. Both were dedicated and outspoken Christian men. Yet both exemplified and lived out their Christian belief in diametrically opposite ways. One of my friends could never quite escape the vociferous superficiality of external spiritual appearances. He was a great talker about spiritual things. The other, a true and lifelong spiritual mentor and my elder by twenty years, was a quiet man of great inner dignity and few spiritual words. To me his life was always a radiant example of "abiding" in the vine of his Lord and Master. Few men have influenced me so greatly in the principles of kingdom living. He is a man whom I know without a doubt was greeted with the words, "Well done, good and faithful servant."

More recently we said good bye to my mother-in-law, Judy's mother. She lived a long and full life, and died as she slept in our home in her own bed.

During the final interview with the hospice intake nurse who came to the house to explain the rules and procedures of hospice, Judy turned to her mom and said, "You don't obey rules, do you?"

"Never have and never will," replied her mother in a weak voice.

She was a spunky lady to the end!

It struck me as an interesting, though actually a sad thing for a lifelong Christian to say within a few days of her death. All the more so because she was proud of it. Judy's mother was always thoroughly involved in all the activities of church life—teaching Sunday school, playing the piano, bazaars and committees, Vacation Bible School, social events, organizing and bringing food...the life of the party, the classic "church mom" who had been a chaplain's assistant in the Coast Guard during World War II. But when it came to the inner components of spirituality, that aspect of her life became an increasing mystery to us. During her last years, as Judy tried to pray with her or speak of spiritual things, she was met by a brick wall of non-response. Had her mother ever *grown* substantially in the Lord through her life? Judy never knew. This one of the final statements to come out of her mouth expressing pride in her independent spirit perhaps reveals a poignant fact about her outlook on spirituality in general.

Did she *want* to grow? Had she made an effort to strip away the old man, to put to death the spirit of the flesh? It seemed rather that she was content with the way she was. Not only content, but proud of her feisty independent spirit.

Yet my mother-in-law always considered herself a strong Christian. She lived a good and upright life. Like my friend above, she "believed" all the right things, so to speak. But the question Judy and I could not escape as the end of her life neared was what had been going on *inside* her. Had she been a growing, self-denying follower and disciple of Christ?

Judy and I found such questions raising themselves, not in a judging spirit, because we loved Judy's mother and admired many things about her. In those aspects of life where she was indeed growing and self-denying—as we beheld so vividly in Judy's father prior to *his* death—we wanted to perceive them accurately as well, and learn from them and thank God for them.

We asked such questions, as I did of my friend who had died a year before, because we wanted to be mentally diligent to learn from these life-experiences. We wanted to know our *own* selves better as life's transitions come also to us. Are *we*—Judy and I—spending *our* lives emphasizing truly eternal things as Christians? Or have counterfeit superficialities of seeming spirituality entrapped us more than we realize?

The death of Judy's father, of my two friends, and then Judy's mother, brought home to me the wider implications of the question whether she was so unusual among the millions of those who consider themselves "good Christians."

Self-denying growth isn't really at the top of the list of emphasized components of "Christianity" in most churches today.

Those lists are quite different and may produce very different results than the Christlikeness that our faith is supposed to work into the depths of our characters.

Then the further question arose in my mind, whether most Christians even know what true Christian growth and maturity are.

I fear the answer is often no. Their pastors and priests and teachers are not teaching them adequately or correctly. Mental diligence is not a high priority. Throughout the history of the church there has, in fact, been much wrong teaching in the church about what spirituality actually *is*. Because of it, dozens of factors of seeming spirituality masquerade as indicators of maturity which actually possess no power whatever to conquer the sin-tendencies within us. These false indicators do not produce the character that Jesus and Paul spoke of as identifying the life-fruit of God's sons and daughters.

Because our perspectives are filled with so many incomplete notions concerning what comprises spirituality, we need to boldly and honestly examine some of the more prominent of them. Recognizing what spiritual maturity is *not*, we can then apply ourselves diligently to discover the essence of how true spiritual growth *does* take place.

To do so requires mental and spiritual *diligence*—the hard work of separating the wheat from the chaff. Without this application of discerning, thoughtful, prayerful diligence applied to our beliefs, Peter's warning is clear: blindness and shortsightedness is the inevitable result.

This chapter might have well been headed by the word "immaturity." I would rather, however, focus our attention on the diligence that *prevents* immaturity from infecting the walk of faith.

THE FIRST CENTURY— COUNTERFEIT PARAMETER OF SPIRITUALITY 1:
SALVATION AND BELIEF

Looking back through the centuries of the church, one does not see much importance in the years immediately following the Apostolic age placed on the personal aspects of spiritual growth. The church was in such an age of expansion throughout the Mediterranean world that the emphasis was on *belief* itself. Confronting people with the Christian *ideas* (the life and teachings of Jesus Christ) so they would acknowledge belief in him was paramount. Apologetics became the primary form of communication to accomplish this goal.

Quickly we observe the first counterfeit indicator of spiritual maturity to rear its head. The word "counterfeit" should not mislead us. Salvation and belief are important, indeed foundational. But it is a question of what they are intended to do. Belief, even when it leads to saving faith, cannot in and of itself produce spiritual *maturity*. Neither can salvation—as belief, repentance, and saving faith merge as one—of itself produce *maturity*. It produces salvation and leads to eternal life. Spiritual maturity, however, emerges later, over time, and is something else entirely. They are not "false" in themselves, they are false *indicators* of maturity. Spiritual maturity is simply something they are not able to accomplish. These are the kinds of insights it requires diligence to see. Lazy minds will not see them.

Though admittedly a weak analogy, the life preserver that hauls the drowning man into the vessel of salvation will not equip him to succeed in his job after he is safely back on shore. Life preserver and job skills are both important. But they are fundamentally different things.

Likewise...belief and maturity are fundamentally *disconnected* components of spirituality.

Belief and salvation may be necessary as *foundations* for growth, but they do not *produce* growth.

CENTURIES 2-4— COUNTERFEIT PARAMETER OF SPIRITUALITY 2: *DOCTRINAL ORTHODOXY*

Because the first few centuries of the church were so volatile and full of conflicting claims and interpretations, combating false ideas became a critical concern of church leaders. This increased the necessity to inform both believers and unbelievers of the facts about Jesus and the tenets of Christianity. They had to inform them *truly*.

The first several centuries of the church, therefore, saw an imperative emphasis not only on belief, but also on the *correct doctrines* of belief.

Everywhere people were pouring into Christianity out of other religions and philosophical systems: Judaism, Greek and platonic philosophy, Roman secularism, paganism. In every case, converts had to be taught the radically different ideas presented by Christianity—that God had become man and had died and risen again to life to demonstrate how atonement was made for sin, and bring to life the potentiality of that atonement for every man and woman.

Even that central teaching, however, was not sufficient to preserve doctrinal purity. As Christianity spread, many tangential offshoots such as Gnosticism developed. These polluted Christianity's essential truths with remnants of paganism as well as Roman and Greek philosophies, necessitating all the more that the ideas of Christianity were *properly* understood.

Very quickly after Paul's time, therefore, his writings—though emphasizing a complete and rounded Christian walk—came to be read primarily in a *doctrinal* context. Paul's numerous injunctions and commands to practical Christian obedience about lifestyle, attitude, unity, and Christlikeness all slipped into the background as his "theology" was more and more scrutinized...and scrutinized as theology detached from his more practical expositions.

The great debates of the second through fourth centuries were ones of theology and doctrine. As these disputes solidified doctrinal correctness into the great creeds of the Church, *doctrinal orthodoxy* gradually emerged as yet another potential false indicator of maturity.

In the same way, it may be argued (though I think this remains a legitimately debatable point) that doctrinal correctness is a *foundation* for growth, but it will not *produce* growth.

CENTURIES 2-4— COUNTERFEIT PARAMETER OF SPIRITUALITY 3:
LEARNING AND KNOWLEDGE

On the heels of this came perhaps the most deadly and mischievous false indicator of all, which has remained a cancerous evil within the church ever since.

This heresy—it must be called nothing less—began early. Not only did the second through fourth centuries produce an emphasis on doctrinal orthodoxy, out of the thirst for that orthodoxy grew the assumption that *knowledge*, founded on correct and orthodox belief, was the means by which to grasp and understand truth. The great Christian thinkers of this era—dozens of men like Justin Martyr, Irenaeus, Tertullian, Origen, Eusebius, Augustine, and Jerome—wrote multitudinous volumes of such quantity as to stagger the imagination. As the refinement of Christian theology expanded, these massive works were studied in great detail in the intellectual centers of Christendom. The major councils of the times were convened to discuss a myriad of ideas and resolve theological conflict and settle on what constituted orthodox belief. Christian schools and universities and libraries were established to expand the studies of theology, as Christian ideas slowly replaced those of classical Greece as the intellectual framework for western culture. Most of the institutions of higher learning throughout western civilization have Christian origins. *Education* became a huge adjunct to the spread of Christianity, and has continued to be so to the present day—from missionary schools in jungle outposts to colleges and universities.

This was an enormously positive development. Obviously the great ideas of Christianity have been the most influential set of ideas in history to influence the world for good. No objective historian would contest that fact. Yet it was also a development that brought in its wake a lethal implicationary result.

This is the heresy—that knowledge produces, even *equates* with spiritual maturity. The more learned a man or woman in doctrine, theology, and the content of Scripture, the more mature he or she must necessarily be. In the minds of millions, spiritual growth is quite literally defined as: *Increasing knowledge about spiritual things*.

Knowledge equals spiritual stature.

This heresy has continued through the centuries and is more prevalent today than ever in obscuring the true parameters of maturity behind a suffocating cloud of spiritual dogma and information. We surely today represent the most knowledgeable generation of Christians that has ever lived. Whether we are the most spiritually diligent in discerning what produces Christlikeness is another matter.

Again misunderstanding will be all too easy. It is a question, however, of what study and knowledge are capable of. I have an insatiable appetite for all things historical and theological. I love to study the past and its ideas! I love Christian theology. To me there are no more *exciting* fields of inquiry. While all around me I see the men of our time seeking pleasure in hundreds of entertainments offered by our leisure-satiated culture, few of those entertainments exercise an allure upon me. Set me down with a book of truly original ideas about the character of God, some passage of Scripture, or an interesting moment of history, and I am in heaven!

The words of 2 Peter 1:5 exhort us toward spiritual knowledge: *With diligence supplement your faith...with knowledge.* Paul repeatedly exhorts us similarly. The Proverbs extol the *knowledge* and *understanding* of the principles of God.

But I am not so foolish as to assume that such study makes me more able to love my neighbor, forgive one who has betrayed my trust, or relinquish my self will.

The heresy is not in the quest to learn and understand. The heresy is wrongly imbuing spiritual knowledge with the capacity to produce wisdom. That capacity it does not have

George MacDonald says it clearly, "God forbid I should seem to despise understanding. The New Testament is full of urgings to understand. What I cry out upon is the misunderstanding that comes of man's endeavor to understand while not obeying. Upon obedience must our energy be spent; understanding will follow." [33]

Learning and knowledge are also fundamentally disconnected from maturity on the two sides of their respective balance scales. Load on the scale an encyclopedic knowledge of every Christian idea or doctrine or theology...stack up a pile of books a hundred feet high...yet the opposite side of *maturity* will not move a hair's breadth.

Are we diligently paying attention to what church history has to teach us. Only so will we recognize the truth that the one is simply incapable of producing the other.

CENTURIES 3-6— COUNTERFEIT PARAMETER OF SPIRITUALITY 4:
THE CHURCH, ITS PRIESTHOOD, AND ITS TRADITION

Concurrent with the development of doctrinal orthodoxy, between the third and sixth centuries the institution of the church gradually rose to dominate the spiritual landscape in a way altogether out of proportion to anything we can find in the gospels. Constantine's sanction of Christianity as what effectively amounted to an official religion of Rome in the fourth century led to a massive church building program throughout the Roman Empire. Huge ornate cathedrals rose over the roof lines of its major cities. Their rites, traditions, masses, liturgies, and priestly hierarchies became more and more elaborate, to such an extent that early Catholicism came more to reflect Old Testament Judaism—infused with the glamour and glory and pomp and wealth of classical Rome at its height—than the Apostolic Age. Money poured into church coffers. Robes of gold and exquisite finery replaced Peter's humble fisherman's garb. A powerful worldwide "religion" of might, politic, and influence was underway.

Truly it came to be known as the *Roman* church. But was *Rome* or the *gospel* its foundation?

It was not long before the Roman church itself became the authoritative institution whose priesthood, structure, and tradition replaced God as the focus of honor, veneration, and obedience. Allegiance to the sacred institution and its creeds, rituals, and steadily more legalistic observances came to define spirituality. The priesthood, rather than the Holy Spirit, became the conduit of grace.

Dozens of examples might be cited as indicative of a structural bloating that replaced the living reality of "the Rock" whom Jesus commanded to feed his sheep. Surely no more glaring example exists than the confessional, wherein the priest takes upon himself the sin-absolving intermediary role, even to the point of allowing himself to be called by God's title, rather than urging his flock to go directly to the true *Father*, through the rent veil into the Holy of Holies, with *Jesus* as the intermediary. It is a practice that conflicts with everything the incarnation of Christ represents, a reversion to Old Testament legalism where God is unapproachable by sinful man without the priest acting in his stead.

This trend of the "church" and its priesthood usurping God's place is by no means merely a Catholic delusion of spirituality. Its implications infect Protestantism to a greater degree than many are aware. In hundreds of ways, church tradition throughout the spectrum of Christendom similarly keeps God at arm's length within a shrouded Holy of Holies, a misperception not merely furthered by the Catholic confessional but equally by the professional ministry and holiness doctrines of Protestantism.

Though the glaring pitfalls of Catholicism and Orthodoxy of the middle ages, as well as the excesses of the reformers of the 16th century, are not hard to observe, we still suffer from the false illusion that the buildings to which we attach the name "church" contain life in and of themselves. We still delude ourselves with the hope that their services, masses, worship, Bible studies, campaigns, ministries, projects, causes, and innumerable activities somehow produce spiritual maturity. We continue to imbue our pastors and priests with far more "intermediary" functionality than God intends. We have been slow to apprehend the *true* nature of God's clergy, priesthood, and leadership—"one thirsty sinner telling another where to find water." Many of God's pastors and priests understand their position as humble servants to God's flock and truly are desirous of washing the feet of their congregations. Yet in many cases their people make wrong assumptions about the nature of their role, making such sacrificial service impossible. These crippling and cancerous misperceptions, therefore, are as much to be laid at the doorstep of the laity as the clergy.

In more subtle ways than we imagine, the church continues to reinforce the old covenantal falsehood that a relationship of distance and inapproachability exists between God and his people.

THE MIDDLE AGES— COUNTERFEIT PARAMETER OF SPIRITUALITY 5:
PRAYER AND THE DEVOTIONAL LIFE

After the fall of Rome in the fifth century, when the church lost much of its prestige and political influence, and with orthodoxy and the structure of the church in place, monasticism expanded to give the medieval church a new distinctive character. In solitary cloisters and monasteries throughout the world of the church, often in deserts and lonely places, spirituality turned inward.

This balancing swing of the pendulum away from Constantine's programs of grandeur and spectacle, emphasized what is called the devotional life as a practice to feed and nurture the inner life and the soul's oneness with God. The pursuit of the resulting spiritual disciplines reached its zenith after the twelfth and thirteenth centuries—prayer, Scripture reading, fasting, meditation, celibacy, poverty, simplicity, confession of sin, self-denial, lifetime service to the church, abandonment of possessions, ministry to the poor, and so on.

These practices nurtured and practiced by medieval monks, nuns, and desert Fathers and Sisters, infused the church with a wonderful tradition of wholehearted and lifetime devotion to God, bringing the Spirit of God into the innermost places of the soul. In a sense we might look upon this era and renewal of personal reality in faith as a second golden era (after the first century) in the church's development.

Many of the contemplative writings from this era are still read today as aids and encouragements in the devotional life. From the journals and thoughts of these saints of old we have gained enormous wisdom into the inner life of the soul's communion with God. Properly understood, they are capable of contributing enormously to spiritual growth. For the dedicated practice of these devotional disciplines, we owe the monks, mystics, and monastics of ages past great honor. Furthermore, out of their lives of solitude in the middle ages were the Scriptures preserved and passed down to us.

Indeed, it is not uncommon for the enthusiastic and totally committed Christian young person to look upon such a life through eyes of idealism, thinking nothing could be so wonderful as to be alone with God, reading and studying his Word, with one's whole life devoted to prayer and meditation. Girls decide to become nuns. I went through a stage at about twenty-two of dreamily contemplating becoming a sort of Protestant monk and mystic.

Life always has a way of intruding into such dreams! Hopefully we each retain a germ of the idealism from the visions of our youth. I will always feel leanings toward this devotional and contemplative component of spirituality in my own walk. Indeed, in one sense we may indeed approach the spiritual bull's eye through some of these inner devotional practices. Prayer is far more likely to produce growth than is stagnant theological orthodoxy. Therefore, these devotional disciplines are far more capable of tending toward spiritual maturity than the early indicators we looked at. They well may lead to growth.

But the spiritual disciplines do not in themselves *insure* maturity. Study of Scripture may remind me to forgive one who has wronged me. Prayer, fasting, and meditation may convict me of the necessity of doing so. Reading a devotional book may further press that urging upon me.

But they will not accomplish it *for* me. Only obedience—my *choosing* to forgive—can do that.

It is in the *choosing* and the diligent *doing* that growth toward maturity comes.

THE REFORMATION— COUNTERFEIT PARAMETER OF SPIRITUALITY 6:
STUDY OF SCRIPTURE

With the advent of the Reformation in the 1500s came a fresh emphasis on study of the Bible. Martin Luther, John Calvin, and other leaders of a "reform" movement that went in many directions, very rightly sought to return the church to Scripture as its foundation. Out of this emphasis nearly all branches of Protestantism became rooted in the conviction that truth is to be found in the infallible and inerrant Word of God.

They were absolutely right. Not only is study of Scripture a vital component of belief and faith, the Scriptures also provide a framework for us to understand spiritual maturity. Yet like the previous counterfeit indicators, they allow a misperception to creep in. Every week do we not hear comments such as, *I am learning so much about the Bible...I feel like I am really growing in the Lord.* In fact, such a statement is not one of maturity at all but of immaturity, and a *false* perspective of God's work. It reveals a distinct *lack* of mental diligence to properly understand the role of Scripture in the life of the Christian.

In the years following the "monk" phase of my early Christian life, I was filled with a passion to study the Bible. I read and underlined and made notes in the margins and devoured books of

Bible study. I was so proud of myself when I first read the Bible completely through! The two or three Bibles I was using at the time are filled with underlines and quotes and lists and sayings and reminders. I really *loved* God's Word! Psalm 119 described my feelings to perfection.

A young man came through the area and was part of our collegiate Christian group at the time. His knowledge of Scripture was vast, like nothing any of us had ever encountered. He was only in his twenties, no gray and erudite scholar. But whatever subject came up, his encyclopedic brain pulled out a dozen appropriate passages to quote. He could cite entire chapters from memory. We who listened were left with our mouths hanging open. It was astonishing. I know there are people who have memorized the entire New Testament. This guy was the closest to such I have ever encountered.

I was in awe of his gift. I have to confess...I envied it. I couldn't think of anything more wonderful than to have the whole Bible at one's command as he did.

But slowly an incredible realization began to dawn on me. This young man was also one of the sourest, grumpiest, and judgmental people in our group. When listening to him quote various passages at length, you always had the idea that you were being preached at by one who considered himself a spiritual giant while all around him sat a collection of spiritual lightweights. In truth...I *was* a spiritual lightweight. But the whole dynamic was unsettling. Knowledge of Scripture notwithstanding, was this really the kind of individual I wanted to emulate?

Within a year he was gone. I never saw him nor heard anything about him again. In retrospect, I realized that I had never once seen him smile.

For me, therefore, the question is very personal: Is scriptural knowledge *in itself* indicative of maturity? The memory of this passing acquaintance is ever with me—and the judging expression of gloom and doom as he quoted the Bible at the rest of the neophytes listening with our jaws dropping in amazement.

Such individuals exist in every church and Christian group, whose knowledge is vastly superior to mine and probably to yours. No doubt some of them are beyond us in spiritual maturity as well. Hopefully in most cases such study and its resulting knowledge *does* produce growth of the right sort. But all too often, don't we secretly wonder whether inward growth toward the character of Christlikeness is moving on the same track?

I raise such a question not in a judging spirit, but as a reminder not to fall into the same trap myself. Every one of us is susceptible to it! The lure of placing our knowledge of Scripture on a pedestal, even if only in our own minds, is always present.

It means *nothing*...if I don't do what Jesus said.

Indeed, the very Bible we revere tells us in a thousand ways that studying its pages and principles to the point of memorizing its words cover to cover will move the scale of maturity not at all...without obedience.

THE REFORMATION— COUNTERFEIT PARAMETER OF SPIRITUALITY 7:
GRACE—JUSTIFICATION BY FAITH

With Martin Luther's nailing of his *Ninety-Five Theses* to the door of the Wittenberg Cathedral door in 1517, and his reaffirmation of the scriptural foundation of justification by faith, a major corrective shift rocked Christendom back toward its New Testament origins. Immediately, however, the enemy of God's purposes caused the theology of Luther's insight to swing *too* far in the opposite direction against the works of Catholicism that had preceded it. Out of the Reformation thus also grew the false doctrine that grace *alone* is capable of producing spiritual maturity.

How many times have we heard the expression, *Only by God's grace.* It is one of evangelicalism's common stock phrases. In reality, however, it exposes a cancerous false doctrine.

The deadly conclusion is that the role of the "justified" and "sanctified" believer living in grace is *passive*. Grace sanctifies and makes us mature saints of itself. *God's* is the active role, not ours. Grace is *everything*.

Justification by faith *is* a stupendous life-transforming truth. But we need to be clear about what growth *is*, and what it is *not*.

How does growth occur? Grace only makes growth *possible* in the potential of spiritual reality. But it does not *produce* growth.

The falsehood that grace can and does produce maturity by divine fiat deadens an understanding of true maturity in many unseen ways. It is based on the notion that sanctification *just happens*. Once we accept Christ as savior, God "acts upon" us from the inside. It is the Holy Spirit's function, not ours.

This overreaction against works can be traced all the way back to the early days of the Reformation. The *Westminster Shorter Catechism* (1647) terms sanctification "the work of God's free grace, whereby we are renewed in the whole man after the image of God, and are enabled more and more to die unto sin, and live unto righteousness." [34]

Every verb construction is passive. We don't have to *do* any renewing, we don't have to *die* to sin, we **are** renewed and **are** enabled. It's all done for us. We are acted **upon** by this mysterious outside force called "sanctification."

As highly as he is respected among fundamentalists, J.I. Packer has done the church no favors by his teaching on this subject. He has in fact worsened the misunderstanding of true growth toward spiritual maturity behind high-sounding words that have a subtly destructive result. He writes:

"The concept is...of a divinely wrought character change freeing us from sinful habits and forming in us Christlike affections, dispositions, and virtues. Sanctification is an ongoing transformation...and it engenders real righteousness within the frame of relational holiness. Relational sanctification, the state of being permanently set apart for God, flows from the cross, where God through Christ purchased and claimed us for himself." [35]

It's all God's doing. We just stand back passively...and let the Holy Spirit change us. It happens automatically. Discipleship on the easy-does-it-plan.

But is it quite so simple? We find nowhere in the teachings of Jesus this lack of personal accountability in the matter of one's own growth.

When Peter blew it, Jesus didn't put his arm on his shoulder and say, "Hey, no problem, Pete. The Holy Spirit will engender real righteousness within a frame of relational holiness in you after a while. Just wait a few years and you will experience a divinely wrought character change that will free you from your sinful habits."

Jesus was a little more direct with Peter than that! He zeroed in with more precision toward choice and personal accountability.

All the passivity inherent in this counterfeit teaching of diligence is not based in the gospel of Jesus Christ. It is based in the wishful thinking of desiring spirituality without paying the personal, self-denying, self-sacrificing price demanded by the altar. To borrow from the title of Dietrich Bonhoeffer's classic book, it is based on the fleeting and spiritually ignorant hope of *avoiding* the cost of discipleship.

The obedience Jesus commanded was no passive obedience. When he finished the parable of the good Samaritan, he didn't look at his listeners and say, "Okay now, study this principle and memorize this story so you can quote it and add it to your bank of scriptural knowledge, and over time a divinely wrought character change will engender righteousness within you. No need for you do anything. Maturity will just happen in time,"

He said, "Go and do the same."

With Jesus there is always a DO. That *do* of diligent obedience is the key to unlocking the *true* indicators of growth into maturity as Christian men and women.

OUR OWN TIME—MODERN COUNTERFEIT PARAMETERS OF SPIRITUALITY:
TOLERANCE, EXPERIENCE, MINISTRY, WORSHIP,
AND MY OWN PERSONAL BLIND SPOTS

The heading above might more aptly read: "In *my* life—counterfeit indicators of maturity."

At this point the self-examination becomes brutally personal. Do we have the courage, are we willing to be bold and diligent thinkers, to turn the spotlight on ourselves?

We will each be pulled and lured and swayed and urged toward our own personal and private roots of self-righteousness. What entices *you* to think more highly of yourself than you ought will most likely not be what makes *me* think more highly of myself than *I* ought. The counterfeit indicators with which we each have to wrestle will be different and personal. Only you and I can say what falsehoods have infiltrated our assumptions and thought patterns about our own supposed maturity.

For one it may be the ability to speak to crowds with dynamism and charisma. Such is no cause for pride or self-righteousness for me because I am singularly *not* endowed with such a gift. Put me in front of ten people and I become a cowering, stuttering child! But I have learned over the years what it takes to write a novel. So if writing a novel should somehow become elevated to pedestal stature, at that point I might be especially susceptible.

What makes *you* think you are more mature as a Christian than you really are?

What makes *me* think I am more mature as a Christian than I really am?

One of Soren Kierkegaard's books is as valuable for its title as for its content. It is simply called *On Self Examination.* Those are three words we ought to hammer into our brains so they jump up in front of us like a pop-up book every time we open the pages of our Bibles.

Bold thinkers are diligent and prayerful self-examiners.

Along with your personal counterfeit indicators and mine, it is also possible to identify several widespread false indicators of spiritual maturity that have arisen in the last hundred or more years, largely within evangelicalism.

The first is an emphasis on *experience and the manifestation of spiritual gifts,* initially emphasized by the Pentecostalism of the early 1900s. The Charismatic Movement of the 1960s broadened the base of this worrisome perspective to the point where most of evangelicalism now equates spiritual maturity with spiritual experience and its related visible manifestations. The catch-phrase, "Have you experienced the Spirit-filled life?" in seven short words encapsulates the enormous misapprehension that has led so many thousands to a false impression of maturity in the Christian walk. Experiential manifestations of God's life with us may be *real*—I would not be supposed to doubt *any* method by which God may choose to work and reveal himself. But manifestation and experience are singularly poor indicators of maturity. In some cases they may actually point in just the opposite direction. It is not unusual that those most dependent on signs and wonders, experiences and emotions, validations and confirmations, are actually the most *immature* as Christians.

In the first decades of the twenty-first century, *tolerance* is stepping forward as symbolic of the new church. Its proponents think to make the Christian life palatable by accepting and embracing everything and anything. Maybe we've been a little too hard on sin all this time.

Growing out of widespread renewal in the evangelical church, in recent times, two related emphases on *ministry* and *public worship* have similarly undermined in whole new ways the perspective of a new generation of millions about the nature of growth.

We watch one who is highly expressive in musical worship, and we wrongly imbue that expressiveness with the implication of maturity. It is *not*, however, always the most expressive in worship who exemplifies maturity. Why do the *Proverbs* so honor silence, keeping one's thoughts to oneself, and controlling one's emotions, if such qualities are not indicators of maturity? Throughout the Bible, it is more often quiet, humble, soft-spoken, self-control that is extolled as a mark of virtue, not emotional expressivity. Scripturally, therefore, the loudest and most expressive in worship may be showing off little more than his or her spiritual immaturity.

It gives us something to think about.

Likewise, many observe those individuals who are said to be in "ministry," so called, and assume that this "ministry," so called, is an outgrowth of spiritual maturity.

Not necessarily.

The obsession to attach the word *ministry* to anything and everything one wants to do, thereby heightening its external spiritual cachet, results in as many cases from *immaturity* than from a lifetime of wisdom.

In fact, the more mature a Christian man or woman, the *less* likely he or she is to start a program or attach a high-sounding label to his or her work. Is this obsession to puff ourselves up with labels of spirituality but one more example of what Jesus called doing one's works, or performing one's worship, to be seen of men.

One wonders whether God is impressed with the "ministry" label.

How much talk do you hear about the ministry of obedience...or the ministry of cleaning toilets...or the ministry of going to work faithfully every day...or the ministry of duty...or the ministry of helps no one knows about...or the ministry of invisible sacrifices...or the ministry of unseen works of kindness...or the ministry of cleaning up after an incontinent bed-ridden relative?

That we don't observe the word ministry attached to such fundamental components of the Christian walk might tell us something about the over-spiritualized use of the term. Diligence, not ministry, leads to Christlikeness.

Many such counterfeit indicators of spiritual maturity exist besides these few we have considered. We must each search our own hearts to discover those perhaps worthy aspects of spirituality (profitable in themselves) that we erroneously imagine to be signs of maturity. This imperative inner quest of boldly-directed, diligent self-examination is one we each will conduct in our own closet of prayer.

False Notions of God's Purposes

"Verily, God must be terrible to those that are far from him; for they fear he will do, yea, he is doing with them what they do not, cannot desire, and can ill endure. Such as many men are, such as all without God would become, they must prefer a devil, because of his supreme selfishness, to a God who will die for his creatures, and insists upon giving himself to them, insists upon their being unselfish and blessed like himself. That which is the power and worth of life they

must be, or die; and the vague consciousness of this makes them afraid. They love their poor existence as it is; God loves it as it must be—and they fear him.

"The false notions of men of low, undeveloped nature both with regard to what is good and what the Power requires of them, are such that they cannot but fear, and devotion is lost in the sacrifices of ingratiation: God takes them where they are, accepts whatever they honestly offer, and so helps them to outgrow themselves, preparing them to offer the true offering, and to know him whom they ignorantly worship. He will not abolish their fear except with the truth of his own being. Till they apprehend that, and in order that they may come to apprehend it, he receives their sacrifices of blood, the invention of their sore need, only influencing for the time the modes of them. He will destroy the lie that is not all a lie only by the truth which is all true. Although he loves them utterly, he does not tell them there is nothing in him to make them afraid. That would be to drive them from him for ever. While they are such as they are, there is much in him that cannot but affright them; they ought, they do well to fear him." [36]

SIXTEEN
LET US GO ON TO MATURITY
True Indicators of growth in the Life of Faith

"Therefore, let us go on to τελειοτητα (maturity)...
—Hebrews 6:1

τελειοτης: TELEIOTES—*Maturity*

TELEIOTES technically means perfection. It derives from TELOS— *achievement, fulfillment, completion, the final step, the supreme stage, crown, goal, result, conclusion, full success*...and ultimately *perfection*. It is a dynamic word, not static or passive, indicating movement and growth *toward* all these ends: the culmination and consummation of an energetic and living process of development.

When the writer of *Hebrews* exhorts Christians to "go on to TELEIOTES" or maturity, he is actually challenging them to step all the way up into the fulfillment of Jesus' astonishing command in Matthew 5:48, "Be perfect, as your heavenly Father is perfect." The word TELEIOTES is closely linked to the obviously related word TELEIOSIS. In both words, but especially in TELEIOSIS, which is used in Hebrews 7:11, the sense of a *process* is clear—actualization, a maturing conclusion. The fulfillment or completion is evident that is the end result of a "growing into" perfection. It is perfection, therefore, that is *attained* rather than inherent by nature. God's perfection, for example, is inherent in his nature. The perfection we are called to is a maturity that must be grown into. TELEIOTES more clearly stresses the accomplishment of the end. It is used also in Colossians 3:14, as well as in the Greek Old Testament in Proverbs 11:3, where it is often translated integrity. Another related word, KATARTISIS, means a "making fit," translated in 2 Corinthians 13:9 as *improvement*. Also related is the word TELEIOS, which simply means *adult*—a grown-up, one who is physically mature and complete.

In light of the above, the progression from Hebrews 5:11-6:1 becomes especially intriguing. The chapter break artificially divides what the author clearly intends as a single thought-progression: "About this we have much to say which is hard to explain, since you have become dull of hearing. For though by this time you ought to be teachers...you need milk, not solid food; for every one who lives on milk is unskilled in the word of righteousness, for he is a child. But solid food is for the TELEION (mature/adult), for those who have their faculties trained by practice to distinguish good from evil. Therefore let us leave the elementary doctrines of Christ and go on to TELEIOTETA (maturity/perfection)..."

WITH ALL THE COUNTERFEIT PARAMETERS OF SPIRITUAL GROWTH we looked at in the last chapter so prominent in the tradition and teaching of the church, what then are the *true* indicators of maturity? How does real and effective fruit-bearing growth take place? What does successfully develop and nurture the wisdom and humility of character that Jesus and Paul pointed to as exemplifying the life of faith?

Most Christian believers who enter their spiritual schooling in a church environment are soon confronted with the imperative of what is called spiritual growth.

It is not a mere option. The writer of *Hebrews* urges his listeners to go on from the elementary doctrines of belief to TELEIOTES (τελειοτης)—translated usually as "maturity" but more accurately *perfection*.

It is a high thing to require of Christians. Good heavens, we're only human...what does he expect anyway!

The writer of Hebrews echoes Jesus' own words: *Therefore, be perfect as your heavenly Father is perfect.*

Perfection! Who can ever measure up to *that*?

Yet there are both passages in black and white and, as the saying goes, we have to deal with it.

DIFFERING PARAMETERS OF GROWTH

The emphasis on spiritual *growth*, while perhaps more strongly emphasized in evangelicalism, is a uniform requirement of the Christian faith, as Hebrews 6:1 attests. All segments of Christendom, though unique in specifics, share this common perspective that the Christian life is a *progressive* one: Belief leads to salvation, which leads to baptism, which leads to church involvement, and so on, after which *many* diverse elements of spirituality are given differing weight and priority value by various denominations and churches.

From the very beginning of my own active walk with God at eighteen or nineteen, I was confronted with this emphasis. A Campus Crusade For Christ seminar drummed into us the fundamentals of "How to grow spiritually" as a post-salvationary component of the famous Four Spiritual Laws. One of my most underlined books of those days was the Miles Stanford classic *Principles of Spiritual Growth.* I also devoured Francis Schaeffer's *True Spirituality,* Watchman Nee's *The Spiritual Man,* and of course Lewis's *Mere Christianity* and many other books with common themes related to growth.

Most serious Christians develop their own individual parameters to define and measure it, and their own guidelines to indicate how growth occurs into "maturity." Many of these, as we saw in the previous chapter, are intellectual and experiential in nature, originating out of two centers of human uniqueness, the mind and the heart.

GROWTH—ESSENTIAL TO SPIRITUALITY

The emphasis on growth is a correct and proper priority for Christians. Indeed, a careful study of the New Testament illuminates the fact that growth toward spiritual maturity *may* actually be more important than salvation itself. This is not a point that would be profitable to pursue in detail. When talking about *fundamentals* little advantage is to be gained by attempting to assess the relative value of one essential over another. *Both* salvation *and* growth are essential. The two are so intrinsically intertwined that, perhaps with the exception of the deathbed conversion, neither salvation nor growth can exist without the other.

Both Jesus and Paul spoke at great length about the process of spiritual *development.* Jesus' foundational teaching, upon which he said "all the parables" were based, was the parable of the sower— growth from seed into mature fruit-bearing plant—a teaching bolstered by the related "growth" parables of the mustard seed, the yeast that makes dough expand, and the vigilant farmer whose grain "grows night and day."

The gospels and the letters of Paul are full from beginning to end with commands and adjurations to *grow,* to *develop,* to *mature* as spiritual beings. Indeed, such commands are far more numerous than commands urging salvation.

The very world around us—a gigantic parable of life—shouts *growth* from every blade of grass to the majestic redwood. If we are not conscious of growth everywhere and in everything, we're simply not paying attention.

It is fascinating, however, that most *aren't* paying attention to this principle in the area of growth that matters most—increasing maturity within themselves.

PEOPLE DON'T CHANGE

It is a remarkable fact that people don't usually change. A teenager with a temper becomes a forty year old with a temper. A critical newlywed becomes a critical retiree. A low self-image at fifteen becomes a low self-image at fifty. A selfish thirty year old becomes a selfish sixty year old.

Wonderfully, this is *not* a universal truth. Many people *do* slowly through life conquer their "besetting sins" and weaknesses. Surely true victory over human weakness takes place within Jesus Christ's church more than anywhere else precisely because of the transforming power of the new life that the Holy Spirit makes possible.

Taking mankind as a whole, however, even taking Christendom as a whole, such transformation occurs in a relatively small percentage of individuals. For most, weaknesses cling like Saran Wrap around the soul. We tend to adapt as we age to our individual weaknesses, learning to mask anger, criticism, envy, pride, and self-centeredness *without* attacking such defects of character root and branch, and taking steps to get rid of them permanently. The temper of the forty year old won't be so explosive and socially destructive as that of the teenager. But the root response, the innate character flaw, may be as deeply rooted as ever.

We don't get rid of them, we just learn to hide them.

Personality and temperament, of course, are always with us. God made each of us with temperamental uniquenessses that remain all our lives. These combine to define who we *are*. A morning person will always be a morning person. An extrovert will remain an extrovert. A shy person will always tend toward soft spokenness.

These traits, and hundreds like them, are unique to temperament. Some enrich our lives and we rejoice for them. Others make life more difficult and we must learn to cope with them and adapt to the negative aspects inherent in them. It is *hard*, for example, to be a shy person. (Take it from one who knows!) This does not make shyness a negative personality trait, still less a sin. Yet it is something which has elements that must to a degree be overcome in order to function effectively in a world generally geared for a majority which is more outgoing.

We all are blessed with a multitude of such inborn traits and temperamental tendencies for which we owe God thanks. Positive traits are nothing to feel proud of—they are gifts from God to humbly and thankfully acknowledge. Negative personality traits are not sins—they are likewise gifts from God intended for our development as individuals of character.

Along with these, sin operates within us from the moment we are born. It attacks inborn weaknesses *and* strengths, and subtly urges selfishness and pride and anger and jealousy and envy upon us. As very early we begin yielding to sin's whispers, other character traits become part of us too that are neither inborn nor inevitable, but that we *choose* to allow to take hold within us. We might simply call these habits. As we grow and continue to give in to selfish impulses, they become ingrained attitudes and behavior.

In the matter of these sin-traits rather than personality-traits, we *do* have a choice. It is different than being shy or extroverted. These hidden weaknesses of character *can* be corrected and changed.

Yet the fact is, even in these areas where fundamental change *is* possible...we generally don't change. The roots of our cherished sin-yieldings go deep. We are not eager to suffer the pain of yanking them out.

Furthermore, most of us resent the challenge toward improvement or betterment. We resent it because intrinsic to such challenge is the obvious implication—if I am in *need* of improvement, that indicates a *lack* or weakness or insufficiency of character in how things stand at present. That is not an admission we want to make. We don't spend much time in front of the mirror of character. "Conviction of sin" used to be one of the reasons why people came to Christ or joined the church. The words are still used, of course, especially at altar call time. But they have mostly become an anachronism from an earlier era. Not many people in our own day have the faintest sense of what it means to be "convicted of sin." We live in an age of self-esteem, of *I'm-okay-you're-okay*, of self-expression and self-confidence. For generations we've been taught to feel pretty good about ourselves. Church has become an increasingly social institution rather than a training facility whose purpose is the hard work of rooting sin out of the intrinsically sinful human heart.

Salvation itself doesn't alter this equation as much as one might think. Salvation tends toward external modification of belief, lifestyle, viewpoint, and opinion more than it addresses internal changes of character. Not only do our personality-traits remain with us, most of our sin-traits also come along for the ride. Perhaps they put on more respectable clothes after a salvation experience or new commitment to Christ or the church. But they're still there, deep down, and not about to give up what has so long been a comfortable home.

And thus...mostly people remain who they are and have always been. Surface spirituality doesn't change that fact. It is supposed to change it. It is *intended* to change it. But the reality is...it usually doesn't.

The reason is simple: Most people are pretty content. They like themselves the way they are. This includes Christians as well as non-Christians. People *can* change. But most don't want to. We don't live in an era in which people think of themselves, in the words of John Bunyan of old, as the "chief of sinners."

P.G. Wodehouse's flagship character Bertie Wooster lives in mortal dread of marriage because of his aversion to what he calls being "molded" by the female of the species. Though couched in the guise of humor, Bertie's reflections sum up the attitude of most men and women.

You know how it is with these earnest, brainy beazels of what is called strong character, Wodehouse says through Bertie's voice. *They can't let the male soul alone. They want to get behind it and start shoving. Scarcely have they shaken the rice from their hair in the car driving off for the honeymoon than they pull up their socks and begin moulding the partner of joys and sorrows, and if there is one thing that gives me the pip, it is being moulded...I like B. Wooster the way he is. Lay off him, I say. Don't try to change him, or you may lose the flavour.*

Whether husbands and wives should engage in the business of molding one another is a question best left for others. But most of us don't like the idea of God molding us either.

Yet such is the essence of what life is about—being molded, shaped, matured, and perfected by God.

We come into life as self-indulgent creatures. The primary business of life is to *grow* into God's selfless sons and daughters.

Thus, in many ways, our churches and their programs are at odds with what is *God's* primary purpose in the world. He is trying to accomplish one thing (Hebrews 6:1). They are busily engaged doing all sorts of *other* things.

No wonder we don't have a keen understanding of what this

thing called τελειοτης even is.

If we want a preliminary perspective on what comprises growth, we might describe it as the process of rooting out and conquering a lifetime of self-induced and self-perpetuated sin-traits, in order that our inborn God-given temperamental-traits might shine out as they were intended, to make us unique, fruitful, productive, victorious children of God.

I find this fact remarkable, however, that I am well beyond sixty with many of the same flaws and weaknesses of character that I had at twenty. In some ways it is even worse now because I am so much more keenly aware of them.

Why don't we change? Why have I not progressed as much during the past forty years as I wish I had? Why is my flesh still so dogged and persistent in the same areas that plagued me at twenty?

When I say that people don't change, it's not because they *can't*, it's because they don't want to. But we *can*.

Judy and I witnessed one of the most remarkable transformations we have ever seen in Judy's own father in the last years of his life. It was a remarkable testimony to the fact that change *is* possible, if we want it bad enough. A generally moody man with an occasional temper that caused Judy and her sister to walk on eggshells in their younger years, at some point in his 70s after his retirement, their father began watching Mr. Rogers on television. An odd thing, perhaps, but wonderful in its effect. Gradually his spirit sweetened. Expressions of affection became more frequent. The two daughters began hearing comments from their father such as, *I like you...I accept you*, during their phone calls home. I saw many letters and cards in this increasingly tender father's hand to my wife which ended with the words, *I love you!*

My father-in-law spent the last fifteen years of his life working hard to allow Christlikeness to emerge from within him, to be accepting and kind, to put others first, to speak with grace and generosity and love. It is often said that we become either sour or sweet in old age. Judy's father became sweeter than any of us had ever known him to be. Even in his final hours of life he was doing what little remained in his power to bring a smile to the faces of those around him. It is an example I will never forget.

Yet sadly such effort is rare.

Why do Christians carry the same traits, habits, and shadowy corners of pride, self-centeredness, and anger through life—hidden and masked though they may be—just like everyone else? Why do so few of the human species "go on to maturity" in the way we noticed happening in the life of Judy's father to produce "thirty, sixty, and hundredfold fruit"?

Besides the innate self-centeredness of the fleshly human creature, one significant factor in the glaring lack of fulfillment of Hebrews 6:1 must surely be much wrong teaching in the church through the years of just what spiritual maturity actually is.

DIVISIONS OF HUMAN EXPRESSION

The human constitution has been divided by philosophers and theologians alike into body, soul, and spirit. The Bible also makes a distinction between the heart, soul, mind, and strength. Much Christian theology and secular psychology for two thousand years (and the Greek philosophers were busy about it long before the Christian era) has been an attempt to probe and understand the human psyche and the human condition in light of these distinctions.

Our purpose here is not to attempt to unravel the interrelated functions of human distinctiveness. It is important, however, to establish the existence of distinct regions of uniqueness within us as men and women where we behave differently. Understanding these, even in a rudimentary way, helps us clarify both why counterfeit indicators of maturity tend to ensnare us, and also gives us insight into the *true* mechanism of the growth process.

From the *mind* or brain proceed thought, logic, reason, learning, the ability to draw conclusions and think abstractly. Out of what we metaphorically call the *heart* proceed feelings, emotions, joy, sorrow, empathy, anger, frustration, happiness, jealousy, and so on.

In the parlance of today they are described as right and left brain functions: the *cognitive* and the *emotive*—the intellectual center where we *think*, the emotional center where we *feel*.

Obviously cause and effect exists between the two. Ideas cause joy. Thought produces emotion, and emotion produces thought. Anger and jealousy, as felt *emotions*, can be caused by *intellectual* conclusions we have drawn about what happens to us.

These two realms, however, do not thoroughly explain our responses. Life does not function merely out of the brain or the heart, but from what we *do* with our thoughts and feelings.

Thus a *third* region of personhood is in its own way far more important than these two. It is a region of power and purpose, strength and dynamism.

It is here where the underlying message of discipleship in the gospels begins to shine forth with radiance and clarity.

THE REALM OF WILL

If one examines the words of Jesus, one finds few commands addressed either to the *mind* or the *heart* in matters of discipleship. Instead Jesus nearly always addresses the *will*.

One can obey only by *choosing* to obey, by *choosing* God's Will over one's own.

The will, that realm of volition within the human consciousness, is the region of obedience. The will is the only place where obedience can take place. It is only in the *will* where the obedience commanded by Jesus can be given.

Thus, it is to the "will" we must look to discover the answer to the question how spiritual growth takes place.

There is no physical place we readily identify with the will like we do the mind and heart. it has no hemisphere of the brain where its work is done. It is elusive and invisible. Perhaps it is the point where right and left sides of the brain join, for surely both cognitive and emotive come together when volition engages to make what we call a "choice" or a "decision."

But the will chooses on its own. The will is its own master.

In that sense, the *will* is supreme among the three. It may use *information* from the mind and *feelings* from the heart (*Logic* tells me such and such...I *think* this is a good idea...I *feel* such and such...my *emotions* urge me in this direction.) But the will is free to make its own decision.

We cannot always control thought or emotion. Both come to us unbidden. They flee just when we want them most—thoughts vanish, emotions fade.

But the *will* is at our control. We can *always* choose.

Mind and heart subserve. The will rules.

It is no wonder, then, that Jesus always addresses the will as the seat and origin of spiritual growth, power, and wisdom. The brain can fill itself with spiritual information. Emotions may be able to keep some personalities operating on full octane.

The *will* is the only realm within our beings capable of transforming character.

Therefore Jesus speaks to the will: *If any man would be my disciple, let him deny himself, take up his cross, and follow me.*

τελειοτης: THE TRUE STANDARD—OBEDIENCE

What, therefore, produces growth within a child of God into the maturity of Christlikeness?

The answer is not really so difficult to find. To do so we must return to the words of the Master.

Jesus said, "If any man would be my disciple, let him deny himself...and follow me...If you love me you will obey my commands."

Obey my commands.

Obedience to his commands is the *only* standard Jesus raises for what *Follow Me* means.

To repeat: Jesus raises but one standard—*obedience.*

Not only is it the only standard of growth and maturity, it is the only standard by which being a *Christian*, a "follower of Christ," is determined. A Christian is one who *obeys*—that is, "follows"— Christ.

MacDonald is as clear as his Master:

It is the one terrible heresy of the church that it has always been presenting something else than obedience as faith in Christ. [37]

The question then becomes: *How* does obedience to the commands of Jesus produce growth into spiritual maturity in a way none of these other aspects of spirituality are able to?

If obedience is the only standard, how does it work?

By doing as Jesus did, and obeying what he taught, we conform ourselves to him. It is a simple matter of transforming habit patterns by practice. Grace and knowledge don't change habit patterns. Practice does. We strengthen the character-muscles of obedience *by* obedience.

Obviously, then, we have to read our New Testaments to find out what the commands are, to familiarize ourselves with what Jesus told us to do.

Then we do it. After years of such obedience...maturity is the result.

GO AND SIN NO MORE

How often in his encounters with people does Jesus sidestep every potential counterfeit indicator of spirituality with a probing command addressed directly to the will.

What could be more pointed than: *Go and sin no more.*

No excuses. No pampering the poor victim with justifications. No church program. No doctrine. No requirement of orthodoxy. No engendering a real sense of righteousness within a frame of relational holiness. No passive grace.

Sin no more. *Choose* to sin no more.

Jesus' commands are direct, practical, down-to-earth, and grow out of the seat of choice within the human constitution: *The will.* They are not commands only to be *thought* about. They are not commands merely to be *felt*. They are commands to be *done*.

> *Commit no sexual sins.*
> *Be at peace with others.*
> *Do good to your adversaries.*
> *Pray for those who mistreat you.*
> *Give more than you are asked for.*
> *Be kind.*
> *Don't judge.*
> *Say what you mean.*
> *Avoid outward spirituality.*
> *Settle disputes promptly.*
> *Forgive.*
> *Practice my words.*
> *Love one another.*
> *Care for those in need.*

Unbelievably direct, personal, and practical. And always...the *will*. And from George MacDonald:

> *The highest creation of God in man is his will...It was not for our understanding, but our will, that Christ came...In choosing and obeying the truth, a man becomes the true son...Man is not lord of his memory or his intellect. But the man is lord of his will, his action...The highest in man is neither his intellect nor his imagination nor his reason. All are inferior to his will...By actively willing the will of God, a man takes the share offered him in his own making, his own becoming. (Selections from various works)*

GROWTH AND MATURITY

At this point we can put all this together to draw some important conclusions about "growth" into spiritual maturity.

In its briefest form, maturity can be seen as *Making wise choices that fall in with God's intended will and the commands of Jesus*

To live in the Will of God, one must know what that Will is. To expand our perspective further, then, maturity emerges out of the capacity to discern God's Will and then to make wise behavioral decisions and choices of attitude and response that are in accordance with that Will—in other words, *living obediently in God's Will.* True spiritual growth is the lifetime progression toward that end.

Growth, therefore, is *invisible.* Emotions are constantly on display. Intellectual knowledge is easy to demonstrate. Making a *choice* of obedience, however, *away from Self* and *toward Christlikeness,* is a private and holy moment that by definition occurs in a region hidden from all but God's eyes.

Summarized:

Spiritual *growth,* for the Christian, is evidenced by the gradually increasing capacity to discern the true Will of God, and then by the desire and capacity to live in that Will—to choose, behave, and respond in accordance with God's Will, in obedience to the commands, and as demonstrated by the example of Christ.

Spiritual *maturity* thus emerges out of growth into Christlikeness of motive, attitude, response, and obedience to the Father's Will, and will be demonstrated by visible humility, quiet wisdom, and Godly character.

THE DYNAMIC OF GROWTH

How does all this take place? *Why* do obedient choices produce growth?

Because the will is the "muscle" of spirituality. Like any muscle, it must be trained and strengthened. As it is trained, its capability increases to make obedient choices in harmony with God's Will.

Father, what would you have me do...not my will but yours be done are therefore the underlying prayers of growing and mature spirituality.

This is what it means to *choose* to be a son or daughter of the Father by the action of the will. Self denying choices point the will toward Christlikeness. The pressure exerted on the will in a given direction reinforces that directionality. It is simple training and habit formation. The more times we yield to anger, the easier it is for us to yield to anger. The more times we say, *I'm sorry,* the easier it is to say *I'm sorry.*

With moment-by-moment practice of obedience, the *will* becomes increasingly capable of mastering *mind* and *heart,* compelling them to obey what the Master commanded.

Humility, wisdom, and spiritual maturity are the lifetime results.

TOOLS FOR GROWTH

It is time now to remind ourselves of the topic of the previous chapter, and look again at the components of spirituality which we considered there.

Recognizing them previously as potentially counterfeit indicators *of* growth, we are now free to embrace them as wonderful aids *to* growth.

All the elements we discussed earlier are intended to produce spiritual growth toward maturity.

To obey the commands of Jesus obviously requires correct belief about him. *Belief*, then, when it leads to obedience, produces growth.

Study of the Scriptures, when it leads to right choices in line with the Will of God produces growth.

Grace and spiritual *knowledge* are mighty assets to bolster wise choices toward Christlikeness.

All the devotional disciplines turn heart and mind toward the things of God. None in *themselves* produce growth. But when the will is obediently engaged with them, powerful results follow.

The very components of spirituality that can be so misunderstood, therefore, also contain potent reality as tools God is able to use in our lives to grow us into mature sons and daughters. When joined with the will, he imbues them with miraculous power to transform and elevate the human species into oneness with his own Father heart.

Again we see the important progressivity of 2 Peter 1:5-7 at work: For this reason, diligently supplement your faith with virtue, and virtue with knowledge, and knowledge with self-control, and self-control with steadfastness, and steadfastness with *godliness*..."

A Lifetime of Choices Produces Spiritual Maturity

In perhaps what is the single most important contribution of C.S. Lewis's insight to Christian thought, he illuminates in very practical terms the *mechanics* of spiritual growth, how and why it is produced by obedience. Lewis's remarkable passage explains the dynamic of this wonderful and miraculous process:

"*Every time you make a choice you are turning the central part of you, the part of you that chooses, into something a little different from what it was before. And taking your life as a whole, with all your innumerable choices, all your life long you are slowly turning this central thing...into a creature that is in harmony with God, and with other creatures, and with itself, or else into one that is in a state of war...with God, and with its fellow-creatures, and with itself...*

"*That explains what always used to puzzle me about Christian writers; they seem to be so very strict at one moment and so very free and easy at another. They talk about mere sins of thought as if they were immensely important: and then they talk about the most frightful murders and treacheries as if you had only got to repent and all would be forgiven. But I have come to see that they are right. What they are always thinking of is the mark which the action leaves on that tiny central self which no one sees in this life but which each of us will have to endure—or enjoy—for ever...The bigness or smallness of the thing, seen from the outside, is not what really matters...*

"*Good and evil both increase at compound interest. That is why the little decisions you and I make every day are of such infinite importance. The smallest good act today is the capture of a strategic point from which, a few months later, you may be able to go on to victories you never dreamed of. An apparent trivial indulgence in lust or anger today is the loss of a ridge or railway line or bridgehead from which the enemy may launch an attack otherwise impossible.*" [38]

As we often observe, the germ of Lewis's insight into the progressivity of growth is found in his predecessor and mentor George MacDonald, who writes:

"*He regards men not as they are merely, but as they shall be; not as they shall be merely, but as they are now growing...toward that image after which he made them that they might grow to it. Therefore a thousand stages, each in itself all but valueless, are of inestimable worth as the necessary and connected gradations of an infinite progress. A condition which, of declension, would indicate a devil, may of growth indicate a saint.*" [39]

"*A man may sink by such slow degrees that, long after he is a devil, he may go on being a good churchman...and thinking himself a good Christian. Continuously repeated sin against the poorest consciousness of evil must have a dread rousing.*" [40]

"*Margaret's...was a true history. Even in the midst of monotonous circumstances, it described individual growth and the changes of inner progress. Where there is no change, there can be no history. And since all change is either growth or decay, all history must describe either progress or retrogression.*" [41]

Part 5

God's Eternal Symphony

Maturity as a Christian is not defined by superficial beliefs or practices, but by apprehending and living by God's highest truths—
learning to hear the music of his eternal purposes.

Key Scriptural Concepts:

Confirmation, Logos

SEVENTEEN

BOLD THINKING APPLIED TO SCRIPTURE

Four Confirming Fences To Validate Accuracy, Prevent Error, and Lead To Higher Truth

> "...in the defense and βεβαιωσει (confirmation) of the gospel."
> —Philippians 1:7

βεβαιωσις: BEBAIOSIS—*Confirmation*

BEBAIOSIS indicates an authoritative establishment of validity. In secular Papyri from the ancient world it is found frequently to signify the final settlement of a business transaction. Its technical meaning is to establish, make firm, secure, hold fast, keep truth, guarantee.

The origin of the word comes from BAINO, meaning *fit to tread on*, in other words *having a firm foundation*. From this beginning derive the associated images of reliability, certainty, validity, strength. The connection to *legal validation* remains always present, and that truth is validated *as* truth because of the confirmations associated with it. Then follows the sense of witnesses validating such truth, which is the sense in which we will explore the meaning in this chapter.

I AM SUFFICIENTLY A TRADITIONALIST, believing rigorously in the "inspiration" of Scripture, to say that I believe all truth can be *found*, and must be *founded in*, God's written revelation. Secularists scoff at such a statement because they have not made the attempt to discover the Bible's High Truths, only to judge it by low (and often wrong) misinterpretations. However, only those who dedicate themselves to seek for Truth like a treasure buried in a field will find what the Bible truly has to offer mankind.

Though all truth may be founded upon the Bible, it is not a book that can be read and understood in a vacuum. How often have I heard certain Christians tell me with pride that they read "nothing but the Word of God," supposing such a posture to indicate heightened spirituality.

GETTING AT SCRIPTURE'S HIGH TRUTH

To interpret the Bible's truth correctly, we need outside help. Though the Bible may contain the elements of all truth, it is not sufficient in itself always to reveal the totality of that truth. When we embark on the quest to read the Bible boldly, guided by the Holy Spirit rather than doctrine, one of the insights that follows is that the Holy Spirit uses additional means (outside help) to reveal truth. In that sense, the phrase "guided by the Holy Spirit," if we mean *only* by the Holy Spirit, is a misnomer. To get to truth, the Spirit of God uses *many* factors.

The "outside help" that clarifies and focuses the Bible's Truth is not necessarily extra Scriptural at all. The outside helps, as I call them, are woven throughout Scripture as invisible warp and woof threads holding the narrative and teaching together. But the non-cliché phraseology may cause some to struggle at first to see the scripturality behind the confirming factors we will examine. In fact they are the tools the Holy Spirit himself uses to reveal truth to our brains and hearts.

The Word of God is the mighty bedrock of truth. Without it we would know very little about God and his purposes for his creation, and we would know nothing about Jesus. But the fruit yielded by the biblical soil is extremely variable. Thus, the interpretation of what the words of the Bible mean must be subjected to other confirming and validating criteria.

There is a more important reason why we need outside help to assist us to get at the Bible's high Truth. Much of the Bible concerns itself with "specifics." We need to translate those specifics up to the high plateau of "general" Truth. The *words* of specific passages and one-dimensional *applications* often do not in and of themselves apprehend high Truth as God means us to understand it. We can talk in ponderous tones about "nothing but the Word of God." But then what do we do where the Bible is unclear, contradicts itself, or when a non-literal or symbolic interpretation is required?

If an elder is to be "the husband of one wife," what does that mean? One wife *at a time*...or one wife *throughout all a man's earthly days*? Does 1 Tim. 3:2 preclude a divorced man from church leadership? Does it preclude women from church leadership...or single men? Knowing the Greek inside out does not resolve it, for Greek scholars do not all agree on controversial passages. Paul's words will be interpreted in whatever way a given reader desires.

Unbelievably, Judy and I know an outspoken Christian man who interprets 1 Tim. 3:2 as *of <u>at least</u> one wife,* saying that the original Greek supports polygamy. Well might the man interpret it thus—he has two wives! What an example of how Christians twist God's words to suit themselves, even while maintaining great piety about "standing on the rock of Scripture."

The Bible is inspired, but it is not always clear, not always literal, *and there are always higher meanings.*

THE FOUR FENCES

Four factors are enormously helpful in illuminating scriptural truth.

- —DUTY
- —THE CHARACTER OF GOD
- —THE UNIVERSE
- —COMMON SENSE.

These four factors imbue Scripture's Truth with harmony and consistency. They act as confirming gauges to clarify its ambiguities and prevent interpretation from running wild without restraint. Interpretation of Truth needs boundaries. Truth, as Lewis said of Aslan, is no tame beast. Neither is truth static. Its interpretations extend in many directions. We need standards by which to weigh the veracity of those interpretations. Taken together, these factors operate in a wonderful symphony of consistency.

They can be viewed as four confirming fences surrounding the field of Truth which we enter through the doorway of the Bible. The fences help us interpret the principles of Scripture correctly as we seek God's high eternal Truth. All four fences must be in good repair, otherwise interpretations will drift into error, falsehood, or into the fenceless relativism of modernism which says, "Hey, truth is anything you want it to be...everyone draws his or her own fences, and where you draw them doesn't matter because ultimately absolute Truth doesn't exist anyway."

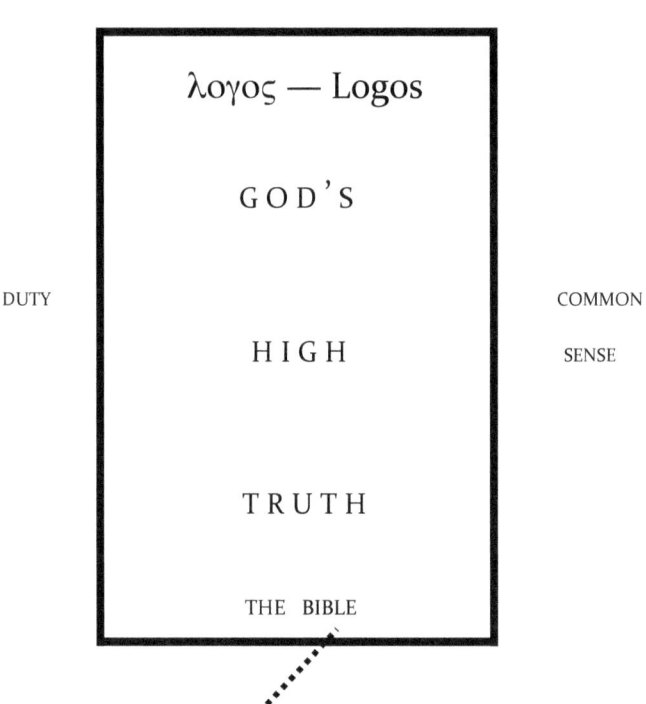

When I call the field of truth in this diagram the Logos, I do not mean merely the Word of God as the specific words of the Bible, but the complete λογος, the *Logos*, the full scope of what God *means* in the Bible—a difference which may be greater than many realize. The Bible itself is merely the gate *into* the field. The fences put the High Logos Truth of the Bible into broader perspective, elevating the Bible's specifics up to the high level of the *Logos* intended by the Father.

To confirm any proposed interpretation of Scripture, therefore, we must ask:

—*Does the Bible say it in both general and specific?*

If so, then the four fences of confirmation come into play to help us accurately interpret the Bible's truth:

—*Does the character of God substantiate it?*

—*Is it reflected with consistency in the world?*

—*Is some action or duty or obedience inherent?*

—*Does it make sense?*

When the Bible seems to indicate a meaning that *violates* any of these five (including contradicting itself), we must prosecute our inquiry further.

For example, we have learned that the Christian polygamist I mentioned, while married, had an affair. When the young woman became pregnant, he then took her for a *second* wife. In other words, his disobedience to a scriptural command forbidding adultery led to his polygamist interpretation of 1 Tim. 3:2. The fence of *duty* and *obedience* in his life is clearly in shambles. Thus his interpretation cannot be relied upon. In disobeying the one command, and then trying to justify it, he was led into error in his reading of Scripture. The fences do not *confirm* his interpretation.

The fences of confirmation have helped us toward greater understanding of this erroneous interpretation.

TRUTH AND MEANINGLESSNESS—AN EXAMPLE

Those who put the Bible's perfection, inerrancy, and literality on a pedestal don't realize how much untruth can actually be supported from statements made in the Bible when one attempts to read it in a one-dimensional vacuum.

Is the Bible "true"? Is *everything* in the Bible true?

Consider Ecclesiastes 1:2, in which Solomon writes: *Everything is meaningless.*

There it sits on the page of the Bible in front of us—a statement that is patently *un*true. Though these words were written by the wisest man in the world, it is a false statement. Even the relativism of modernism, therefore, has scriptural support straight from Solomon's mouth.

Here is an instance where interpretiveness rather than a literal reading is required. Now it will be the evangelical, along with everyone except the most confirmed nihilist, who will explain away the literal words on the page. If it is not interpreted with latitude, Solomon's words would render the whole Bible pointless, and existentialism the highest truth (by proclaiming the absence of truth) in the universe.

But there is not really such a great mystery here. The fence of *common sense* places Solomon's words into perspective. We inherently understand the latitude we must bring into our reading of the passage.

Moreover, meaninglessness violates everything we know about the *character of God*. Solomon's words are not consistent with who God is. With God everything has *tremendous* meaning! On every page of the Scriptures we see God's efficiency. Nothing is wasted. Everything from God's hand has multiple impact and purpose. Everything he does is creative and productive and alive with eternal usefulness and significance. There is no idle time, no idle words, no idle parts of his creation.

Likewise, Solomon's words violate *duty*. If everything is meaningless, what is the point of obedience? Throughout the book of Proverbs, Solomon himself stressed over and over the lifelong benefit of diligence and duty. *Everything is meaningless* violates his own teaching.

Furthermore, the statement violates the *universe*, where unmeaning and chaos are the last terms by which any thinking scientist would describe a created world that is wonderfully ruled by order and harmony, from the concert of the planets to the organization of the cell.

A quick and cursory examination of the passage reveals that the *literal* words on the page violate all four fences. The literal words are *not* confirmed as they stand.

Therefore, we must look deeper into Ecclesiastes 1:2. From the incompatibility of Solomon's words to the four guidelines, we do not conclude that the Bible is untrue, only that we haven't yet arrived at the full meaning God intends in the book of *Ecclesiastes*.

The fences don't necessarily make meaning clear. They only alert us to potential inaccuracies in our perspective. Not certain inaccuracies...*potential* ones. Not inaccuracies in the Word of God...but in *our perspective*, in our lack of full understanding or knowledge.

FIRST FENCE OF βεβαιωσις:
DUTY

Of the four fences, duty may be the most difficult for the modern mind to understand, especially alongside what might sound more familiar to evangelical ears such as a term like "obedience," which represents a key element of duty though not the totality of it.

Duty is a complex word with many shades of meaning. In brief its essence parallels its sound—*do*. Duty involves *doing* something simply because we're supposed to, not necessarily because we want to or feel like it.

A lengthier definition might include: *That which a person is bound, morally or legally to do; the obligation to follow a certain line of conduct; obedience and submission to something or someone greater; what is required; responsibility, the binding force of what is right.*

Duty is doing one's job, so to speak, persevering in life's calling, faithfully doing what you ought to do. That is why much of what duty embodies is not necessarily fun. In duty we find the tremendous word *ought* raised to high stature in the economy of God.

I love William Barclay's self portrait. He says, "I can and do work...I know I have a second class mind, but I can sit down and work. I don't make the slightest claim to inspiration in preaching or writing. I only claim to have gone to work as any working man must go." [42]

His statement to my mind embodies duty and shows what mighty use God can make of it. Obviously the application is clear. We are duty bound as Christians to behave in certain ways, to do certain things, to order our lives according to certain guidelines. Our responsibility is to do what God puts before us. Much of what is put before us is not necessarily pleasant. It is simply our duty. Thus it is our calling in God to fulfill it...simply because we *ought* to.

The entire Bible points toward practical outworking of faith. We've got to *do* faith, not merely *think* faith, *act* out faith practically, not just *talk* out faith. *James* and *Romans* always function hand in hand. Faith *and* works.

By identifying duty as one of the four fences that confirm Truth, the point isn't that every passage of Scripture contains a clear command to a specific action. The Scriptures don't work like that. One-dimensional interpretations always lead to legalism.

However, we must bring to bear on our attempt to understand Scripture the realization that all God's truth, and all accurate interpretations, will—sometimes in subtle ways—inherently *tend toward duty*. Again, all right reading of scriptural truth will point in some way toward duty. If an interpretation does not confirm duty, we are reading its meaning incorrectly.

Everything is meaningless, if true, far from tending toward duty, would only *discourage* duty. If everything is meaningless, why do anything? Nothing matters. Lethargy and inaction are the obvious results. Meaninglessness points *away* from duty.

On the other hand, if everything *has* meaning, then what we *do* becomes of tremendous significance. Duty is intact, the fence secure.

Correct reading of Scripture always has this result—encouraging me to *do* things well, to obey, to do my *duty*, because such is important to God.

Because the fence of duty is violated by the words, "Everything is meaningless," does that mean we throw out Solomon's words and ignore them altogether?

By no means. The apparent violation of the fences means we must seek deeper understanding beyond what the words *seem* to say. The specifics must point to some higher general truth of the Father's *Logos* as yet unperceived. The violation of the fences forces us to probe deeper. We must move from low things to high things. We must look to High Logos Truth to rightly imbue this passage with God's intent.

When we do, we see that Solomon, like the polygamist, had so shattered his own fence of duty, taking 800 wives and disobeying God's commands at so many points, that his whole perspective of truth disintegrated. By his disobedience, he was no longer able to see truth correctly, or even judge between truth and falsehood. Out of that upside-down perspective emerged his statement, "Everything is meaningless," as a warning of the ultimate result when we do not live by God's principles.

The wisest man in the world lost his wisdom in disobedience. Solomon himself had become the fool of his own proverbs.

The higher truth, the *Logos* that God means in the book of *Ecclesiastes* now comes into view: *Live in obedience to God's commands or foolishness, ruin, and meaningless will result.*

A CONTROVERSIAL EXAMPLE

Let us consider 1 Thessalonians 4:17, where the four fences of confirmation also force us to probe beyond surface explanations.

The words are, "We who are still alive and are left will be caught up together with them in the clouds to meet the Lord in the air."

What the literal words *seem* to mean (at least many have told us they mean) is that at the second coming believers alive on the earth will follow believers who have already died, and will fly into the sky, to meet Jesus as he descends from a literal heaven located in the sky above this physical earth. Driverless cars careening off freeways and pilotless planes crashing to earth are all part of the literalist scenario.

But are we not forced to see in this common interpretation a tendency *away* from order, obedience, and duty. If suddenly all Christians will be taken out of this world in a literal twinkling of an eye, what motivation is there to do our duty in the things we have been given to do? If I may be snatched away tomorrow without warning...what does duty matter?

More motivation may exist to share our faith, perhaps. But in the way of personal responsibility toward the small things of life—planning ahead, and a hundred such practical injunctions from the book of *Proverbs*, the common evangelical interpretation tends to discourage attentiveness. Throughout history, some of the *least* responsible citizens of every age have been those who have believed so strongly in an impending second coming that they disengage from society because of it. So immediately we encounter a serious difficulty in attempting to confirm the literal interpretation. Literality lands us in a morass of inconsistencies. If any interpretation of any doctrine is true, including the second coming, it should tend toward *greater* diligence and duty in our daily tasks and responsibilities.

It is not that we are thus free to discard such a passage. It is at this point that we must climb higher, and try to boldly listen for what the High Logos has to reveal. The four fences of confirmation prompt us to carefully and thoughtfully examine the implications of the literal words, in order to probe the *high* meanings God intends. Only so can we translate those specifics up into the realm of *Logos*, God's high Truth. To my mind, many common interpretations of the end times do not do so. They are specifics-based, not *Logos*-based. They violate the fences.

The high meaning of 1 Thess. 4:17 is not something we need attempt to resolve at this time. We do not hold the literal interpretation up to bold thinking scrutiny in order to set some other interpretation in its place. This is one of many mysteries in God's Word whose fullness we do not yet comprehend. But I believe one day that the high *Logos* of this passage *will* be revealed, and may be much different than that which presently fills many books on the subject.

SECOND FENCE OF βεβαιωσις:
THE CHARACTER OF GOD—TRUTH OF THE HIGHEST ORDER

That Scripture must conform to the character of God is so obvious it hardly needs be said. If the Bible is *God's* revelation, certainly it must conform to the character and nature of who *God* is and how he works. It is easy to lose sight of this obvious truth, however. Over the years much of theology *has* lost sight of it.

A great deal within theologic orthodoxy stems from just this dichotomy, originating out of the teachings of men of lower character than that of God himself, the Being Jesus addressed as his *Abba*.

God's so-called *wrath* is one such example, proceeding out of the minds of certain ancient church fathers and later reformers and their response to their spiritual adversaries more than out of the nature of the Father of Jesus. The Old Testament emerged out of a primitive time and a tribal culture. Many of its writings inevitably use warlike imagery as a result. Jesus made clear that the old has become new, and that he came to reveal the Father as one in all ways with himself. Yet many Christian theologians through the centuries have not adequately made that transition in their portrayal of God's Fatherhood.

God is holy, to be sure, and the Bible clearly speaks of his wrath. But our interpretations of what is implied are so horrendously at odds with what the character of Jesus' Father *must* be, that we have to probe deeper to discover what is really meant. We have to translate literality and one-dimensional interpretations up onto the higher plane of the *Abba-Logos*.

Our interpretations must scale those heights.

The mountain peaks of eternity beckon!

HOW GOD WORKS

Not only in our reading of the Bible must we remain scrupulously attentive to who God is, we must with equal wisdom look to the way God works. It is not that God always works in exactly the same way. But neither is the outworking of his plan random. He operates in a generally consistent manner to accomplish his will. Aberrations in his general M.O. are just that—unusual and uncommon.

When the unusual occurs, we rejoice. But we can never forget that it is the exception. We cannot *expect* God to act by exception. As we read Scripture, then, we need to read with the expectation of God's *usual* method.

One of the ways in which God normally works is to carry out his plans *slowly*, over a long time. With God, the *instantaneous* is an exception.

Thus we must never *expect* God to act instantaneously. Our interpretations should always start from the foundation point of a slow and *non*-instantaneous reading of passages that point to God's intent. When we read in Romans 5:4 that "endurance produces character," we need to read it *expecting* this process to be a long and slow one, and not expecting God to infuse character into us overnight.

Mankind needed redeeming while Adam and Eve walked the earth. Yet it took God thousands of years to ready the world for the coming of his Son. People died in sin during those thousands of years as God made preparation for redemption. But God is *never* rushed. He did not send his Son to the world until "the fullness of time."

When Jesus came, he spent thirty years in preparation. God worked his divine will through the *slow* processes of human development. In all of what God does through his natural creation, growth is slow.

Of course God *can* work speedily. It is just not his usual way. The fence of God's character dictates that 99% of the things in his plan will be accomplished slowly. We could literally cite hundreds of scriptural examples—Noah's slow preparation for the flood, God's seemingly slow and delayed fulfillment of promises to Abraham and Sarah, the 400 years of Israelite bondage in Egypt while the people prayed and prayed and prayed for deliverance. This highlights one of the reasons why we must be very cautious about praying for instantaneous miracles—whether financial, miracles of healing, or other kinds of instant solutions to life's needs, pains, and anxieties. God's plans and purposes are simply never rushed.

When we subject 1 Thess. 4:17 to the validating scrutiny of how God works (slowly), we discover in the common interpretation an explanation of events involving a very different method (*instantaneous* transformation of believers.) If we are not immediately jarred by this incongruity, then we are not sufficiently aware of the large and consistent themes of Scripture. I do not find myself jarred because I *disbelieve* in the prophetic word of 1 Thess. 4:17 regarding something that will take place in the future, but because I sense something intrinsically at odds with the way God's purposes are usually carried out. The very words "twinkling of an eye" should alert us—if we are reading with a bold thinking mind and a careful eye—to the possibility that we may in this instance be encountering *symbolic* rather than *literal* language.

The bold thinker does not question the common interpretation from doubt or disbelief, but because he or she is being prompted by the Holy Spirit to scale the mountains...and listen to the higher things God may have to say...and pay attention to who God is.

Those of bold thinking faith will find nothing fearsome in such a challenge. It may even be that such doctrinal sacred cows as (for evangelicals) the rapture will be the stumbling block that will separate the bold thinking men and women of Logos Faith from the boys and girls who are satisfied with superficialities.

Those who object and say that we are explaining away Scripture only reveal their own unawareness of the Bible's larger themes, and God's *frequent* use of the symbolic in his Word to convey his High Logos Truth. Why so few evangelicals consider that the words of 1 Thess. 4:17 may be symbolic in the same way as are the words "crucifixion with Christ" and "circumcision of the heart," may remain a mystery for years to come.

Clearly we do not know for certain whether "twinkling of an eye" is symbolic language. It may represent one of those 1% of cases where God will *not* work according to his normal pattern. But we cannot be cavalier in making such an assumption without much prayer and bold thought. God's *normal* method should cause us to wonder if these words imply more than what seems apparent by a literal reading.

God *can* but does not *usually* do things "in the twinkling of an eye." What is the high *Logos* intended here. Truth is present…but what is that truth, and on what level is it to be apprehended?

What is in the *Abba*-heart to accomplish?

THIRD FENCE OF βεβαιωσις:
THE UNIVERSE MUST REFLECT GOD'S TRUTH

Truth must also reflect, not just who God is and how he works, but what he has *made*. Everything that proceeds from God's hand must flow in harmony and consistency.

Such harmony may not always be immediately apparent. But if we dig deep enough, such harmony always exists. As the Jews recall to mind daily, *The Lord our God is* ONE.

In the same way that God normally works slowly, he ordinarily works through the natural laws of his created universe. He is not bound to, but he *usually* does. Nearly every spiritual lesson of the Bible, including most of what Jesus himself taught, comes through the natural outworkings of the physical world.

Miracles are not God's customary mode of getting things done. They serve the purpose of occasionally arresting our attention, but are not intended as everyday occurrences. Those who preach that God wants to work a miracle in your life every day badly misread the Scriptures, the nature of God, and the very purpose of miracles.

God carries out 99.999% of his broad sweeping plan in the lives of men and women through life's normal processes. LIFE itself is a grand miracle. Once set in motion, it continues on. God's plans and purposes are incorporated and drawn up into it, *without* a frequent supplementation of additional miracle. It is only rarely that God choses for "miracle" to interrupt the flow of his ongoing *natural miracle* of life.

So those pietists who ask (as a friend of mine used to do every time I saw him) what miracle God has done for us today are only displaying their own ignorance of God's method. God *doesn't* do miracles in our lives every day. His revelation and the maturing of his sons and daughters is produced through obedience not miracle. The universe functions by Supernaturalism, to be sure, But it is High Logos Supernaturalism, not miraculously giving us parking places because we pray for them.

To continue our look at 1 Thess. 4:17, we need to address the fact that though occasionally God suspends natural law—the sun standing still, a floating ax head, Jesus and Peter walking on water, the healing of diseases and afflictions— *ordinarily* he does not. Sickness usually runs its course. Most people are *not* healed by instant miracle, but by the slow, "natural miracle" of the body's recuperative power, or by the high-Logos miracle of death and transformation into perfect health. Both natural recovery and resurrection into eternal life are miracles, but they occur through the working of *natural* law.

The rapture, as commonly envisioned, necessitates a suspension of natural law. It could no doubt be interestingly debated whether the rapture defies gravity or not. At what point do the bodies of believers become glorified and therefore weightless? But certainly the simultaneous mingling of the earthly and heavenly realms, with visions of cars without drivers crashing into telephone poles, airplanes without pilots... these go against God's *normal* and natural method.

Such images derive from a comic book mentality, but are not consistent with biblical patterns. They have great appeal because they are bizarre. Serious students of the Bible, however, recognize how widely they deviate from consistent high-Logos scriptural patterns and Truth.

It is not that God *cannot* work in this way. If it serves his purposes then God will certainly suspend natural law. The point is only that we are on solid scriptural ground to inquire whether more *Logos* meaning might exist beyond the literal words. We are not seeking hard and fast conclusions, only inquiring whether we are encountering one of those places in the scriptural mountain where the *Logos* meaning God intends lies buried in a rich vein of gold unseen from the surface.

FOURTH FENCE OF βεβαιωσις:
COMMON SENSE, THE IMPORTANT LOST VIRTUE

Why has common sense been lost as a valued component of spiritual maturity? Unbelievably, to occasional evangelical theologians the words, "That doesn't make sense," are welcomed as a badge of honor. On the basis of a misreading of "the cross is foolishness" to the world, and "I will destroy the wisdom of the wise," and other such passages, they demean the very common sense God has given us by which to discern, validate, and confirm truth.

Is it any wonder the world thinks us unthinking, backward, and one-dimensional when the *violation* of common sense has become a *virtue*?

Our minds, hearts, and intellects, however, have been given us by the Creator as tools to assist us in understanding truth.

The Bible is not the only revelation we have been given. We have also been provided "internal" revelation which we must use shrewdly to evaluate truth. The conscience and the intellect are not aspects of our fallen nature as some Calvinists would have it, they are characteristics of our created-in-God's-imageness that he gave us to use in our pursuit of truth.

God gave the conscience to point toward *duty*.

God gave the intellect and the heart to combine—emotions and thoughts together—to produce what I call *divine common sense*.

A brief example will hopefully clarify how we are to use both in our pursuit of truth, though it is far too scripturally complex to pursue in depth.

The prevailing theology says that God is a good God of forgiveness and love, but that he will punish unrepentant sinners for eternity. This dichotomy pits two opposites together and says that God will act in both ways at once. This clear violation of common sense is one of the great stumbling blocks against the Christian faith in the world.

Christians dismiss the difficulty with "God is higher than our ways," Calvinists adding that common sense is a function of depraved man's sinful condition and therefore cannot be trusted.

Without attempting to resolve the dilemma in detail, we merely note that common sense has been given us by God, like the conscience, for the discovery of truth. It is no more depraved than my hand. Sin can corrupt any of God's gifts—my hands, common sense, the conscience, the created world, the love between a man and a woman...sin knows no bounds. But intrinsically those gifts come *from God*. We either spoil them or submit them to his use.

Therefore, as bold thinking sons and daughters of God, praying to have the mind of Christ developed in us, turning over our hearts and intellects to the Holy Spirit—we submit common sense to him too. In all humility and honesty, we then say, "*Infinite love and forgiveness toward all men and women*, operating alongside the *eternal punishment of sinners*, appears to violate common sense." In doing so we are exercising a *reliable God-given indicator* in wondering if something is missing in the commonly given interpretive-equation.

Common sense tells us nothing *for certain*. Common sense is not *itself* truth, it is only a potential confirmer of *Logos* truth.

Having submitted their brains and intellects to the transformation of the Holy Spirit's work, bold thinking Christians rely on common sense to keep them oriented toward truth. When they become aware of defects in the prevailing old-covenant interpretations of God's character, methods, and ultimate purposes, they are not afraid to take their questions to God.

Then they pray:

Thank you, Lord, for illuminating your being and purposes through all the tools of revelation you provide— through my brain, my conscience, the world you have made, and from that in my heart which knows that you must be higher and more loving than men's low theologies. Thank you for pointing me to more...reveal the heart of your Abba Logos to me yet more fully!

It is such scriptural conundrums as these—the rapture, God's wrath, eternal punishment, and many more with which each of us wrestle in our own prayer closets—that bold thinking Christians learn prayerfully and courageously to explore. Though in the end they may come down on different sides of many diverse and complex doctrinal issues, they yet respect one another for the common quest toward High Logos Truth.

LITERAL AND SYMBOLIC OBEDIENCE

To this point we have examined the four fences of confirmation chiefly as urging us beyond *superficial* meanings toward more *spiritual* ones? However, they apply equally in the opposite direction. They may just as well uphold and confirm *literal* interpretations.

When Jesus said, "Do not judge," "Forgive your enemies," and "Do as you would be done by," he meant no more nor no less than exactly what he said. He clearly intended obedience in such cases to be literal. All four fences confirm, in these examples, the necessity of a *literal* obedience. To interpret any of these as "symbolic" and to invest the imperative of forgiveness with some ethereal "higher" meaning would violate the fence of duty just as surely as a literal meaning might in some other instance.

We note again why bold thinking must operate in all directions at once—toward literality and toward high Logos symbolism...as each is confirmed by the four validating fences.

The Bible is no one dimensional document. How can it be—it is the revelation of God himself!

In John 13:15, after washing His disciples' feet, Jesus said, "I have set you an example that you should do as I have done for you."

Does Jesus mean we *literally* are to serve one another, to take the humble position, to wash one another's feet?

Or is Jesus speaking symbolically and figuratively here? Is this a *Circumcise your heart* passage (symbolic), or a *Do as you would be done by* passage (literal)?

What is called for—*symbolic* interpretation or *literal* obedience?

Judging from our response, it must be the former. How many pastors, teachers, and priests have you witnessed on their knees washing the feet of their people? A few, perhaps, but it is not a widespread practice for which Christ's church is generally known.

Jesus said, *You should do as I have done.* But common practice points to the conclusion that most Christians do not take this passage as one where literal obedience is required.

Why do so many insist on a *literal* interpretation of 1 Thess. 4:17, but a *figurative* interpretation of John 13:15?

In actual fact, this passage also reveals the wonderful multi-dimensionality of the Bible—washing one another's feet is a principle that is imbued with *both literal and symbolic* meaning! The more we see the application of *both* meanings together, the greater each becomes on its own.

All Scripture can be subjected to the confirmation of the four fences to get beyond one-dimensional interpretations and to probe more deeply into the rich ore of God's High Truth.

MIRACULOUS SUSPENSION OF GOD'S NORMAL METHOD

God occasionally breaks in from *above* the fences, forcing us up and out into unseen, heavenly dimensions altogether unperceived on the two-dimensional plane.

These breaks into a higher dimensionality of truth are not "exceptions" at all, but only confirmations of truth on the ultimate level of the *Abba-Logos*

Do the incarnation and the resurrection, for instance, violate natural law and common sense?

Of course. The resurrection immediately forces us to examine its stupendous claim more carefully. Our perceptive inquiry must drive us higher toward the *Logos*.

Considered at a higher level, we might ask: Does the resurrection violate *truth*? If a man rose from the dead, as historical evidence verifies, then perhaps something higher is at work. Perhaps to understand it we must escape the bounds of two-dimensional thinking altogether and enter into a higher realm.

The whole purpose of studying scriptural specifics is to drive us to find God's High Truth. God is constantly goading and impelling us higher into the scriptural mountains where his Symphony of eternal purpose is playing. What seems an inconsistency at one level, if you pursue it far enough, drives you ultimately to the far more profound truth that the Man who rose from the dead could be no other than the God who created natural law, death, common sense, and everything else, and who is therefore the only One capable of making them all submit to his purposes!

In apprehending the higher meaning, we have found the *Logos* himself!

The Bible Leads to the Logos of God

"The Bible never deals with impossibilities, never demands of any man at any given moment a righteousness of which at that moment he is incapable; neither does it lay upon any man any other law than that of perfect righteousness. It demands of him righteousness; when he yields that righteousness of which he is capable, content for the moment, it goes on to demand more: the common-sense of the Bible is lovely." [43]

"Sad, indeed, would the whole matter be, if the Bible had told us everything God meant us to believe. But herein is the Bible itself greatly wronged. It nowhere lays claim to be regarded as the Word, the Way, the Truth. The Bible leads us to Jesus, the inexhaustible, the ever unfolding Revelation of God. It is

Christ "in whom are hid all the treasures of wisdom and knowledge," not the Bible, save as leading to him. And why are we told that these treasures are hid in him who is the Revelation of God? Is it that we should despair of finding them and cease to seek them? Are they not hid in him that they may be revealed to us in due time—that is, when we are in need of them? Is not their hiding in him the mediatorial step towards their unfolding in us? Is he not the Truth?—the Truth to men? Is he not the High Priest of his brethren, to answer all the troubled questionings that arise in their dim humanity?....There is more hid in Christ than we shall ever learn, here or there either; but they that begin first to inquire will soonest be gladdened with revelation; and with them he will be best pleased, for the slowness of his disciples troubled him of old...The Son of God is the Teacher of men, giving to them of his Spirit—that Spirit which manifests the deep things of God, being to a man the mind of Christ. The great heresy of the Church of the present day is unbelief in this Spirit. The mass of the Church does not believe that the Spirit has a revelation for every man individually—a revelation as different from the revelation of the Bible, as the food in the moment of passing into living brain and nerve differs from the bread and meat. If we were once filled with the mind of Christ, we should know that the Bible had done its work, was fulfilled, and had for us passed away, that thereby the Word of our God might abide for ever. The one use of the Bible is to make us look at Jesus, that through him we might know his Father and our Father, his God and our God. Till we thus know Him, let us hold the Bible dear as the moon of our darkness, by which we travel towards the east; not dear as the sun whence her light cometh, and towards which we haste, that, walking in the sun himself, we may no more need the mirror that reflected his absent brightness." [44]

EIGHTEEN

TOWARD THE HIGH *ABBA*-LOGOS

Learning to Hear the Symphony of Eternity

"In the beginning was the λόγος (Word), and the λόγος (Word was with God, and God was the λόγος (Word)...
And the λόγος (Word) became flesh and dwelt among us, full of grace and truth; we have beheld his glory, glory as of the only Son from the Father."
—John 1:1, 14

λόγος: LOGOS—*Word*

LOGOS is one of the most complex concepts in biblical studies. Its importance is clear in its use more than 300 times in the New Testament, with both spiritual and secular connotations. In all Greek word studies and theological dictionaries, more space is devoted to the idea of the LOGOS than nearly any other scriptural word. Its original meaning is not actually "word" but of a *collection* or a *counting*, from which comes the sense of *list* or a *catalogue*, then gradually *language, narrative, speech, discourse, proverb, written account, tradition*.

From these beginnings, LOGOS came to signify *teaching, discourse,* then *revelation, rationality, the process and origination of thought*. Gradually in Greek philosophical literature it took on yet higher meaning, as a thing apart from and higher than man—the power of reason on a cosmic scale. The human LOGOS was but one small part of the higher universal cosmic LOGOS. As the concept continued to develop, the LOGOS took on more spiritual overtones—God, God's revelation, the mediating reason and word and creative power by which God makes himself known, the divine agent of knowledge. Even the idea of the LOGOS being the "son of God" had appeared in Greek mythology prior to the time of the Apostle John. The Jewish philosopher from

Alexandria Philo (c. 20 B.C.-c. 50 A.D.) wrote extensively about the LOGOS in an attempt to unite Judaism with Greek philosophy. In his writings, the divine LOGOS comes from God as a mediating figure between God and the temporal world—even representing humanity as an advocating high priest who governs the visible world in place of the invisible God. It may thus well be that Philo was instrumental in John's developing thought which ultimately he gave to the world in the first chapter of his gospel.

It is clear from such backgrounds why both Jesus and the Bible are referred to as the "Word." In both are fulfilled God's teaching and Will, the full LOGOS of his written and living revelation.

WE TALK A GREAT DEAL ABOUT TRUTH. We talk about knowing truth, discovering truth, proclaiming truth, living by truth. Yet when all is said and done, the thing we call *truth* remains fairly subjective.

Some will respond, "Ah, but we know that God's Word is the only truth. No truth is to be found outside the Scriptures." Such a statement calls to mind C.S. Lewis's observation when discussing the word "Christian": "Now this objection is in one sense very right...very spiritual...It has every amiable quality except that of being useful." [45]

Of course it is perfectly accurate to say that God's Word is truth. It is also a useless comment if that is as far as it goes. The devil is in the details, or, in the case of Scripture, in the interpretation. It's not quite so easy as making a blanket statement about the truth of the Bible. Even when it comes to a matter as fundamental as salvation, clichés about "the truth of the Bible" don't get us very far. The New Testament has been "interpreted" to yield many distinct (and sometimes almost completely opposing) "doctrines" of salvation.

It would seem that Pilate said a mouthful when he asked Jesus, "What is truth?"

Something beyond proof texts is needed.

THE FAR OFF SONG

When I first began to read the Bible seriously at the age of about eighteen or nineteen, I quickly encountered a methodology concerning the Bible, a way of approaching Scripture that would dominate my study, the spiritual training I received, and how I communicated my beliefs, for two decades.

It was the method of the learned and underlined text, the

memorized phrase or sentence or principle to meet every doctrinal query one could pose, and to resolve every situation in life.

"The Bible has the answer for everything," I was told. And these learned texts—neatly categorized, referenced, and noted at the back of my Bible—systematized those "answers" in an orderly and unambiguous way. The intended result was that I would know *what* I believed, *why* I believed it, and *where* to find the scriptural evidence, documentation, and proof of that belief.

This method of study was satisfying for a few years. I found it rich and rewarding. I loved the truths of the Bible and found them invigorating and full of life. I did my best to order my life according to them. My Bible became worn and underlined and full of sayings and quotes and lists and brief notations about various passages. At that age I took more than a little pride at how well-used my two or three favorite Bibles and testaments began to appear.

Yet gradually hints began to creep in as I read—like faint echoes of a melody from far over distant mountains which, by the time they reached me, were but broken fragments of a grand and magnificent symphony—of higher and more lofty themes that existed in God's heart than could be revealed by the surface specifics of Scripture.

As I sat with my Bible in my lap, flipping through its worn and well-annotated books, scarcely a page without a note or underlined passage, it slowly began to dawn on me that I might continue to study and study and study for the rest of my life—to the point of underlining the entire Book!—and still miss the big picture of what God's Word truly *meant*, if I remained inattentive to that distant symphony filtering faintly toward me from the high places of God's eternal purpose.

As much as I loved the details of Scripture that had been the focus of my study till then, they were no longer enough.

I had begun to hear fragmentary echoes of a higher song. I knew I needed to climb to loftier outlooks in my understanding. To do so would require a new scriptural quest of a different nature than what had dominated my study till then. It would require a reorientation. It might require revised methods, a fresh outlook, a bold approach. But I wanted to hear the symphony as God meant me to hear it. All my references and underlinings I now realized were mere "notes" of a higher song—important notes, yet *individual* musical tones. I saw that my previous study had been but the learning of elementary sounds and scales. But a symphony was being played. And the hunger continued to grow stronger to hear that symphony in more of its fullness.

What eternal music was God himself playing, high beyond the vistas visible from where I had yet ventured in my reading of Scripture? What music did *all* the notes together actually make?

It was at this point that I began to recognize an important principle. It was a little fearsome. I realized that a graduation day had come. I saw that to discover the music of the high places, I had to launch out, in a sense, on my own—beyond what I had learned and been taught, even perhaps moving in my research beyond those I had looked to as mentors during my years of spiritual grounding. I had to embark on a journey of scriptural investigation in which I would rely on the Holy Spirit, the Spirit of Truth, as my guide, rather than the learned doctrines of men.

Thus began my own quest to read the Bible more expansively—reading not for its superficialities, not to underline, not to add more words and phrases and proof-texts to my storehouse of knowledge, but reading rather for the big picture...to hear Scripture's high symphony.

In attempting to apprehend God's high truth, for some years I have employed the phrase "high Logos truth" to clarify my focus in this quest. It is the name I eventually gave to the symphony.

THE HIGH ETERNAL "WORD" OF GOD

By the phrase *high Logos truth,* I intend no dogma, no list of doctrines or principles, but rather a mindset, a perspective, an outlook that seeks God's purposes rather that what may be more immediate, smaller, temporal attempts to lay hold of them.

All Christian doctrines have within them the possibility of both high and low, temporal and eternal, interpretations. As but one example, we know that unity is something God values and that Jesus commanded. Many years ago in our area, five local pastors became inspired to seek more unity between themselves and their congregations. What followed was an exciting time of sharing that resulted in several large five-congregation gatherings. Everyone was excited because *unity* was happening. Unity, unity, unity was on everyone's lips.

These developments were good, wholesome, productive, invigorating, and enlightening.

But they were temporal. Within five years those five churches were as disconnected as before. As I write, none of the pastors have been involved locally for years, at least two, possibly more, are with the Lord. Their churches are *completely* changed from those days.

That "unity" was but a passing blip on the screen.

This exposes the limitation of interpreting God's high truth with temporal application. When we read John 17 and our hearts are warmed by Jesus' prayer for Unity among *all* his followers for *all* time and *throughout* all time, we know that he means something higher, grander, more expansive and eternal than merely two or three gatherings of a few churches. Jesus was praying for God's high, eternal WORD regarding Unity in the universe to be accomplished and fulfilled (brought to TELEIOTES, *perfection*) in his disciples and those who followed them. He was looking toward eternity as he prayed. His vision was for the fulfillment of God's high eternal Will.

It is for this reason in my writings that I speak of unity and *Unity*, of the church and the *Church*, of truth and the *Truth*. There are *small* expressions of *high* truths. The gathering together of the five churches was a true expression of lower-case unity, but was not in itself capable of apprehending the high upper-case eternal Logos *Unity* for which Jesus prayed. In the same way, the multitude of temporal churches that fill the world are not yet capable of being called the high eternal *Church*, which will one day be Christ's bride without spot or blemish.

Do we know of a certainty every element that will make up that Unity, or all the characteristics that will be radiantly visible in that Church? Of course not. We cannot yet see into eternity. But we know that a high eternal United Church *will* exist (in the fullness and perfection of the word,) and that God is laying the groundwork for it even now.

We faintly hear some of the music of Unity and the Church and Eternity's Redemption...but only brokenly and distantly.

As we therefore attempt to distinguish between lower-case applications and Upper-case Truths, we are looking ahead to the time in God's plan when all things will be brought to completion and perfection.

It is to highlight this progression that I entitled this chapter *Toward* the High Logos. We are on a journey. We are progressively *learning* to see with more and more eternal insight. We are attempting to scale the mountains from whose peaks some of that high Truth is faintly visible. It is the same reason, after a hiatus of a dozen years, that when I felt God's urging again to begin writing non-fiction in an attempt to illuminate the character of God in the same way I had attempted to do in my fiction, I used the imagery of a spiritual quest "out of the valley" and "up the mountains" in the book *A God To Call Father*. [46]

I am convinced that all the doctrines of Christianity, whose small and limited lower-case definitions we revere, are in reality but temporal outer clothes by which men have dressed up truths too high and expansive for them to grasp. When God's High Logos Truth is revealed, the clothes will fall away. We will then see with high mountain vision. We will at last apprehend the bigger picture. We may discover that it was there all along, if only we had been willing to believe big-enough things of God. At last we will see what Jesus actually *meant*.

No longer will we revere the explanations, for we will see the Truth inside them.

Understanding the high themes and hidden mysteries of Scripture in this way, along with the practicality of obedience, is the primary challenge of the Christian faith. Indeed, it is such a great challenge that many even of the most diligent of Bible students never manage to penetrate but the bare surface of God's mysteries. Instead, most satisfy themselves throughout their Christian lives with superficial interpretations of what God intends as deep and eternal truths.

Many scriptural surface readings do indeed contain value in their own right. Hundreds of its literal commands and practical principles and proverbs provide wisdom for daily life exactly as read. The Bible has truth to reveal at *whatever* level we come to it. But God also commands us to search out his Word for the profound *high* themes that Scripture reveals to those who prayerfully and humbly seek to discover them.

Big things cannot be reduced to small definitions. The big picture I speak of cannot be summarized in a three-point sermon, each with three sub-headings...tidy, succinct, quotable. Formulas to define God's ways—the lifeblood of the normal method of reading the Bible—are the very limitations and confines we are thinking boldly to escape. Formularizing high Logos Truth is as futile as trying to tie a string around a rainbow and haul it around so you can look at it whenever you like. It can't be done. You have to stand back and let the wondrous thing fill your heart with wonder.

That is how God's high Truth should impact our lives. We can't *define* it. We can only approach it with prayerful wonder.

Of a certainty, all I can say about the symphony called *God's High Logos Truth* as it concerns any specific doctrine—the incarnation, salvation, creation, the rapture, hell, the trinity, the Old Testament slaughters—is that I hear its far-off melody that tells me all will be good and infused from beginning to end with the loving character of God.

God must mean more than my eyes can see, and all will come right in the end.

In that high knowledge, I am at peace.

WHY LOGOS?

One of the Bible's most imaginative and visionary authors was the first to coin the term *Logos* to embody the essence of God's high symphony of eternity.

Can there be any two more powerfully begun books in all the Bible than *Genesis* and *John*?

Both begin with the identical words, *In the beginning.* Many of John's readers, *all* his Jewish readers, would have instantly recognized his link to the opening of the Pentateuch by the use of these three words.

In the beginning…—Genesis
In the beginning…—The Gospel According to John.

But then John takes a dramatic and unexpected twist.

Rather than, "In the beginning, *God*…" John shifts the attention *away* from God.

He makes the astonishing claim that something *else* existed in the beginning with God, that at the beginning of all things…God was not alone.

It was a revolutionary idea.

John calls this something else the λογος, the *Logos*. Our Bibles translate it as "Word," but in the Greek of the first and second centuries λογος carried far higher and more significant meaning than merely *word*. Logos connoted the totality of divine Wisdom and Reason and Law which governed the universe. Wisdom was sometimes called the mother of Logos. In Greek philosophy, where "God" was seen as transcendently higher and infinitely above the created order, so much so that he had no direct contact with it, the Logos came to be seen as God's mediating instrument both to create in the physical realm and to maintain contact with that creation.

The connection between these Greek concepts and John's first chapter will be obvious. Greeks reading John's first words would have found them familiar. Jews, however, could well have been scandalized at the thought that something—this Logos—was in existence in the beginning with God.

But John goes on to say that the Logos is not a some*thing* at all.

He calls the Logos "him." It is some *one*...a person. Moreover, God created everything in the universe through this Logos-Person.

The brilliance of John's exposition is breathtaking. He is speaking in a way the *Greek* world can grasp in preparation for explaining who Jesus was and what his life symbolized on a cosmic scale. At the same time John is speaking to *Jews* and *Christians*, who will relate to the concept of the *Logos* differently than will the Greek. To them he places the life and work of Jesus Christ into perspective in *their* worlds and frames of reference, illuminating Jesus' relationship with God the Father of the Old Testament and the Creator of the world.

In a single passage of pure luminescence (the depth and breadth of whose meaning yet remains unfathomably complex and impenetrable), John continues his masterful progression by introducing the Logos into the world of men by calling it/him the *light*.

In the creation of *Genesis*, light was the first thing God created: *Let there be light.*

Now John, in an unbelievable twist of literary irony, calls the Logos the *light* of the world, through whom was created everything in the world. In other words, the light *in* the world was created through the Light *of* the world!

The climax to John's brief but timeless introduction literally sends chills through my body as I read it, so perfectly has John's progression from *In the beginning* risen to this majestic crescendo:

And the Word became flesh and dwelt among us, full of grace and truth; we have beheld his glory, glory as of the only Son from the Father.

Now it is not only the Jew whose mouth is hanging open at what John has said, the Greek too is speechless, all his philosophies suddenly fallen to pieces at his feet. His prized philosophical logos has ceased to be an ethereal intellectual theory or esoteric ideal or abstract metaphysical concept.

The Logos has become a man!

The High Symphony of Eternity

In our bold attempts to listen to Scripture's music in new ways, we seek an *approach*, not doctrinal interpretations. The melodies of that Music each will have to discover for himself or herself. Bold thinking gives us a perspective that enables us to do so.

I am reminded of North Wind's far off song:

"I will tell you how I am able to bear it, Diamond; I am always hearing, through every noise, through all the noise I am making myself even, the sound of a far-off song. I do not exactly know where it is, or what it means; and I don't hear much of it, only the odor of its music, as it were, flitting across the billows of the ocean outside this air in which I make such a storm...Somehow, I can't say how, it tells me that all is right; that it is coming to swallow up all the cries...And...that song has been coming nearer and nearer. Only I must say it was some thousand years before I heard it." [47]

About these writings from the yellow wood...

Yellowood House is committed to writings that explore "bold thinking Christianity." Readers will be encouraged to follow the courageous thinkers of the Bible who lived their spiritual lives, not within the secure boundaries of learned formula, but who dared think big about God. Together we will venture into many obscure pathways that lead toward mysteries of God's purposes that can only be discovered by taking the road less traveled.

THE ROAD NOT TAKEN
Robert Frost

*Two roads diverged in a yellow wood,
And sorry I could not travel both
And be one traveler, long I stood
And looked down one as far as I could
To where it bent in the undergrowth;*

*Then took the other, as just as fair,
And having perhaps the better claim,
Because it was grassy and wanted wear;
Though as for that the passing there
Had worn them really about the same,*

*And both that morning equally lay
In leaves no step had trodden black.
Oh, I kept the first for another day!
Yet knowing how way leads on to way,
I doubted if I should ever come back.*

*I shall be telling this with a sigh
Somewhere ages and ages hence:
Two roads diverged in a wood, and I—
I took the one less traveled by,
And that has made all the difference.*

Titles from Yellowood House and other books authored by Michael Phillips can be purchased through bookstores, on Amazon, or at www.fatheroftheinklings.com. More information about Michael Phillips and his works can also be found at that site. Visit Michael Phillips on Facebook (www.facebook.com/michaelphillipschristianauthor) and at the blog www.daretothinkbigaboutgod.com.

THE COMMANDS

Michael Phillips Calls THE COMMANDS *the most important book he has written. Available on Amazon, from any bookstore, or from FatherOfTheInklings.com. For quantity discounts, see "The Michael Phillips Aisle" in "The Bookstore" of www.fatheroftheinklings.com.*

---

[1] George MacDonald, *The Hope of the Gospel*, 1892 "Salvation From Sin."
[2] C.S. Lewis, *Mere Christianity*, "Preface."

[3] C.S. Lewis, *Mere Christianity*, "The Invasion."
[4] George MacDonald, *Unspoken Sermons, Second Series*, "The Truth in Jesus."
[5] C.S. Lewis, *Mere Christianity*, "The Law of Human Nature."
[6] Richard Foster, *Celebration of Discipline*, p. 9.
[7] George MacDonald, *Unspoken Sermons, Second Series*, "The Last Farthing."
[8] George MacDonald, *The Hope of the Gospel*, "Salvation From Sin."
[9] C.S. Lewis, *Mere Christianity*, "The 'Cardinal Virtues.'"
[10] George MacDonald, *There and Back*, Chapter 40.
[11] C.S. Lewis, *Mere Christianity*, "Is Christianity Hard Or Easy?", "Counting the Cost."
[12] C.S. Lewis, *Mere Christianity*, "Is Christianity Hard Or Easy?", "Counting the Cost."
[13] C.S. Lewis, *Mere Christianity*, "Is Christianity Hard of Easy?"
[14] George MacDonald, *Unspoken Sermons, First Series*, "Love Thy Neighbor."
[15] C.S. Lewis, *Mere Christianity*, "Making and Begetting."
[16] C.S. Lewis, *The Four Loves*, Chapter 2.
[17] George MacDonald, *Unspoken Sermons, Second Series* . "The Last Farthing."
[18] C.S. Lewis, *Mere Christianity*, "Nice People or New Men."
[19] C.S. Lewis, *Selected Literary Essays*, "Hamlet: The Prince of the Poem."
[20] C.S. Lewis, *The Allegory of Love*, Chapter 1, I.
[21] C.S. Lewis, *Reflections On The Psalms*, Chapter 11, "Scripture."
[22] For those interested in further reading that *does* plumb the depths, no better expositions exist than George MacDonald's "The Truth" and "The Truth in Jesus," found in *Unspoken Sermons Third Series* and *Unspoken Sermons Second Series* respectively. Both appear in edited form in my edition of MacDonald sermons, *The Truth in Jesus*.
[23] C.S. Lewis, *Mere Christianity*, "The Invasion", "The Shocking Alternative", "The Perfect Penitent."
[24] C. S. Lewis, *Mere Christianity*, "The Three-Personal God."
[25] Dr. Loyal Hurley, *The Outcome Of Infinite Grace*, p. 1.
[26] I apologize that I no longer have the reference for this book. It has been so long since I made note of the quote, not intending to use it in a published edition of this book, that I do not remember either the title nor the author.
[27] C.S. Lewis, *Mere Christianity*, "The Great Sin."
[28] C. S. Lewis, *Letters to Malcolm: Chiefly on Prayer*, Chapter 6.
[29] Elaine Pagels, *Beyond Belief*, Random House, 2003, p. 38.
[30] Elaine Pagels, *Beyond Belief*, pp. 33-8.
[31] C.S. Lewis, *Christian Reflections*, "The Poison of Subjectivism."
[32] George MacDonald, *Unspoken Sermons, Third Series*, "The Creation In Christ."
[33] George MacDonald, *The Hope of the Gospel*, "Salvation From Sin."
[34] The Shorter Catechism of *The Westminster Confession*, answer to question 35, "What is Sanctification?"
[35] J.I. Packer, *Concise Theology*, p. 169.
[36] George MacDonald, *Unspoken Sermons, Second Series*, "The Fear of God."
[37] George MacDonald, Unspoken Sermons, Second Series, "The Truth in Jesus."
[38] C.S. Lewis, *Mere Christianity*, "Morality and Psychoanalysis" and "Charity."
[39] George MacDonald, *Unspoken Sermons, First Series*, "The Consuming Fire."
[40] George MacDonald, *Unspoken Sermons, Third Series*, "The Final Unmasking."
[41] George MacDonald, *David Elginbrod*, chapter 61.

[42] William Barclay, *A Spiritual Autobiography,* Wm. B. Eerdmans, pp. 22-24.
[43] George MacDonald, *Unspoken Sermons, Third Series,* "Righteousness."
[44] George MacDonald, *Unspoken Sermons, First Series,* "The Higher Faith."
[45] C.S. Lewis, *Mere Christianity,* "Preface."
[46] Michael Phillips, *A God to Call Father,* Tyndale House, out of print but available from FatherOfTheInklings.com.
[47] George MacDonald, *At the Back of the North Wind,* Chapter 7.

www.ingramcontent.com/pod-product-compliance
Lightning Source LLC
LaVergne TN
LVHW051039080426
835508LV00019B/1600